METAMORPHOSIS
The
Mind
In
Exile

METAMORPHOSIS

The
Mind
in
Exile

HAROLD SKULSKY

HARVARD UNIVERSITY PRESS
Cambridge, Massachusetts
and London, England
1981

Copyright © 1981 by the President and Fellows of Harvard College

Publication of this book has been aided by a grant
from the Andrew W. Mellon Foundation

Library of Congress Cataloging in Publication Data

Skulsky, Harold. —
     Metamorphosis : the mind in exile.
     Includes bibliographical references and index.
     1.   Metamorphosis in literature.   I.   Title.
PN56.M53S5   809'.915   80-29526
ISBN 0-674-57085-5

SUSANNAE·
CUI PERSEVERE IUDICANTI
ET COHORTANTI AMICISSIME
USQUEQUAQUE HAEC COMPONENS
PLACERE CONATUS
NONNUMQUAM ETIAM PLACUIT ·
AUCTOR OPUS
D · D · D

ACKNOWLEDGMENTS

I welcome the opportunity to thank Pauline Walker for her sterling performance in typing several versions of this manuscript; my friend and colleague Vernon Harward for his happy suggestion that I make room for Marie's werewolf; Mary Ellen Arkin for her vigilant and tactful editing; and Joyce Backman, whose good offices on behalf of my work have left me permanently in her debt. The most profound, elaborate, and long-standing of my obligations in this connection is acknowledged in the dedication.

The extracts from Virginia Woolf's *Orlando: A Biography* (copyright 1928 by Virginia Woolf; renewed 1956 by Leonard Woolf) are reprinted by permission of Harcourt Brace Jovanovich, Inc. I would also like to thank the literary estate of Virginia Woolf and The Hogarth Press for permission to reprint these extracts.

CONTENTS

METAMORPHOSIS
The
Mind
In
Exile

INTRODUCTION:
The Problem
and the Method

EVERYBODY IS FAMILIAR WITH THE OBLIGATORY FAIRY TALE
episode in which the shattering of a spell graphically discloses that an otherwise unaccountable dragon or weasel or
frog has all the while been none other than the missing prince or
princess; or with the figure of myth who is rescued or punished
by an obliging or inconvenient change of sex. This obsessive
fantasy of transformation, read as one sign among others in the
preliterate code, no doubt has a good deal to tell us about
primeval patterns of belief, and perhaps about the hidden grammar of all belief. But this is not, I suspect, why the fantasy has
enjoyed the loving attentions of sophisticated artists in various
traditions and epochs of European literature. The source of
fascination is rather the fantasy itself, taken literally as a condition contrary to fact; for one cannot hope to draw out its consequences without facing certain ultimate and perhaps menacing
questions about what it is to be a person.

Very well, Gregor has become a beetle, Elpenor a swine, Io
a heifer. These particular beasts are persons. Does that make
sense? Surely not, a materialist might well object — any more
than that a statue should survive its demolition, or a tune its
scrambling. Mind, which presumably links the beasts with their
human predecessors, is precisely that material structure and

1

function with whose catastrophic unraveling we are being diverted. Replace the notion of physical process with that of disposition to characteristic behavior, and we have the objection of the behaviorist: the enchanted swine lacks the wherewithal to act or be disposed to act the same as Elpenor; what else could warrant our identifying the two? It is all very well (as we shall find our authors doing) to ascribe the thought of persons to their minds and their behavior to their bodies[1]—as if one thought as one moves, by reference to a part of the whole. But the analogy is unconvincing; surely my mind's thought is my thought by a longer and emptier name. It is, by contrast, a genuine addition to the report of my having moved to say which part of me, or (equivalently) of my body, was in motion. Dualism—ancient and perennial as we shall find it to be—is the delusion of a perverse grammarian.

Thus for both materialist and behaviorist (on whose behalf I have been playing devil's advocate), the fictional premise is a piece of nonsense. It is impossible to comply with a request to conceive of an irreducible domain of mental states and events. Not so for our authors, who are encouraged, by the bias at least of their fictions, to affirm the autonomy of the mental as the ground (if ground there be) of individual dignity and rights, and as the ultimate object of love. Is bias alone the inducement? Is it not rather the pressure of the most conclusive kind of evidence? There are subtle and formidable arguments on both sides, and this, at all events, is not the place to address the issue—only to suggest that it cannot be exorcised by appealing to the truism that persons are the beings that reflect, remember, anticipate, feel, and suffer emotion. Among the crucial doubts that haunt the fantasy of transformation is not the non-issue of whether the human self resides primarily in physical or mental properties, but instead the hardily controversial issue of whether mental properties, under an unsentimental and unswerving gaze, dissolve without residue into physical. To a materialist, no doubt, this prospect holds no terrors. But with literature, as I hope to show, the case is otherwise.

If the fantasy of transformation prompts the literary intelligence to entertain such questions, it is instructive that the converse also occurs; that a serious exploration of such questions may lead one to adopt the strategies of the literary intelligence, and the fantasy of transformation in particular. In the following passage the modern philosopher Thomas Nagel tries to fix the notion of subjectivity — of mind itself rather than merely of the kindred minds in which we acknowledge personhood; and is thereby led to contemplate an imaginative effort more radical than any we shall encounter elsewhere in this study — so radical, in fact, that in the given sense it is doomed to failure:

Bats . . . present a range of activity and a sensory apparatus so different from ours that the problem I want to pose is exceptionally vivid . . . Even without the benefit of philosophical reflection, anyone who has spent some time in an enclosed space with an excited bat knows what is is to encounter a fundamentally *alien* form of life.

I have said that the essence of the belief that bats have experience is that there is something that it is like to be a bat . . . But bat sonar, though clearly a form of perception, is not similar in its operation to any sense we possess, and there is no reason to suppose that it is subjectively like anything we can experience or imagine. This appears to create difficulties for the notion of what it is like to be a bat. . .

Our own experience provides the basic material for our own imagination, whose range is therefore limited. It will not help to try to imagine that one has webbing on one's arms, which enables one to fly around at dusk and dawn catching insects in one's mouth; that one has very poor vision, and perceives the surrounding world by a system of reflected high-frequency sound signals; and that one spends the day hanging upside down by one's feet in an attic. In so far as I can imagine this (which is not very far), it tells me only what it would be like for *me* to behave like a bat. But that is not the question: I want to know what it is like for a *bat* to be a bat . . . Even if I could by . . . degrees be transformed into a bat, nothing in my present constitution enables me to imagine what the experience of such a future stage of myself . . . would be like.[2]

We may note the tacit assumption that it makes sense to speak in such a case of a "future stage of *myself*"; in addition to the dubious category of subjective states, we are being asked to countenance a self to endure them, and to persist despite their substantial and even total alteration. On Nagel's hypothesis, one and the same experiencing self endures the transition between being a person and becoming a bat. It is the kind of notion that the people around Kafka's beetle come to reject. In their developing view, the beetle lacks the claim on them even of being a *former* person—a later and brutal stage of what had once been someone they knew—much less of being a person here and now. Nagel himself cannot do without the notion because of the essential connection between subjectivity and empathy; we cannot grasp subjective experience other than our own without imagining our survival of a transformation—without trying to adopt the relevant point of view: "The more different from oneself the other experiencer is, the less success one can expect with this enterprise."[3]

In his essay on cetology Melville likewise assumes that there are facts about whales that are incomprehensible without immediate acquaintance—facts therefore to which only duly whalelike beings can be privy. But inaccessible as they are in *content*, cetology is incomplete without at least a sketchy account of their *structure*:

Far back on the side of the head, and low down, near the angle of either whale's jaw, if you narrowly search, you will at last see a lashless eye, which you would fancy to be a young colt's eye, so out of all proportion is it to the magnitude of the head . . . In a word, the position of the whale's eyes corresponds to that of a man's ears, and you may fancy, for yourself, how it would fare with you did you sideways survey objects through your eyes . . . You would have two backs, so to speak: but at the same time, also, two fronts (side fronts): for what is it that makes the front of a man—what indeed, but his eyes? . . . Man may, in effect, be said to look out on the world from a sentry-box with two joined sashes for his window. But with the whale, these two sashes are separately inserted, making two distinct windows, but sadly impairing the view . . . Anyone's experience will teach him, that though he can take in an undiscriminating sweep of things at one glance, it is quite impossible for him, attentively, and completely, to examine any two things—however large or however small—at one and the same time; never mind if they lie side by side and touch each other . . . How is it, then, with the whale? True, both his eyes in themselves, must simultaneously act; but is his brain so much more comprehensive, combining, and subtle than man's, that he can at the same moment of time attentively examine two distinct prospects, one on one side of him, and the other in an exactly opposite direction? If he can, then it is as marvellous a thing in him, as if a man were able simultaneously to go through the demonstrations of two distinct problems in Euclid.[4]

Melville here takes it for granted that there are subjective facts about the vision of whales to which a human being can only meagerly approximate by imagining, for example, that his eyes are sightless and that he sees through his ears. It is just this kind of assumption that ordinary folk in some stories of transformation cannot or will not make; part of the alienation of Ovid's Callisto, Apuleius' magic beast, Kafka's Gregor, Marie's Bisclavret, Keats's Lamia, and Woolf's males and females arises because some mental facts, unlike all physical, essentially depend on a point of view. It is logically possible, at least, for animals of different species to conceive of the same physical reality even if their characteristic visual sensations are not the same. By the same token the *ways* in which physical objects appear to them respectively — their mental realities — will be mutually inconceivable; in the subjective domain, reality and appearance coincide. "Does it make any sense," Nagel wonders, "to ask what my experiences are *really* like, as opposed to how they appear to me?" The oppressors of the victims of transformation retort in effect: does it make any sense in that case to talk of experiences at all, as opposed to shape and behavior? The riddle of Mind, in the stories I shall be considering, shades into that of the Other, for the missing clue to both is the status of the subjective — a question that "lies at the heart of the problem of other minds, whose close connection with the mind-body problem is often overlooked. If one understood how subjective experience could have an objective nature, one would understand the existence of subjects other than oneself."[5]

In some of the stories of transformation we shall be studying, the autonomy of the mental is so vigorously proclaimed that there is a curious shift in the burden of proof, and it is the notion of the objective — of physical reality — that is put on trial. Thus in *Lamia* and *Orlando* we find attacks on both naive and scientific realism that tended to embarrass critics of a few decades ago, but that in these days of Kuhn and scientific relativism may be regarded more tolerantly. In the treatments of Ovid and Donne the fantasy of transformation becomes the centerpiece of a powerful absurdist vision that draws morbidly on the same fund of radical doubts, and in Apuleius transformation is erected into a mystical panpsychism.

The fantasy at the heart of the fictions that will interest me in these pages is not, I think, infinitely malleable. By its very nature it forces a confrontation with some or all of a small cluster of concerns associated with the nature of personhood and personal identity. One such concern — the last I shall discuss in this introduction — is the strain in the notion of moral obligation that naturally accompanies uncertainties about what it is to be a person. Can the monstrous beetle's human kinsmen and the werewolf's wife really be expected to sacrifice their happiness to an alien form of life? For the ramifications of this concern in the stories of Kafka and Marie de France I refer the reader to the appropriate chapters; but it may not be out of place to consider here two cases of what might be called transformation in reverse that generate the same concern.

In the first — which is not a fantasy — a she-ape taught to express itself in sign language appears to have risen to personhood, if not humanity, and thereby to have threatened some disruption to our categories both legal and moral. What rights are we willing to grant a creature that reports its feelings?

[Francine] Patterson [the investigator] lives off campus now, and her late arrival causes anxiety to the gorilla, which whimpers and cries, and signs "Sad" when asked how she feels. "Other mornings it will be 'Happy,' or 'I feel good,' depending actually upon how she feels. Once a reporter was here, and he asked her whom she liked the best, me or my assistant. Koko looked at me, looked at my assistant, and then gave the sign for 'Bad question'" . . . "[Patterson] showed some movies of Koko right after she had torn apart a sponge, something she wasn't supposed to do. [Patterson] questioned her very pointedly about the sponge, shaking it in her face. She asked her, 'What is this?' Koko was silent for a moment and then answered, 'Trouble.' And she reached out and embraced Patterson. That's powerful stuff." . . . "Koko looks in a mirror, and if you ask her who it is, she signs 'Koko.' "[6]

Two contrasting responses to such testimony are reported in the journalistic account I am quoting. One (by a juridical theorist) is to the effect that it is no longer legally proper to treat the gorilla as a mere chattel because "when you give it the conceptual apparatus for conscious reasoning, you have radically altered it . . . If it has never been one before, it is an individual now. It has the apparatus for the beginning of a historical sense, for the contemplation of self." The positivist reply to this is that "the animals [that have been taught to speak] are still not human, and the laws [the jurist] would bring to bear are human rights, are they not?"[7]

The criteria of personhood being invoked here are of course hardly clear. Is it a question of behavior? Then it may be thought that neither reasoning nor self-reference is enough to qualify an object for personhood; the accomplishments and potentialities of computers would appear to be a counterexample. Is it a question of inner states? Then one may ask why the gift of speech should be necessary to personhood; cannot Koko have suffered and even thought before she was taught to sign? Or, one may ask, is it a question of fact (behavioral or interior) at all? Are the disputants not rather deliberating whether to include gorillas — at least those that use sign language — in the scope of the noun "person," with all the changes in *our* behavior that conventionally attend such a change in verbal insignia? As often in the literature of transformation, we are in the presence of a conceptual distress that is at the same time a moral emergency.

The same kind of anxiety, I think, is generated by the following hypothetical problem, in which (again by reverse transformation) it is brute matter that seems to have risen to personhood:

M is a synthetic duplicate of Jones's central nervous system. By "synthetic" I mean only that it was constructed in the laboratory. It is not made of metal or of plastic, but of exactly the same proteins, nucleic acids, and other substances as was Jones's. By "duplicate," I mean that the parts are arranged just as the corresponding parts were in Jones's system; let us assume that the correspondence is atom-for-atom. Also, we somehow arrange that what happens in and to M is exactly the same in every detail . . . as what happened in and to Jones's central nervous system throughout Jones's life . . . The question, of course, is whether mental events are among the things which happen in or to M. Better, we can introduce at least a nominal distinction between M, a mere physical thing, and a subject of mental states about whose existence we are asking. We shall call the latter "O" for owner; if O exists, then O "owns" M just as Jones owned his central nervous system . . . In the case of no significant interaction between M and its environment, central state theories [roughly, theories that reduce mental properties to states of the brain] imply that O exists, and behaviorist theories [roughly, theories that reduce mental properties to behavior] imply that he does not.

Assume, as is likely, that we have reason for deciding in favor of a central state theory. Then we also have reason for deciding in favor of the existence of O, the owner of the "disembodied brain."[8]

Now having set the stage, the inventor of the puzzle (the modern philosopher Lawrence H. Davis) proceeds to bring out its moral bearings by asking "whether or not the owner of the disembodied brain enjoys the same right to life we normally accord embodied persons — as opposed, say, to cattle, lame horses, and human foetuses." The answers considered by Davis turn once more, as we should expect, on differing notions of personhood. One such notion involves "possession of a self-concept": "In one recent formulation, this means having the 'concept of a self as a continuing subject of experiences and other mental states,' and believing that one is oneself 'such a continuing entity' . . . If this is all that is needed . . . O . . . would qualify."[9] (We might recall Koko's achievements in this vein.) Another favorable answer, constructed by Davis from some remarks of John Rawls, proceeds as follows:

"The capacity for feelings of pleasure and pain and for the forms of life of which animals are capable clearly imposes duties of compassion and humanity in their case" . . . What is interesting in this passage is the reference to "forms of life of which animals are capable." I am not sure I understand just how they impose duties on us; but if they do in the case of animals, they certainly do in the case of O. For O's form of life is fully human; the fact that the significance of his experiences and the impact of his volitions are totally other than he thinks would seem to be morally irrelevant. It does not follow that it would be wrong to turn off the machine supplying jolts to O's disembodied brain. But we should at least think twice before doing so.[10]

The acknowledgement of O's existence — whether as a sequence of electrochemical or of irreducibly mental events — appears to make it harder to bring oneself to switch M off, though O's incurable solitude and delusion of living Jones's life might form the basis of a case for euthanasia. Once again in this instance a troubling demand is made on the sympathetic imagination, one that goes beyond mere fantasy or *jeu d'esprit* by requiring us to draw the moral consequences of a notion of persons, and hence to commit ourselves to such a notion: what is the ground of dignity—or is the ascription of dignity itself just a game of categories?

In the studies that follow I have approached my texts on the premise that they exemplify the vocabulary, grammar, and semantic rules of particular national languages at particular stages of development and constrained by the conventions of particular genres.[11] This premise seems to me to be both true and important. It is no doubt equally true and important that each such text is partially coextensive with another text written in the language of the individual or collective unconscious; but it is also irrelevant to my present enterprise. Since the languages of the twin texts in each case differ crucially in structure and even in lexicon, one reads the one largely by declining to read the other; to read the unconscious text, for example, one must treat extensive portions of its twin as a matrix of pseudotext designed to hide the message like a pattern in the carpet.[12] It is sometimes maintained that the meaning of the unconscious text is in some sense the real or deeper meaning of its twin, but this is a confusion encouraged by the supposition that the unconscious text is causally prior. Perhaps it is; but it is a different text all the same, and its meaning, be it ever so deep, is peculiar to itself. I persist in thinking, moreover, that the meaning of its twin the literary text, elucidated by careful scholarship, is quite deep enough.

CIRCE AND ODYSSEUS:
Metamorphosis
as Enchantment

THE HOMERIC STORY OF CIRCE INVITES US TO ENTERTAIN THE
fantastic premise that certain men, for a brief interval,
have been made to exhibit all the bodily characteristics of
swine. I believe the poet actively helps us to honor his invitation — to take his premise seriously — by answering some of the
hard questions that arise when we try to grasp the situation.
Can such bodies, in their swinelike phase, be sensibly described
as belonging to persons at all? What justifies us in holding that
the human bodies that end with the swine's creation have the
same owners as the human bodies that begin with the swine's ex-
tinction? Just what sort of evil is the ordeal itself? It is rare — perhaps unique in so public a form of discourse — for an epic poet
to be forced by the demands of his plot to say what he thinks
about so private a version of the sphinx's riddle as what it is to
have a mind, what it is to have a body, what it is to be the same
person from moment to moment, what it is quite simply to be a
person.

In what sense, if any, are these swinelike beings persons?
The general view intimated by the text seems to me reasonably
clear, if not clearly reasonable. We are to suppose that the survival of a person, however whimsical the career of his body, is
guaranteed by the survival of a mind. Mind and body are dis-

tinct enough to have reciprocal influence, and in some respects mind is causally more basic. Circe's potion transforms bodies only after inducing amnesia: "And she mixed up with their food grim poisons, that they might utterly forget the land that fathered them. And when she had given it and they had drunk, then in a trice she struck them with a wand and penned them up in the swinefold" (10.235–238). The Circean power over body, in fact, is typically "beguilement" (*thelxis*) – a power, ultimately, over mind (10.213, 318, 326). Despite their nature, the bodies of the new wolves and lions surrender to the emotional habits of the minds that survive in them: "Nor did these rush on the men, but rather stood up round about, fawning with their long tails. As when a prince is thronged by his hounds as he walks home from the feast, and they fawn on him (for always he brings them dainties to gladden the spirit), so were these thronged by wolves of mighty claw, and by lions, fawning" (10.214–219). We are told in so many words that in the new swine "mind was steadfast as before; so wept they as they were penned up" (10.240–241), and it is immediately obvious to Circe that the resistance of Odysseus' body to her charm is due to the resistance of a mind unfathomably devious: "But you – in your breast is a mind that cannot be enchanted. You, then, are Odysseus the master of stratagem, whose coming on the swift black ship, on the homeward path from Troy, was ever foretold me by the slayer of Argos, the god of the golden staff" (10.329–332). As for that god, we may be sure that his devious mind is still at work in the body of the scant-bearded youth who greets Odysseus on his way to Circe's palace, just as the grace of Persephone allows the mind of Teiresias its living energy within what is no more than the mockery of a body: "The blind prophet whose wits are steadfast, for to him in death Persephone has granted a mind, to him alone awareness; and the others, shadows racing" (10.493–495).

It is of course genetically impossible, as perhaps the Homeric poet himself would have agreed, for human bodies to become exactly like those of swine. It is the kind of thing that does not happen; but the story would be pointless if we could not conceive of what things that do not happen would be like if they did. In this respect at least, Circe's spell is a fantasy that has a chance of entertaining us because we have a chance of entertaining it. The survival of mind in the changelings, by contrast, for some readers both ancient and modern, fails to happen not only in the actual scheme of things but in any conceivable scheme of things at all. A human mind in a porcine body is as unserviceable for the uses of fantasy as a five-pointed sphere. But such worries are presumably groundless; for on the view we are considering the Homeric poet, whose ascertainable notion of mind in fact rules it out, can hardly have reserved a place even in a fabulous universe for minds that are no more than contradictions. We not only should not but cannot take the text literally, for it has no literal meaning.

Now it may be that the changeling mind is a sort of nonsense, though I have yet to achieve the threatened bafflement. But if it is nonsense, I think the Homeric poet cannot be acquitted of talking it, or of treating it as central to the picture of the human condition that forms its context. It will not do, for example, to reject a literal reading on the ground that Homeric claims about mind are really about how bodies are likely to behave under standard conditions. "The ancient commentators," we are told, "say that what is preserved in such persons [as the victims of Circe] is the mind not as a whole but only in respect of friendliness to humanity. Hence the fawning [of Circe's wolves and lions on the approaching crew]. In the same way Pindar's dolphins, 'though men no longer, have not left behind their man-befriending life.' " In this vein, one scholiast reasons as follows: "If their minds persisted, how is it that Circe is nonplussed by Odysseus' failure to change [in mind]? Perhaps she is talking about their new savagery; or the solution may be a matter of style: when she says 'a mind is in your breast that cannot be enchanted,' what she means, without circumlocution, is 'you cannot be enchanted.' Or perhaps the steadfastness of mind in the crew has to do not with the whole mind but only with gentleness."[1] The short reply to this line of argument would be that gentleness is not a part but an expression of mind, which cannot be accurately described even in part by listing items like tail wagging. It is true, as Kurt von Fritz shows, that Homeric terms roughly answering to mind (noös, noema, phrenes) often simply name the capacity to perform acts of evaluation (noesis), and that such acts are associated with characteristic gestures;[2] but the terms also apply to what carries on noesis unobservably,

or is prevented from doing so: "a man's mind darts about . . .
and yearns for many things"; "his mind had other urges"; "utter
your grief, do not hide it in your mind."[3] In this Homeric usage
mind is clearly presented to us as the organ and not the function
of thought, despite von Fritz's contention that if the Homeric
Greeks had drawn the distinction (which he denies) "they would
probably have considered the *noös* a function rather than an
organ."[4] The point of Circe's remark about a *noös* impervious to
enchantments, for example, is "that Odysseus' clearness of mind
has not been affected by her magical art."[5] But this is surely
mistaken; even in Greek one does not put the clearness under
one's spell but the mind.

If the human mind is an organ of thought as the human
hand is of manipulation — if it is, for example, the brain by
another name — then once again porcine bodies with human
minds are no more the stuff of fantasy than of fact. The question now is whether Homeric *noös* is to be glossed according to
the lights of a materialist. The objections of ancient commentators seem to take this for granted — as if the blind singer in his
wisdom could not fail to be a good Aristotelian or Stoic — and
some modern scholars argue in a similar vein: "*Noös* means the
interior, virtually neurophysiological force that sets a human
being in motion, determines his actions, but remains invisible,
and to be known must first be manifested."[6] It is useful to contrast this assessment with the older view of Rohde: "We often
find mentioned side by side with the 'midriff' [*phren*] and in the
closest proximity with it, the *thymos*, a name which is not taken
from any bodily organ and shows already that it is thought of as
an immaterial function. In the same way many other words of
this kind (*noös, noeîn, noëma, boulé, menos, mêtis*) are used to
describe faculties and activities of the will, sense, or thought,
and show that these activities are thought of as independent,
free-working, and incorporeal."[7]

One might easily object, on behalf of the other reading,
that these activities are presented in the Homeric text as so
many operations of the *phren*, which Rohde himself describes as
"the seat of all the functions of mind and will." The term, after
all, is very often either coordinated with *noös* or used in
equivalent contexts, and the mind itself, if located at all, is invariably to be found in the breast. But the objection is not very

formidable; as a psychological term *phren* does not accommodate a materialist interpretation. Amputation of the diaphragm is clearly not in question when we hear of someone who becomes *aphron*—who loses his *phren*—in frenzy or infatuation: "Here in turn did Zeus son of Kronos take away from Glaukos his *phrenes*"; "Which of the gods now has set in your breast a fruitless resolve and taken away your prospering *phrenes*?"[8] Perhaps the name of the organ is being converted here by metonymy into a name of the organ's function: "The gods have deprived you of your intelligence." But the organ is no more a material object than the function. "Soul and specter there are in Hades' mansions, but *phrenes* altogether there are not."[9] Yet in the sense that now concerns us, the dead Teiresias' *phrenes* are "steadfast" in what is now at best a fluid and at worst a shade (10.493ff.). And Teiresias, as Rohde observes, is not the only dead soul, stripped of bodily organs, that the gods allow a *noös* in perpetuity: "The almighty power of the gods is able in special cases . . . to preserve for individual souls their consciousness [*noös*]; in the case of Teiresias as a reward, in the case of these three [namely, Tityos, Tantalos, Sisyphos], objects of the gods' hatred, in order that they may be capable of feeling their punishment."[10]

I see no good reason, then, to disagree with the ancient critic who concludes that Odysseus' unfortunate shipmates had "fallen into such a state as to retain a human soul, but with its mind [not] awake." The alternative readings, I think, are mistaken but far from negligible, for as I shall point out in later chapters, the charge of literal nonsense haunts the literature of metamorphosis, often as the pretext of a powerful wish: "If only one could part the breast and having looked into the *noös* lock the breast up again," as the Athenian banquet song has it—if only the mind were, at least in principle, a public object.[11] The fantasy of the mind in exile is redeemed from harmless grotesquerie in large measure because it is the natural focus of speculative anxieties in contention: that the mind is no more than another native of the material universe; that in such a universe it is a resident alien to whom the fraternal rights of citizenship are forever denied.

In assimilating fantasy to epic the Homeric poet seems to have taken into account his hearers' limited patience with the fabulous. His problem is an episode that hinges on what is, in the causal sense at least, a glaring impossiblity. This is an embarrassment; but a likelihood can be conjured up rhetorically by indirection—by distracting our attention from the whole matter of causation. In Aristotelian terms, a story can balance rather more securely on an impossibility that contrives to be likely (in the rhetorical sense) than on a possibility that seems unlikely. "The transformation into pigs," as Denys Page shrewdly remarks, "is the one unrealistic element in the tale of Odysseus and Circe; it is therefore reduced to the smallest possible measure." Circe's rigmarole does not bear thinking about, and for the same reason the audience had better not be troubled about the pharmacology of *môly:* "The detail of the manner in which the hero neutralizes the magical arts of the sorceress is, as a rule, a treated at some length in versions other than the *Odyssey* . . . The matter is wholly omitted by Homer . . . The most obvious and likely explanation is to be found in the poet's desire to suppress the purely magical elements in the folktales which have been adopted by the story of Odysseus."[12] The result of this well-timed reticence is an impossibility that can pass rapid muster as a likelihood. In the Near Eastern analogues of the Circean transformation (which are perhaps also its ultimate models) this tactic is out of the question, for the entire point is the efficacy of magic. The point of the Homeric metamorphosis, by contrast, is what is entailed by the sheer fact of transformation; its antecedents are not only incredible but beside the point.

For the Homeric poet—if I am right—mind, like personhood, is an irreducible feature of the world, and the virtue of fantasy is that some intimate features of the terrain of fact can be properly mapped only from the vantage point of the counterfactual. One such feature is the distinctness of properties that have their actual instances in common. Suppose, in particular, that the class of things with a human mind is in fact indistinguishable from the class of bodies with such and such a structure, so that whatever happens to be in one class falls into the other as well. We say that the classes are one and the same. But on our supposition, having a mind is likewise indistinguishable from having a physiological property, for whatever has either one has the other. Shall we not say about the indistinguishable properties what we said about the classes, that they too are one and the same? Only, one is inclined to think, if there is no logical possibility of their differing in their instances—only if there is no possible world in which a thinking thing lacks the given physiological property, or something that has the property is without a mind. To exhibit such a possible world is to illuminate the actual world as well.[13] Mind cannot be a physiological property at all if in the court of Circe it proves, without absurdity, not to be such. It is by his way with the unreal that the Homeric poet discloses a profound, and no doubt unexamined, conviction about the real. Of course it remains a question whether the conviction is warranted—whether the tale does not tip into absurdity; this suspicion perhaps is the special force of the tale for us. For the first hearers, in their innocence or wisdom, the question probably did not arise.

Allegorizers from antiquity on have claimed that the shapes of Circe's victims are simply emblems of their moral condition. This reading would give mind an autonomy and causal importance commensurate with what I take to be its rank in the Homeric scheme of things, and perhaps there is some slender basis for moralization in the text. For example, Odysseus hesitates to mount Circe's bed in view of what she has done to his comrades—"lest when I am stripped you make me base and void of manhood [anenor]" (10.300); to have lost the shape of man—to become anenor—is evidently to be base or evil (kakos): Circe's power, then, is the power to corrupt. And the magic beasts in which she specializes resemble species to which moral exception is taken by folklore—scavengers and predators (10.213, 433). But if their behavior is any indication these beasts are distinctly unbestial; and on the moralizing interpretation of beastly shape, the poet has allowed himself an odd gaffe when he chooses the following simile for one of the few moments in the episode when human beings express an emotion that the poet clearly admires:

I went back to the swift ship and the strand of the sea [after encountering Circe]. Then on the swift ship I found my trusty mates mourning heavily with a burgeoning of tears; and as when the herded cows are coming to the fold having had their fill of forage, and all together the meadow-dwelling calves cavort round them in greeting and the fences no longer hold them, but with a din of lowings they run round their dams—so my mates when they laid eyes on me poured themselves out in tears. And their mood seemed to them as if they had come home to the land of their fathers and to the city of rocky Ithaca where they had been bred and born.   (10.407–417)

The poet wants a touchstone of loyalty and warm affection; casually—or is it pointedly?—he shows us dumb animals. If the crew's loss of human form is merely the natural expression of some vice they are indulging, it is, once more, odd that it should so entirely depend on Circe's artifice, and should surprise them in an act as innocent as the consumption of a porridge.

The fact is that the context of the episode is a series of repellent vignettes of a barbarity and meanness and folly that show not the least tendency to alter the shape of their human practitioners: the envy and avarice of the crew untying the sack of winds (10.38–45), the moral cowardice of Aiolos grimly banishing a suppliant convicted of bad luck (10.72–75), the cowardice and disloyalty of Odysseus' kinsman Eurylochos (10.255–269, 431–435), the cowardice and stupidity of Elpenor (10.550–560). The *Odyssey* is the story of a traveller who "has seen the cities of many men and come to know their *noös*" (1.3); the frequent vileness of that *noös*, as it is portrayed in the sequence of which the visit to Circe is a part, is shown to be easily compatible not only with a human shape but with the institutional trappings of a civilization.

These comforting appearances, in fact, are the bait of the nightmare that gradually engulfs Odysseus on his visit to the Laistrygonians. We are lulled at first with a distant view of quiet industry near "the lofty capital of Lamos," where "a sleepless man could earn double hires, the one herding cows and the other pasturing the gleaming sheep (for hard by each other are the roads of night and day)" (10.84ff.). The narrative eye acknowledges the harbor framed by a "white calm" (10.94), "carts hauling timber to the citadel from the high mountains" (10.103–104), and the Achaian scouts happening on "a maiden before the city drawing water in an urn . . . for she had come down to Artakia, fair-flowing spring" (10.105, 107). Trapped in the idyll, we find ourselves presently watching the good burghers consuming their "unlovely banquet" of men, "spitting

them like fish" (10.124) as the "evil blare rushes upward along
the quay, of the rending of men and the splintering of ships"
(10.123). An ancient critic modestly advises us to notice "that it
has availed the Laistrygonians nothing to be disposed in a com-
monwealth, that is, to have a city-state; for even so, they
themselves are neither just nor gentle."[14] It is true that character
for the Homeric poet is rooted in the *noös* and not in
physiology, but if we cannot do without a bestiary emblem of
assorted moral depravity, there is much to be said — much that
is said by the poet himself — for the featherless biped. Circe's
magic, in this context, can hardly be a debasement; it is easier to
think of it as a promotion.

The episode of Circe is part of the long account of his afflictions given by Odysseus at the court of the Phaiakians, and
since his factual grasp varies with the demands of epic narrative,
there is sometimes an ironic margin of error between what he in-
fers and what his story implies. The fluctuation is clearly
enough marked. Odysseus does not infer, for example, but
knows immediately and in detail, how Circe dealt with his crew
inside her palace, and in the same way he reports outright that
the old minds persist in the new bodies. On the other hand, he
gets a specific, though ambiguous, warrant for his notion of
Circe's generalized malice (10.317): he has it on the authority of
the masquerading Hermes that Circe's magic is evil (10.288), but
he is never told just why Circe keeps her private menagerie, or
what Hermes can have meant, if he really thinks her malicious,
by repeatedly telling her of Odysseus' impending visit (10.330–
331). Is Hermes, as elsewhere in the mythic tradition, a double
agent?

The point is not, of course, that Circe scrupulously draws
the line at celebrities; only a solemn vow, extorted by a show of
murderous intent on Odysseus' part, will protect him from a
second attempt to enchant him. But it is equally clear that the
poet has not favored us with a malevolent witch. The comrades
restored "knew me and clung each to my arms, and there came
up in us all a voluptuous keening to which round about the
mansion set up a dismal clangor. And the goddess herself was
moved to pity" (10.388ff.). "When they [the reunited crew] saw
and marked one another face to face, they wailed and mourned
with the mansion throbbing around them. And standing by me

she spoke aloud, the bright goddess: 'Zeus-descended son of Laertes, cunning Odysseus, now at last keep down the strong grief. I too know how greatly you have been tortured on the teeming sea, and ravaged by cruel men on the dry land . . . But now, thinking always of your hard exile is leaving you juiceless and spiritless, there is no moment of joy for your spirit, you have endured so much" (10.453–459, 463ff.). " 'O Circe, fulfill the promise you made to me, to send us home. Already the spirit is eager in me and in the other mates who wear out my heart with grieving around me when you are away.' That is what I said. And she replied, the bright goddess, 'Zeus-descended son of Laertes, cunning Odysseus, do not stay any longer at my house since now it is against your will' " (10.483–489). The poet has taken pains to show that whatever the reasons for Circe's obvious compulsion to entrap, neither malice nor cold mischief is among them.

One crucial reason, I think, is explicit in the text: "Again they became men, younger than before and fairer and grander to behold" (10.395–396). The ordeal of transformation, far from being a corruption, is an initiation and cannot end with the mere restoration of the earlier shape, or with anything short of the means for a new beginning. Circe reveals her victims, not in the shape they lost, but in the shape to which they have meanwhile been ascending. The catharsis is achieved, fittingly enough, by assimilation to the form of an animal that is a familiar vehicle of ritual cleansing in later Greek cults, and perhaps, if we follow Frazer's conjecture, of mystic regeneration as well:

To explain the rude and ancient ritual of the Thesmophoria the following legend was told. At the moment when Pluto carried off Persephone, a swineherd called Eubouleus chanced to be herding his swine on the spot, and his herd was engulfed in the chasm down which Pluto vanished with Persephone. Accordingly at the Thesmophoria pigs were annually thrown into caverns to commemorate the disappearance of the swine of Eubouleus. It follows from this that the casting of the pigs into the vaults at the Thesmophoria formed part of the dramatic representation of Persephone's descent into the lower world; and as no image of Persephone appears to have been thrown in, we may infer that the descent of the pigs was not so much an accompaniment of her descent as the descent itself.[15]

There is at the very least, it seems to me, a significant parallel between the transfiguration of Odysseus' men by their interval of totem incarnation and the splendid emergence of the totem goddess from her cyclic withdrawal into Hades. It is Circe's office in the Homeric scheme—her *moîra*—to serve not only as the oracular daughter of the sun but as the celebrant of this mystery; just as it is Hermes' office to refrain from interfering until the mystery is accomplished, and to prepare Circe for the arrival of a visitor reserved for mysteries even more august. Circe and Hermes are messengers of the same secret order, with complementary powers and duties, and the transformation over which they preside is not a fable of debauchery but a sacrament.

The ancient moralization of the text whose Christian curator and advocate is the twelfth-century Archbishop Eustathius acknowledges the prominence given by the poet to the theme of the distinctness and dignity of mind, but regards that theme as incompatible with the premise of transformation; it is the mind that turns bestial and the body that retains its humanity, despite the poet's apparent claim to the contrary. Hermes, after all, tells Odysseus that his comrades have been penned up "like pigs" (10.283), not that they *are* pigs. "The phrase 'like pigs,' " says Eustathius, "corroborates the allegorical reading we advanced a little earlier, to the effect that those who succumb to Circe, the type of pleasure, have not literally become pigs, but 'like' (that is, as if they were) pigs, because their way of life is swinish."[16] Two centuries later we find the Jewish biblical exegete Saadia Gaon resorting, under similar doctrinal pressures, to a similar method of disposing of Nebuchadnezzar's shagginess "as of eagles" and claws "as of birds," and of the angelic warning that "like as oxen will he crop the grass": "Do not suppose that he has become a donkey or wild ass, but rather that he has gone mad and become as dull as a beast, and that from filth, sweat, and droppings his hairs have flourished like the feathers of eagles and his nails like the claws of the bearded vulture and frigate bird that tread on their claws."[17]

Such speculations are often worth taking seriously, if only because they themselves take the text seriously enough to attend to its details and to the possibility that these are not otiose. One might contrast the response of a modern critic to the nuance that exercised Eustathius: "The words implicitly deny that they

[Odysseus' men] have been transformed into pigs; only the man who is not a pig can be shut up 'as if he were a pig.' This is simply a fault in the phrasing, and Odysseus assumes that Hermes has asserted what in fact he has implicitly denied, the transformation into pigs."[18] But the phrasing is not at fault, for the change that is the central datum in the story cannot be a change of species. Species is determined not merely by shape but by individual history. No matter how porcine these offspring of human beings have become, their past, and especially their pedigree, decisively count against their being classified as pigs. By the same token, no matter how human the past and future of these porcine beings may be, their present counts irrevocably against their ever being classified as men. The poet's faulty phrase, in short, is exact and significant, just as Eustathius takes for granted; the changed comrades are indeed pigs only "as it were" — and for that matter, human only "as it were." What we learn eventually is not that they ever stopped being human, but that they never began. Their transformation has retroactively defrauded them of a species — or rather, it has disclosed the fact that they are in a class by themselves. Personal history has branded their accursedness and sanctity into their very essence.

I have been arguing that the story of the transformation is a tribute to the unique status of mind in a world of bodies, and that the ensuing transfiguration gives the tribute a religious inflection. But the poet takes a moral interest in mind as well. Odysseus is embarked, as our reluctant proxy, on a quest for the mind of the peoples he visits, and though in the current episode one can hardly avoid a dominant impression of bitterness, it is also possible to make out a corrective pattern, a tribute to mind as the ultimate ground of the moral. For the story of Circe's magic is also the story of Odysseus' response to it, and he is spared the magic at least partly so that both stories can be told.

What we are shown is an adept at choosing in the absence of hope who twice hesitates between survival and suicide, and twice resolves on life. His comrades untie the winds, damning themselves and their captain to indefinitely prolonged exile: "Waking up I cast about in my pure spirit whether to fall from the ship and snuff myself out in the sea or to endure without a sound and be still among things that live. But I bore up and

stayed where I was, lying on shipboard with my head covered"
(10.50–54). Odysseus has rallied his men and himself with the
assurance that "we will not yet, though we grieve, sink into
Hades' mansions before the day dealt out to us comes on"
(10.174–175); when Circe informs him that Hades' mansions are
precisely his next port of call, "my nerve snapped, I sat on the
couch and cried, and my heart was no longer willing to live and
see the sunlight. But when I had had enough weeping and roll-
ing about I answered her and said: 'O Circe, who will be our
pilot on this journey?' " (10.495–501). Odysseus regards the roll-
ing about of others with the same compound of understanding
and detachment; the Homeric dialect, in fact, leaves an
idiomatic pause in the text for a dismissive shrug: "They wailed
shrilly, with an outpouring of tears; but [and here the shrug, as
if to say: they could ill afford it] — for no deed [*prêxis*] was doing itself on their behalf while they wept" (10.201–202; see
10.567–568).

It is entirely fitting that Hermes should be instructed to
save the connoisseur of *prêxis* (doing, enterprise, turning a profit) — this transcendent opportunist whom Circe instantly
recognizes as *polytropos*, the versatile one par excellence — from
being deprived of the wherewithal to exercise his chief talent.
And what is that talent if not the Protean art of disguise, of a
kind of self-transformation that manages at the same time to be
the purest affirmation of a self that, in its inalienable unity,
transcends intact the phases it passes through? It is perhaps
equally fitting that Odysseus and not Hermes — the hero and not
the god — should be the agent of his crew's deliverance, and that
Odysseus' freedom should at the same time depend on a sacred
herb, "hard to dig out, but the gods can do everything" (10.306).
"This *môly* that Hermes discloses by rational inquiry," as
Eustathius remarks, "is not accessible to human beings by virtue
of their mere humanity, for it is a good divinely bestowed."[19]
Eustathius is perhaps thinking of the partnership of nature and
grace in Christian theology, but I suspect that the Pauline
scheme is in fact not nearly so close to a partnership of the
human and the divine as the pairing of Hermes' deference to
Odysseus with Odysseus' reliance on *môly* in restoring his crew.

The principle involved is announced by Zeus in what
amounts to the proem of the epic: "It angers me to think how

mortals blame the gods. For we are the source of evil, according to them. But they themselves, by their own willful malice, have pain beyond their portion [*moros*]" (1.32–34). For its heroic recipient, the *moros* is both a limit and an opportunity, the raw material of action; he is measured by what he does with it, even if his doing is condemned by luck to be no more than an act of the mind. And such a doom will be the rule rather than the exception, for epic is not a divine comedy but a history of inevitable disintegration, however briefly and gloriously arrested. The Homeric poet bears witness to the urgent importance of the human story, the authenticity of the values he celebrates. He is no absurdist—no Ovid *avant la lettre;* but he is a pessimist. Ultimate hope is extracted from his message only by doing it violence. The men who emerge renewed from Circe's spell will butcher the oxen of her father the solar god and pay by being swallowed up in the whirlpool Charybdis, carrying their sacred monstrosity with them into the void.[20] Odysseus himself, according to the tradition of the epic cycle, will be murdered by a son whose mother is no less than Circe. And the incorporeality of mind affirmed by the fantasy of its exile in the magic beast will not save it, as Odysseus is allowed by the poet to see for himself, from the squeaking parody of survival that awaits it in Hades.

OVID'S EPIC
Metamorphosis
as Metaphysical
Doubt

I HAVE TRIED TO SHOW THAT THE FANTASY OF TRANSFORMATION supplies the Homeric poet with an epitome of his conviction that the mind, however mortally linked to physical objects, is not itself such an object or any part of one. Ovid's conviction is the same, I think, but his use of the fantasy is very much more complex. One measure of this difference is that certain episodes in his vast poem of transformations, read out of context, are consistent with an anti-Homeric view: that mind is merely a random attitude of matter, one of the subtler shapes that emerge from the tireless doodling of the cosmos. We are specifically invited by the opening declaration of intent to contemplate "the change of shapes into new bodies" (1.1–2) — that is, of old bodily shapes into new — whose underlying incoherence and caprice are exposed in the vision of the original chaos, where "nothing kept its shape and the elemental qualities aborted each other" (1.17–18).[1] The same theme of absurd flux recurs shortly after in the grotesque reversals of the flood, with its tree-perching dolphins (1.302), aquatic tigers (1.305), and anchors biting into the greensward (1.297). Such revolutions are after all to be expected in a scheme of things whose elements, as we are reminded toward the end of the poem, are cyclic stages in the aimless thinning and thickening of matter: "They all come out of each other and decay into each other . . . and not one of them keeps its form, but nature, the improviser of things, draws on some shapes to mend others" (15.244–245, 252–253).

Among these short-lived chemical improvisations are the successive states of our labile bodies, and of the labile selves with which the poet sometimes seems to identify them: "Our own bodies too suffer a continual and unresting change, and the thing we were or are is not the thing we shall be tomorrow" (15.214ff.). Life and awareness in general, presumably, are beholden to the same physical processes as are the creatures half of mud, half of flesh arrested in various stages of ripeness by the recession of the Nile (1.416-437); or the Etruscan prophet Tages whose embryo was a clod in a ploughed field (15.553–559); or the generation sprung from giant-gore, whose mind was so nearly a function of matter that "you would know they were born out of blood" (1.162); or the whole deteriorating series of generations that ends in our own ancestral age of stone, a pedigree of which our habits are so many "proofs" (1.415). "Dank steam engenders all things; a harmony of antagonisms is fit for teeming" (1.432–433); and it may well appear that by the same token Anaxarete's stony cruelty (14.758) and the acid scoffing of Apulus (14.524ff.) are not merely figurative kin to the materials into which the offenders eventually disappear.

The disappearances themselves often seem to carry the equivalent suggestion that the persistence of the self is the persistence of a certain sort of body; but then many of the transformations are macabre travesties of the process of dying. The mother of the Heliades tries to tear away her daughters' bodies from the trees they are gradually becoming, "and with her hands breaks off the yielding branches, but from those places drops of blood trickle as from a wound. 'Have mercy, mother, I beg you,' cries out the wounded one, whoever she is, 'have mercy, I beg you. The body you are mutilating in this tree is mine. And now farewell'; over the last words comes the husk of the tree" (2.359-363). Before the dragon shape engulfs him Cadmus calls out: "Come to me, my wife, come to me, wretched as you are, and while something is left of me, touch me; take my hand while it is a hand, while the serpent has not taken possession of all of me" (4.583ff.). Clearly when there is nothing left of his familiar shape there is nothing left of Cadmus either. If the fantasy of transformation is often presented as a surreal kind of death, it is not surprising that at least once a surreal kind of death (by plague) is presented as a fantasy of transformation: "First the innards are scorched, and the sign of hidden flame is a flushing, with breath drawn in gasps. The tongue is rough and bloated with fire, the parched mouth opens to the warm winds, and the heavy air is caught at gapingly. They cannot abide a blanket or any covering but lay the vitals down on the hard ground, nor is the body cooled by the earth, but from the body the earth seethes" (7.544–560).

The generation of stone comes alive at the outset, like Pygmalion's bride, by what amounts to a chemical change in mortuary sculpture: "As indistinct as it was reminiscent, a human shape could be seen, but like the inchoate shape of unfinished marble images — yes very like roughhewn statues. But of those statues, the moist earthy part was diverted to the function of the body; what was hard and stiff changed into bone; the veins that were, remained and kept their name" (1.404–410). The random pulsations of matter virtually guarantee that, later in the poem, unfortunate descendants of the same generation are killed by a cruelly ingenious reversal of the process. The doomed Aglauros, for example, finds that she cannot get up from her chair:

She fights to rise with the trunk of her body upright, but her knee-joints are rigid, coldness eddies through her nails, her bloodless veins whiten, and like the evil cancer that keeps on spreading and creeping and adding the uninjured members to the marred, so by degrees a deadly winter came into her breast and shut up the pores and passages of life. She neither tried to speak nor, had she tried, could have cleared any path for a voice. Now stone was occupying her throat, her face was petrified; there she was now, bloodless, a statue of one in a seated pose. (2.822–831)

The transformation of Atlas into a mountain becomes the occasion for analyzing the dissolution of a person as an intricate pairing and exchange between counterparts, in which death is portrayed as a mockery of life: "The beard and hair go into forest, the shoulders and hands make chains of hills, what was a head is the peak atop the mountain, the bones turn into rock" (4.657–660). The same apparently reductionist impulse under-

lies the meticulous observation of the Ismenides as they stiffen
from suicidal grief into its monument:

> The most faithful of them all said: "I will follow my queen into
> the sea" and, poised for her dive, could not move in any direction but
> was fixed and mortised into the ledge. A second, trying to continue
> beating the breast, felt the rigor of the arms she tried. That one over
> there, having stretched out her hands by chance toward the waves of
> the sea, stretches out her hands, now as a thing of stone, toward the
> waves of the selfsame sea. As for this one, as she was clutching and
> tearing the hair from her head, you would have seen the instantaneous
> hardness of the fingers in the hair. The attitude in which each was sur-
> prised is the one in which she is arrested.   (4.551–560)

Perseus' use of the Gorgon's head against his marriage rivals is,
again, an excuse for variations on the same nightmare: "Even
then [Phineus] was struggling to look away, when his neck grew
rigid and the optic fluid solidified into rock. But the terror of the
mouth and the imploring expression and the hands palms upward and the vulnerable attitude were left in the marble" (5.232–
235). Treated this way, the fantasy of transformation tends to
reduce death to still life and life to death in motion. The distinction will seem less radical than the infatuated Pygmalion
supposes.

Transformation, however, is not always the end of self in
Ovid; in fact, the instances I have been considering obscure the
quite general agreement between the Ovidian and the Homeric
versions of the fantasy in rendering transformation as the ordeal
of a persisting awareness. For Ovid too, this awareness is not a
physical process. "The universe still wanted an animal more
sacred than these, one that could contain the depth of mind and
be lord over all the others. Humanity emerged—whether that
artificer of things, source of a world better [than it had been],
made this being of divine seed, or the newborn earth, just divided from the zenith, still harbored seeds of the sibling sky and
Prometheus mixed her with rainwater and fashioned her in the
image of the all-wielding gods" (1.76–83). (As we shall see, there
is probably more than a dash of pious fraud in this effusive
humanism.) The crucial and pervasive assumption is the
Homeric: the properties of having a mind and of having a certain sort of body may invariably coincide without thereby

needing to be the same; the possibility of their *not* coinciding is far from unthinkable, for a reader of Ovid's poem is in the business of thinking it repeatedly. This is evidently the sense of Pythagoras' remark, toward the end of the poem, that "we are not bodies only but winged souls too" (15.456–457). In particular, it will be unhelpful to talk of mind, like the Peripatetics, as the body's form; on Ovid's showing there is no more reason to call one a form than the other, and if the Peripatetic idiom expresses a truth, we should be prepared to concede the symmetrical truth that the body is the form of the mind. Ovid's Pythagoras distinctly prefers the latter way of talking: "As the pliant wax is stamped by new shapes and does not remain as it has been and does not hold the same shapes but is the selfsame thing for all that, so the soul by my doctrine is always the same but passes into one shape after another" (15.169–172). The shapes of the soul are the successive bodies with which, like wax, the soul is imprinted. The mind, in short, is a palimpsest of embodiments.

To serve this conception, the poet typically shows us a kind of transformation that corresponds no more to death than to life. This is why it is the appropriate answer to Myrrha's prayer: "You divine wills, if you exist at all, that open yourselves to those who have owned their guilt, I have deserved a grim punishment and do not refuse it. But lest I contaminate the living by survival and the dead by being dead, thrust me away from both kingdoms and, changing me, deny me life and death" (10.483–487). One major critic explains that "only a third realm, the realm of inanimate nature, could accept her unwelcome presence," and that in what follows "Ovid insists on her loss of consciousness."[2] But this quite misses the horror of what actually happens.

First Myrrha's pregnant body, with one exception, changes into a tree: "Already the growing tree had bound her heavy womb and had engulfed her breast and was beginning to cover her neck, but she did not bear with the delay. She crouched down to meet the coming wood and let her features sink under the bark. Although she has lost her former senses along with her former body, she weeps, and warm drops trickle from the tree" (10.495–500). Unfortunately for the victim, however, to lose one's former senses is not to be insensate: "The misbegotten child had grown under the trunk and was looking for a way to extricate itself from its mother. The pregnant belly distended itself in the center of the tree. The mother was racked by the burden. The surges of pain have no words to utter them, Lucina cannot be called by the voice of one in the act of bearing. Yet the tree resembles one in labor, and huddles in a stutter of sobs, awash in streaming tears" (10.503–509). Myrrha's former awareness is lost to her not because her pain is no longer really pain but on the contrary because now it is quintessential; the only organ she has left is filled with it. Ovid powerfully succeeds in showing us a tragic monstrosity, a tree with a mind entirely given over to inarticulate suffering. Ovidian transformation of this kind is deformity and alienation driven to the limit of the imaginable — solitary confinement by one's own body.

And normally what the Homeric poet asserts of *noös* is precisely what Ovid asserts of *mens*. In the grinning bear (2.481) Callisto's "former mind remained" (2.485), but her "power of speech is ravished away" (2.483), and her terrified son prepares to kill the approaching brute that "looked as if it knew him" (2.501, 504). In the deerlike Actaeon as his hunting dogs plunge after him, "nothing was left but his former mind" (3.203), along with a travesty of speech that serves only to condemn him, like the Homeric victims, to the status of an anomalous object, a metaphysical castaway in a class by itself: "He groans, and the sound he makes, however inhuman, is no sound a deer can utter" (3.237ff.). If anything validates his abortive claim that "Actaeon ego sum" (3.230), it is this isolated awareness. In the end the dogs "stand round him in a ring and, sinking their jaws in his body, tear to pieces, under the image of the false deer, their master" (3.249–250).

"The essence of Actaeon's tragedy," we have been told, "is that he combines an animal form with a human mind . . . He tries to communicate his identity to his dogs and his friends . . . and thereby only intensifies the agony of his terrible death." Callisto's story resembles Actaeon's in showing "a transformed human being . . . exposed to destruction from unsuspecting kindred and friends. The difference is that here the ultimate disasters are avoided."[3] But even if the perfunctory divine machinery by which Callisto is saved could be viewed, in a sophisticated narrative, as more than a sarcasm, brute physical disaster is a coarse measure of the "essence" of tragedy. The crucial objection, however, to describing either story as a tragedy is that these nightmares are not very much like tragedies at all; it is far easier to view them, in fact, as antitragedies in which the liturgical duties of recognition and purgation are mischievously neglected, or as comedies of invincible error in which the joke of mistaken identity is on all of us. For the "ultimate disaster" with which both tales are concerned cannot be avoided because it is not an event; it is the incurable solitude of mind of which the groaning pseudo-deer is merely the sardonic emblem.

The edge of cruelty in the comedy of transformation is sharpest, perhaps, in the farcical account of Io's reaction to her bovine incarnation: "Her effort to utter a moan achieved a moo. The sound that scared her to a frenzy was the sound of her own voice. She came to what had been her favorite playground, the banks of the Inachus; at a glimpse in the stream of her new horns [and muzzle], she took a violent fright and fled in panic from herself" (1.637–641). Restored after much suffering to her former shape, "she fears to speak lest, heiferwise—she moo" (1.745). It is not enough to say that "the effect of the cow on the woman is highly comic."[4] The object of this clever cartooning is deep alienation resulting from a sudden and thoroughgoing deformity; the humor we are being treated to here, in short, is gallows humor, and the focus of the narrative irony is the fact that among those who are prevented by Io's deformity from making full contact with her is Io herself. The effect of the cowlike body on the person it belongs to transcends comedy because the ground of the distinction between body and person eludes Io. And in this respect at least, she is not alone.

There is a sense in which Ovidian transformation, were it possible, might perhaps be expected to cure rather than cause the alienation Ovid uses it to portray. I am, let us say, deeply in doubt about you. We differ in ways that matter to me, and I cannot satisfy myself that a certain expression of yours means the same thought or feeling as it invariably does in me, or indeed that it expresses any thought or feeling at all. On the assumption that causal laws are uniform everywhere (a risky assumption in Ovid, as we shall see), I can translate this question about your expression into one about mine. If I were like you in the ways in which we now differ, would my expression still be regularly attended by the same mental event as in my actual condition? If so I can conclude that our current likenesses are sufficient conditions for the law of expression and feeling that I happen to be able to observe directly only in myself; I am now warranted in supposing that I know your mind when I note your behavior. I can of course begin to develop this warrant step by step by assimilating myself to you in each missing respect and seeing (in myself) whether the psychophysical law continues to hold, and no doubt I can find the means to make some of the required changes; but for countless others, my experiments in self-revision will proceed only with the collaboration of a sorcerer — unless I inhabit Ovid's imaginary universe, where one would at least expect that the desired assurance about other minds is no further away than a convenient transformation and an obliging god.[5]

Ovid's imaginative experiments, however, are disappointing in this respect. In the case of Phaethon's doubts about his paternity, for example, his father Apollo is more than an obliging god; if Apollo cannot convince his son he will lose him: "Are you after a sure guarantee? I am giving you a sure guarantee by fearing for you. My fatherly dread is the proof I am a father. Here, just look at my face. I only wish you could probe my chest with your eyes and catch the fatherly concern inside" (2.91–94). The power of self-transcendence, as it turns out, is not in the gift of Ovid's gods; the grammatical mood of Apollo's wish, even in a divine mouth and a fictitious universe, is the optative of what cannot conceivably be granted. The closest approach in the poem to a transformation that gives insight into otherness is the story of Teiresias' seven years as a woman; but the poet effectively dismisses the myth by putting it in the service of routine misogyny (3.318–333). Where love succeeds, as in the story of Baucis and Philemon (8.620–724), the circumstances are congenial, and where the circumstances are problematic, as with the jealousies of Cephalus and Procris (7.697–752, 797–862), the results are not reassuring. The accompanying transformations, if any, lead either to the usual solitary confinement of the victims (Baucis and Philemon, 8.716–719) or to a sentimental but mindless imitation of rapport (Ceyx and Alcyone as heraldic birds of matrimony, 11.742–748). Baucis and

Philemon, in short, are the exception that proves the rule – the only salvageable (self-transcending) mortals in a world destined for the flood.

But I have been taking it for granted that Ovidian transformation can be a universal solvent of differences, and it cannot. There is a whole range of facts about me – my past – that I cannot change even in imagination; it is imaginable that I was born on a day other than my actual birthday, but not that at some moment my birthday should have become a different day. It is imaginable that Actaeon should stop having his current shape, but not that he should stop having had such a shape. The victims of Ovidian transformation are excluded by their past from understanding, by assimilation, anything but their own forlorn uniqueness; and even here, in the ordeal of Narcissus, Ovid finds unsettling things to show us.

At the outset Narcissus finds himself passionately drawn to a face and body unaccountably but hopelessly divided from his own by the surface of the spring – "not a vast ocean or a road or mountains or city ramparts with barred gates, but trifling water" (3.448ff.). He then finds that the coveted body is his, and that his misfortune is exactly the opposite of separation: "My plenty is what makes me poor" (3.465). Finally, we hear that he would be reconciled to his own death if it did not mean the death of his beloved, with whom he shares not only a body but a soul: "My death is no affliction to me. With death I lay down grief. But this dear one – I could wish he might endure longer. As it is, the two of us, in total sympathy, will die in a single soul" (3.471–473). This final transcendence of lust – one might almost call it altruism – is not unanticipated. Narcissus' frustration is at least as sentimental as it is erotic: "When I laugh you give me a smile; I've noticed your tears too as I weep. And as far as I can guess by the movement of your beautiful mouth you are sending me answers that miscarry before they can reach my ears" (3.459–462). In this "ingenious exercise in paradox"[6] the most ingenious paradox of all is Narcissus' dying conviction that he is pining not for himself but for someone else from whom he does not differ in any respect. In his madness (3.494), Narcissus ends by conceiving of himself and his all-too-intimate companion as an exception to the Law of the Identity of Indiscernibles.[7] But the point of that law is that exceptions – things not the same that

have all their properties in common — not only cannot be produced but cannot be conceived. Narcissus' ill-starred piece of
conceiving is not merely a paradox whose ingenuity we can
relish in detachment, but a piece of subversion. The target is an
intuitive notion of sameness (and selfhood) that for all its
unclarity is hard if not impossible to do without: to be an individual is somehow to be unique, as the partners in Narcissus'
love affair so unhappily fail to be.

Uniqueness may consist (as here) in the totality of one's
properties or only of one's memories or one's locations from
moment to moment; the tampering with such criteria that goes
on in Roman comedy seems to reflect a subversive impulse
closely akin to Ovid's, and a brief look at an exchange in
Plautus' *Amphitruo* may show something about the comic
energy of both. Amphitruo's slave Sosia encounters a duplicate
who shares his intimate memories, and whose itinerary to date,
like his own, is apparently continuous with that of the past individual both claim to be: "By Pollux, you'll certainly never get
me to be anyone else's but ours [that is, the Sosia of this
household]" ("Certe edepol tu me *alienabis* numquam quin
noster siem"). But the oath on the identical twin Pollux proves
ominous; as the double passes one test of Sosianitude after
another, Sosia's confidence gradually evaporates:

By Pollux, when I study that fellow and then go over my own
form, just as I am — I've often looked in the mirror — he is my spitting
image; he also has a widebrimmed chapeau. He has on the same outfit, exactly. His calf, his foot, height, hairdo, eyes nose lips cheek chin
beard neck. The whole thing. Why go on? If his back has whipmarks,
there's no resemblance closer than this resemblance. But when *I think*
about it, I personally *am* certainly the same as I ever was [sed quom
cogito, equidem certo idem *sum* qui semper fui]. I know my master, I
know our premises. I am sound in my wits and my wisdom.

But these mental criteria, too, turn out to be duplicated in un-
nerving detail, and the ironic result — from which Sosia boasted
his immunity at the outset — is a crisis of alienation: "Undying
gods, protect me I beg you. At what point did *I* stop existing —
get changed — lose my shape? Or was it I who left myself to that
fellow but happened to forget about it? Because he is the current
proprietor of the whole image that was mine before."

It is true that the problem is tainted by a deception; the other Sosia is not a double but merely Mercury in disguise. And it is equally true that Latin *alienatio*, in a slave expecting shortly to be masterless — to be in fact of indeterminate status — suggests the hazards of freedom as readily as those of madness. If the speaker's memory has indeed been failing him, then Sosia's master need not also be his; come to think of it — he may be his own master. Yet, taken as a hypothesis, the illusion has given us good reason to suspect that our criteria of identity, as they stand, are themselves illusory. A recent student of such criteria remarks, with justice, that "the problem is a *serious* one. One might think of such factors as memory claims, personality, spatiotemporal continuity, and some kind of causal conditions as responsible for my identity through time; but if I divided, surely each resultant person could stand in all of these relations to the original person."[8] Where is the "seriousness" in all of this? It does not happen, of course, that people divide. And perhaps it always happens that things standing in such relations are identical. But this is cold comfort if, as the visions of Narcissus and Sosia wickedly suggest, our notion of identity itself is inexplicable; if it has no logical connection with the notions on which we fall back to explicate it; if (in short) we do not know what it is to be a self.

The *result* of Ovidian transformation is an intellectual subversion of much the same kind. Typically, individuals of one species turn not into individuals of another, but simply into other species. The effect is achieved by grammatical sleight of hand: singular sentences are allowed to merge into general, proper nouns into common, personal history into natural history. Thus we seem to be learning about Progne and Philomela when we hear that, in the swiftness of their escape from Tereus, "you would think their bodies were being lifted by wings — they *were* being lifted by wings" (6.667–668). Now the narrative abruptly shifts into what at first appears to be the historical present: "One of the two seeks the woods, the other comes up on the roofs of houses." But in the next sentence, what seemed to be the present tense of vivid narrative turns out to have been the tenseless present of zoological generalization; we have been hearing about habitats, not events, and are now informed about characteristic plumage: "To this day the marks of gore have not passed out of its [that is, any nightingale's] breast, and its feathers are stamped with blood" (3.669–670). As for the sisters' enraged pursuer Tereus, "with the swiftness of his grief and craving for revenge he turns into the crested bird whose immoderate beak projects in a lengthy spear. The bird's name [the common noun denoting any member of the species] is 'hoopoe,' and its face seems to be equipped with a weapon" (3.670–674). Again, we watch Picus trying to escape the rebuffed and vengeful Circe: "He is surprised at the unusual speed of his running. He saw feathers on his body, and out of resentment that in his person a new bird is being added to the forests of Latium, he impales the wild oaks with his hard beak . . . The wings absorb the crimson of his robe; what had been a brooch, the gold that had bitten his mantle, becomes plumage, his throat is girded with tawny gold, and no trait of his former self remains to Picus but the name" (14.388–395). As we are reminded at last that "picus" is really a common noun, the alchemy of grammar completes the transformation of the hero, not into a particular woodpecker, but into the woodpecker in general.

Ovid's treatment of the fantasy of transformation undermines the notion of personal identity in still another way. Whether the victim divides like Picus into a new species or joins a familiar one, his new form stands for a passion by which, in the end, he has been fully absorbed. Thus Cyparissus becomes the funereal tree after he rejects all consolation and prays "to mourn for all time" (10.135). "You will be mourned by me, mourn others, and attend those who mourn," says Apollo (10.141–142). Cyparissus has been refined into an archetype of bereavement. Spurned by the god of the sun, Clytie becomes an archetype of unrequited love, the species heliotrope: "She turns to the sun and, changed as she is, is unchanged in love" (4.270). Aesacus has caused the accidental death of Hesperie and is sentenced to be nothing but his own remorse, for the goddess of the sea refuses to connive at his suicide:

The lover scorns to be forced to live in spite of himself, scorns that anything should stand in the way of a soul that would issue from the home of its desolation; and when he has taken on new wings at the shoulders he flies up and again sends his body onto the levels of the ocean. His feathers lighten the fall. Aesacus raves and goes off head first into the deep and assails again, without end, the passage to death. Love has unfleshed him, leaving legs that are one long stretch from joint to joint, and a long neck; his head is a long way from his body. He loves the sea and is named after his habit of diving into it. (11.787–795).

The life of the diver bird is a pantomime of the suicidal impulse to which Aesacus has been reduced.

Again, Erysichthon's bottomless hunger becomes a natural force, "like the sea that receives its rivers from the whole earth and is not filled by their waters, and like the greedy fire that never rejects nourishment, and incinerates countless torches; the more the supply the more the demand, and its gorge is the wider by its very engorgement" (8.835–839). What remains in the end is a hieroglyphic emblem of hunger: "He begins to rip his own limbs to pieces with rending jaws and, in his wretchedness, was building up his body by tearing it down" (8.877–878). The suggestion here, as in all these instances, is that the victim has been refined into an abstraction, in this case of infinite hunger; Ovid tells us that Erysichthon has been embraced "with both arms" (8.818) by the property of Hunger, which is also presented to us as a paradigmatic figure, "in a rocky field uprooting scanty grass with her nails and teeth . . . The skin hard (you could see the vitals through it); the bones were sticking out dehydrated under the bent loins. In place of a belly there was the belly's place" (8.799–800, 803ff.). If a genuine individual cannot possibly be a species, it is equally impossible for an individual to be or become a property. In Chapter 6 I shall argue that Spenser appropriates the same paradoxical transformation to say something affirmative about the nature and destiny of the self. Here the contextual evidence of negative intention, as we shall see, is substantial: the self baffles our categories; the Apollonian injunction to know it is no more than a taunt, for it cannot be known.

I have tried to establish that the fantasy of transformation, in Ovid's treatment, is the story of the self as it endures a catastrophic physical change, a change sometimes attended by a loss of awareness and hence in effect by death; sometimes by the persistence of a mind alienated from all selves including the self it belongs to. But Ovid broadens his inquiry into the tragicomedy of personhood by broadening his notion of transformation to include catastrophic mental change of the sort we are (rightly or wrongly) inclined to classify as an act (in contradistinction to mere events): the act of will or of "making up one's mind" (in Latin idiom, *applicatio animi*). Ovid lets us violate the privacy of a mind in the process of changing itself — or is it rather of being changed? The resulting transformation, in its own way, is quite as arbitrary as the physical transformations that surround it — a mechanical contest of strength among contrary stimuli: "Before the eyes [of Medea as she hesitates between love for Jason and duty to her father] right and loyalty and shame had taken up their stand, and desire was just retreating in defeat" (7.72–73).

As it happens, Medea's resolve turns out to be false, for Ovid's subject is choice in bondage not merely to force but to accident. Thus we are often treated to unstable equilibria masquerading as free will at the point of being exercised. On the verge of incest Myrrha "sometimes despairs and sometimes wants to venture; is ashamed; desires; fails to find what she should do, and like an axe-riven trunk when the last blow is yet to come and it is moot which way it will fall and there is danger from every side: the mind tired out by contrasting wounds tends in its frailty this way and that and takes a measure of stress in each direction" (10.371–376). In the same way Althaea is momentarily poised between vengeance for her brothers and mercy toward her son: "Just as a ship seized by the wind and by a current opposite to the wind feels a double force and is uncertain, heeding both: so Althaea wavers in a wild ambivalence, and by turns subdues her anger and eggs on the anger she has subdued" (8.470–474). Whether human choice is caused or causeless in Ovid — the fiat of leverage or dice — "wrong" choice on his showing clearly cannot be palliated in the Stoic manner as misguided choice; "if I were capable of it," argues Medea with pathetic lucidity, "I should be sane. But I am tilted against my will by a strange force. Desire urges one course, the mind another. I see the better, approve the better — and follow the worse" (7.18–21). Sooner or later in the course of rationalizations that are often comically ingenious, the speakers of Ovidian monologue regularly say or imply with Medea that "no ignorance of the truth is seducing me" (7.92–93).

It would be misleading, however, to join one recent critic in supposing that in such episodes "the unity of the self is destroyed from the inside by the pitting of contrary feelings against each other," or that Ovidian monologues like those of Medea, Scylla, Althaea, Byblis, and Myrrha are to be contrasted with their counterparts in Euripides: "In the Greek tragedian these pieces have a distinct explanatory value, whereas in the Latin poet their essential object is the portrayal of the inner division of being."[9] This line of argument rests on a fallacy; it is true that the same action cannot simultaneously repel and attract a single person in the same respect, but it does not follow, for example, that Medea's simultaneous eagerness and reluctance to help Jason need to be parceled out between two Medeas rather than two expected consequences of such help, the one agreeable, the other not. In general, the mere fact that *mens* and *cupido* (7.19–20) are two functions need not double the self that performs both; necessity simply does not assign properties by the rule of one to a customer. If there were truth in the schizophrenia interpretation of the Ovidian monologues, it is not at all clear why Ovid's precedents in this vein should not yield to the same interpretation. The suggestion of mechanical determination is equally plain in the climactic soliloquy of Euripides' Medea, for example, and as in Ovid the operative psychological term sometimes denotes a faculty or stimulus and sometimes the person under its influence: "*Thymos* [that is, my urge to vengeance] is too strong for my counsels"; "Do not, you *thymos* [that is, do not, vengeful Medea], venture on this work."[10]

It is not surprising to find a version of the schizophrenia theory, if not in Euripidean, at least in Homeric criticism: "At first it might be suspected that *thymos* and *noös* are nothing more than the parts of the soul, such as we know them from Plato's psychology. But these parts presuppose a psychic whole of which Homer has no cognizance." "Homeric man has no unified concept of what we call 'soul' or 'personality.' "; "For Homeric man the *thymos* tends not to be felt as part of the self; it appears as an independent inner voice."[11] But in the Homeric case, the text explicitly disconfirms the schizophrenia interpretation. In each of the *Iliad's* four major deliberative soliloquies the same pair of formulaic lines marks respectively the introduction and the climax of the sequence: "In his depression he spoke to

his valiant *thymos*"; "But why has my *thymos* been talking of
these things with me?"[12] Clearly the "he" of the first line is identical with the "*thymos*" of the second, and the "*thymos*" of the
first line with the "me" of the second. The *thymos*, in short, is
both the speaker and the person addressed; it is simply the self
named by a description that fits the emotional transformation
being portrayed. The fallacy of taking the schizophrenia view
for granted, here as with Ovid, is to suppose that what has more
than one property must be more than one thing. In all three portraits of the will in crisis — Ovid's, Euripides', and Homer's — the
unity of the self is not in question precisely because its lonely
oneness is the essence of its ordeal. Ovid's challenge, in the vision of Narcissus, is not to the unity of the self but to our complacent assumption that common sense or reason enables us to
understand that unity.

The crisis of will, in the tradition I have been considering,
is a catastrophic and arbitrary *transformation* of the self in its
most intimate — that is, its mental — aspect, and this I think is
why Ovid chooses to associate that crisis with the fantasy that
recurs most insistently in his poem. The victim of the Ovidian
predicament in general is naked to the caprice not only of matter but of mind. As we look on at the monstrous Actaeon we are
assured that "only his former mind persisted" (3.203). What follows, in a brief sequence of *erlebte Rede* — a fusion of third-person narrative with first-person frame of reference — is the record
of an abortive inner transformation: "What is he to do? Seek
once more his house, the palace of a king? Hide in the woods?
Embarrassment thwarts the one choice, fear the other. While he
hesitates, the dogs have seen him" (3.204ff.).

There is another dimension to the arbitrariness of the act of
will as Ovid portrays it; the temptation of a Byblis or a Myrrha
would be pointless if we did not agree that the object of their
fascination is evil, and that our way of applying terms like "evil"
is not arbitrary. But this is among the uncomfortable questions
that Ovid's stories refuse to ignore. Is it possible that, like the intuition of personal identity, moral intuitions are not backed by
a rational criterion? Is evil reducible to taboo? What beyond
prohibition, for example, does the wrongness of incest amount
to? Part of the motivation for Ovid's choice of this example was
no doubt the opportunity it offered for the elaboration of dis-

orienting paradox; the partners in incest, like those in the affair of Narcissus, are estranged by having too much in common; "Because he is already mine, he is not mine," Myrrha complains of her father; "nearness itself is my undoing" (10.339-340). Byblis wishes "that the gods might cause us [herself and her brother] to have all things in common but our ancestry" (9.490-491). This flirtation with absurdity, however, is a stylistic reflection of the more fundamental absurdity of a moral principle rooted in a "bond of nature" (10.353) of which nature seems to be strangely oblivious: "Human meddling has passed grudging laws, and what nature leaves free, the grudging laws forbid. But there are tribes, they say, in which son and mother couple, daughter and father, that the affection of kindred may grow by the twinning of loves. Unhappy that I am, that by luck I was not born there, and am injured by the accident of place" (10.329-335).

It is true that Myrrha's argument is self-serving, but the cultural premise on which it turns is a commonplace of ancient anthropology, and there is nothing in Myrrha's speech or its context that discredits her conclusion; on the contrary, the teller of her tale—the Thracian Orpheus—has misgivings about advertising an act that may not, after all, be greeted with spontaneous distaste: "I shall sing ominous things; stay away, fathers and daughters, far away! Or if my songs beguile your minds, in this instance let me lack credit, do not believe the deed was done; or if you believe, believe its punishment as well" (10.300-303). Orpheus goes on to concede in effect that what is unnatural, in the strict sense, is hardly likely to require such powerful deterrence: "If nature, however, allows this crime to appear, I am glad for the tribes of Thrace and for this region of ours; I am glad for this land, that it is far from those domains that begot so great an enormity" (10.304-307). The country that inspires these congratulations is of course the country of the bloodthirsty Tereus, Diomedes, and Polymestor, with whose enormities Ovid regales us elsewhere in his poem; it is a place whose reputation for atrocities, including human sacrifice, makes a huge and pointed joke of Orpheus' complacence; it is also, as we are informed a little earlier, the home of the Thracian pederasty introduced by none other than the complacent speaker himself (10.83ff.), whose idea of a natural act to contrast with Myrrha's abomination is the suicide by which Erigone saw fit to express her grief for her father Icarius (10.450–451). And it would seem that on Orpheus' view of moral failure, which is otherwise stridently explicit, the drunkenness and adulterousness of Myrrha's father, which allowed her nurse to trick him into incest (10.435–443), do not disqualify him from judging his daughter in righteous outrage and trying to carry out a sentence of death (10.474–475). All this is far from encouraging us to suppose that the grounds of moral judgment are anything more universal or less arbitrary than individual taste, or at best the custom of the society we are born into.[13]

The relativistic implications of what Myrrha calls "the accident of place" have a temporal analogue in which Ovid takes a special interest: the transformation in the moral perception of a single society by which a total ethos that has always been the model of the highest good gradually yields to a wholly different notion of how life is to be lived. In the moral sphere, the sorceress to blame for emerging monstrosity is apt to be the caprice of history: "You who are that vanquisher of so many men, Achilles, have been vanquished by the Grecian wife's cringing abductor . . . Now that dread of the Trojans, glory and guardian of Hellas, son of Aeacus, chief unsurpassable in war, has been consumed. The god who made his armor made his pyre. Now he is ash, and what is left of so great an Achilles is some little thing that cannot easily fill an urn" (12.608–609, 612–615). This ludicrous transformation ushers in the age of the new man, the man who contrives to win the armor of Achilles and yet (if we are to believe the rival claimant) is altogether unworthy of the prize.

Ajax' bill of particulars against Ulysses is in effect a baffled protest of the old order against the new. Ulysses is the "preacher of crimes" who instigated the abandonment of Philoctetes (13.45–54), who falsely convicted Palamedes of high treason in revenge for the latter's exposure of his evasion of military service (13.56–60), who deserted Nestor in battle (13.65ff.) and pretended to be incapacitated by his wounds so as to be rescued by none other than Ajax (13.73–81). In his reply Ulysses does not condescend to notice the charge of deserting Nestor or abjectly clinging to Ajax. If he evaded military service to spare Penelope, he has the illustrious precedent of Achilles' similar act of tenderness toward Thetis: "I do not fear at all — if now I cannot ward it off — a criminal reproach that I have in common with so great a man" (13.303–304). As for the alleged betrayals of Palamedes and Philoctetes, if Ulysses' conduct of these affairs was criminal, the generals who sanctioned it at the time are accomplices after the fact, and unfortunately for Ajax, they are also the sitting judges in the present case (13.307–319).

Ulysses devotes most of his rebuttal to his positive claim on the generals' favor: a kind of service to the state that is both indispensable and far too subtle for the likes of his brawny rival. Ulysses has the credit of persuading Agamemnon to sacrifice his daughter to the defeat of Troy, to consider "public utility" and "weigh the honor against the blood" (13.191–192). Ulysses relieved Agamemnon of the trying duty of overcoming the suspicions of a mother "who needed to be got round by guile and not by exhortation" (13.193–194). Ulysses massacred Rhesus and his men in a nocturnal raid (13.249–250) and stole the mystic palladium from the Trojan citadel (13.337–338, 344–345). The mention of this last exploit gives the orator an opportunity to play with a favorite form of argument: "At the moment when I forced Troy to be conquerable, at that moment I conquered Troy" (13.349). By parity of reasoning, since it was Ulysses who recruited Achilles, Achilles' deeds of valor belong to his recruiter (13.171), and since it was Ulysses who talked Ajax out of obeying Agamemnon's premature command to his allies to leave Troy, Ulysses can count Ajax' subsequent prowess as his own (13.236).

The significance of Ulysses' prize, in Ovid's ironic formulation, is that "the power of eloquence was disclosed by the outcome; the arms of a man of valor were won by a man of wit" (13.382–383). Whether they believe Ulysses or not, and perhaps especially if they do not, his masters are bound to appreciate the usefulness of so consummately guileful a sophist; and Ulysses' guile is not limited to sophistry. He is the principal Greek architect of the "utility" to which he habitually appeals (13.188, 191, 211, 215, 362), and it is clear that though he would confine his judges to a choice between his own cultivated intelligence and the philistine dullness of his opponent (13.135ff., 290, 295, 363), the real antithesis to the criterion of utility is the criterion of glory by which "Achilles is equal to himself and feels not the emptiness of Hades" (12.619). But in the episode immediately following the arms debate, Ovid introduces us to an Achilles who feels the emptiness of Hades all too acutely, as the Achaean fleet is about to set sail from Troy: "Suddenly, as grand as he used to be while he lived, from the widely sundered earth issues Achilles; like one who threatens, he was wearing again the look of that moment at which in his rage, with unjust sword, he had made for Agamemnon. 'Are you leaving,' he said 'without a thought for me, Achaeans? Has the gratitude due my valor been buried along with me? Do not do so! And that my grave not be unhonored, let the sacrifice of Polyxena appease the ghost of Achilles' " (13.441–448).[14]

Presumably the point of saying that Achilles looked the same once before when he did something unjust in defense of his glory is to hint that his current demand for glory (on pain of unspecified reprisals) is likewise unjust, and that coming from him it is not at all surprising; glory is no truer a moral measure than utility. But this throws us back on our sentiment that *we* have a measure of our own. No doubt the contrast between the ugliness of Achilles' aspiration and the proud calm with which Polyxena submits to her death is designed by Ovid to reinforce this sentiment. But the whole spectacle is ambiguous. The Achaeans themselves are invited by their fallen comrade to think that Polyxena's death, while profoundly unfortunate, is necessary and even just; this is apparently the view of her weeping executioner, Achilles' son. With executioners who are already weeping, an appeal to moral sentiment does not promise to take us very far. Polyxena herself supplies us with an alternative to such an appeal as well as to glory and utility: the will of the gods, which she says can never be appeased by human sacrifice (13.461). But Polyxena is mistaken; the sacrifice of Iphigenia, for which Ulysses has just been proudly taking the credit, was demanded not by the ghost of a hero but by the Olympian Diana.

Ovid's parody of epic narrative is consistent with the moral relativism I have been trying to illustrate; violence is presented to us as an arabesque of uninterpreted facts among which moral facts (if any) are numbingly elusive.

Look over here: Rhoetus is grabbing up, ablaze from the altar's center, a plumtree torch. He grazes Charaxus' temples on the right side — temples sheltered by tawny hair. Seized like a parched crop by the greedy flame, his hair burned and in the wound singed blood gave a fearful hissing sound such as redhot iron often gives when — drawn out by the smith with curved tongs and lowered into the tank — it screeches all the more and, plunged in the lukewarm water, hisses on. (12.271–279)

By the valor of Pirithous, they say, Lycus fell; Chromis as well by the valor of Pirithous. But both give a lesser glory to the winner than was given by Dictys and Helops, Helops run through by a spear that made a passage from temple to temple, launched through the right ear and piercing to the left. Dictys, slipping down from a cleft hilltop as he flees in panic from the son of Ixion in pursuit, is falling down headfirst. With the weight of his body he broke a giant ash and girdled it, once broken, with his loins. (12.332–340)

To Dorylas I [Nestor] said (for courage gave me strength): "See how much your [helmet] horns yield to my iron"; and I flung the spear. When he could not dodge it he put his hand in the way of the brow destined to suffer the wound. Together with the brow, the hand was impaled. There is a shout; but as he stopped overcome with the bitter wound Peleus (who was standing nearby) struck him with his sword in the middle of his abdomen. He lunged forward and in his fury dragged along his bowels on the ground, and what he dragged he stomped, and what he stomped he ruptured, and snarling up his legs in it, collapsed on an empty abdomen. (12.383–392)

And you, Achilles, do not suppose that Mopsus son of Ampyx was merely an oracle. By the spear of Mopsus the centaur Hodites was struck down and tried and failed to speak, tongue nailed to chin and chin to throat. (12.455–458)

"Now," said Caeneus, "let us test your body with our iron," and down into the shoulders to the hilt he sent his doom-bearing sword, and moved it groping into the vitals and rotated it with his hand, making a wound within a wound. (12.490–493)

One critic complains (as if these were inadvertencies) that Ovid's "death scenes are only grotesque," generating "neither sympathy nor sincere repugnance."[15] But this is surely the point. War is presented to us as a fantasy of transformations — dismemberments so bizarre and indiscriminate and clinically observed as to baffle moral interpretation. Our disapproval (which Ovid no doubt shares) is made to seem an affectation with no more factual import than the queasy reflexes of taste.

The impresarios of our fantasies and transformations in Ovid's poem are demons whose exploits occupy a number of his studied exercises in description. If the orator Ulysses, prepared to speak on both sides of any question, is the saboteur of our confidence in the existence of *moral* facts, every demon illusionist is a Ulysses of the *physical* domain.

Some have the power to pass into more than one shape — as you do, Proteus, tenant of the land-embracing sea. For sometimes they have seen you as a youth, sometimes as a lion. Now a rampaging boar, now you were the sort of snake they dreaded to have touched. Sometimes horns would make you a bull; often you could seem a rock, often a tree. Sometimes you mimicked the face of the limpid waters and would be a river, sometimes you would oppose the water and be a fire. And the wife of Autolycus . . . had no less power. (8.730–739)

Ovid's water demons inevitably share the illusionary talents of their element; Thetis, until she is betrayed by her colleague Proteus, manages to fend off an uninvited lover by the arbitrary manipulation of appearances: "Unless you [Thetis] had resorted to your familiar arts by continual varying of shape, he would have succeeded not only in daring but in doing. But at one moment the bird was you — but he kept holding the bird. At another you were the massive tree — clinging to the tree was Peleus. The third shape was the dappled tiger's; that one scared off the son of Aeacus, and he loosened his arms from your body" (11.241–246). Not inappropriately the same gift runs in the family of Ulysses himself, the great-grandson of the god of thieves and the grandson of the notorious mountebank who steals not only people's goods but (like his wife) their perceptions as well — "Autolycus, the wizard of larceny, who habitually made white of black and black of white, his father's worthy apprentice" (11.313ff.).

The disconcerting suggestion implicit in these episodes becomes explicit in others; for the mind in sleep, it turns out, is an element quite like water, with its own versions of Proteus and the rest. Its presiding "craftsman and copyist of form" (11.634–

638) is the being that goes by the uninstructive name of Morpheus, "the Things of Shapes," and that, for all we can ever know of it, might just as aptly be named Amorpheus, the thing with no essence at all. He is, we are unhelpfully told, the person who wasn't there, just as his triplet Ikelos, "the Resembler," is the evanescent beast (11.638–641), and the third brother Phantasos, "the Imaginist," is the mockery of this or that inanimate object (11.641–643). And it is clear enough that the brothers' multiplicity is as much as mockery as their trade. What the brothers are to perception, the creatures of Fama—the things people tell each other (or themselves)—are to judgment; in the house of Fame "a mingling of truths and fabrications mills about at random" (12.54). The confusion of true and false opinion is matched by the confusion of perception and misperception—by the existence of "dreams that by mimicry come exactly even with real shapes" (11.626). The former confusion is the ground of the ancient skeptical doctrine of *isosthenia*, the ultimate indifference and futility of all issues of fact; the latter is the ground of the tendency in ancient skepticism, perhaps especially that of Carneades, to think of the objects of ordinary sense experience as the fictions of a theory precariously vindicated by mere convenience.

"The logical result of the Ovidian conception," remarks a recent critic, "is a universal doubt regarding the essence of things."[16] I think we may recognize in the triune person of Phantasos the culprit in this tale of the theft of the capacity to believe. The mind is at the mercy of *phantasia*—the continuum of its imagery—and the Stoic notion of a *phantasia kataleptiké*, an image that holds reality in a mental fist, is a piece of hortatory nonsense. (This is the view of Carneades, and Ovid's agreement with him on this and other points, as I shall have a chance to illustrate again a bit further on, is characteristic and important.) Otis has shrewdly remarked that "the horrible death of Pentheus [3.712–733] . . . recalls most pathetically the death of . . . Actaeon. Like him, Pentheus is unable to communicate with his human assailants and, like him also, he is forced in his dismemberment to beg for mercy without the human means to do so . . . Though Pentheus is not in fact an animal . . . he appears as such to the frenzied women."[17] The underlying subject of this recurring Ovidian nightmare, I think, is the hopeless entrapment of mind: like the mind of Actaeon, by the body; like those of Pentheus' tormentors, by appearances. In this connection it is sobering to consider the observation of a recent experimental psychologist that "the physiological data [of the dream state] describe a central nervous system that is in fact behaving as if it were receiving a high level of sensory input from the environment." This imaginary environment — imaginary from the vantage point of the experimenter, at least — "presents an essentially complete visual field . . . Just as in the waking state, all sensory modalities are ordinarily present in the dream . . . with many details in each mode."[18] It is all too tempting to yield to Ovidian mischief here, to remind the experimenter that his observations too are parts of "an essentially complete perceptual field," and to ask him what conceivable observation of his would exclude the possibility that the victim of Phantasos is not his apparent subject but himself.

Phantasos is not the only prankish despot among the Ovidian gods. The dismemberment of Pentheus, for example, is the illusionary demon's work on behalf of Bacchus and represents the latter's notion of penal justice. Juno, again with the aid of hallucination, has Learchus dismembered by his father (4.513-519), and indulges her chronic jealousy by sadistically delaying the delivery of Alcmene's child (9.284, 296, 308-309) and causing Semele to be incinerated by what was to be an act of love (3.263-266). But this latter exploit is merely Juno's homage to the vindictive ingenuity of Diana, whose way of correcting Actaeon's manners is treated by the gods, with an Ovidian shrug, as a debatable issue: "Gossip went both ways; some thought the goddess more violent than was just, others commend her, calling her worthy of her austere maidenhood. Both sides find reasons" (3.253ff.).

With much the same indifference to which reasons are right we find the son of Venus denying that he was the cause of the incestuous derangement punished so cruelly in Myrrha (10.311-312), only to be told a little later that Venus' doomed fascination with Myrrha's son was a judgment on the goddess for the passion of Myrrha (10.524); and again, the same furies that help instigate Myrrha's obsession (on another account of its cause, 10.313-314) are officially charged with its punishment (10.349ff.). Apollo, who questions the justice of Jupiter's sum-mary execution of Phaethon (2.393), further demonstrates his taste for juridical niceties by condemning his challenger in a musical competition to a leisurely death by flaying (6.385–391). But the challenger is paying for having *lost* to the god of the sun; the prize of *winning* a contest (again in artisanship) with the goddess of wisdom is to be struck thrice on the forehead and rescued from an act of mortal despair only to be converted into a creature of immortal despair: "Live on, but keep on hanging" (6.135). Arachne achieves her masterpiece and her doom simply by recording the rapes committed by male members of the pantheon, who use their protean gift for purposes exactly opposite to those of Thetis (6.103–126); and it is one ironic feature of Ovidian theodicy that divine power is defended, if at all, from the charge not of capricious abuse but of limitation.[19] It is not true, for example, as the slanderous Pierides maintain, that the Olympians hid in fear of Typhoeus in the beast avatars of Egyptian cult (5.325–331); and at the same time the freethinking Pirithous is quite wrong to make light of just such divine gifts of concealment: "You think the gods too powerful, if indeed they add shapes and subtract them" (8.614–615). The pious retort of Lelex, "ripe in spirit and years" (8.617), is that "the power of heaven is measureless and unbounded, and a divine wish is a divine deed" (8.618–619).

Divine reward in Ovid is as much a whim of power as divine punishment: the deification of Acis (13.885–886), Ino (4.539–541), and Hercules (9.247), the good luck of Telethusa (9.684–701) and Philemon and Baucis (8.724) show the gods in an appreciative mood, but it is a mood rather than an expression of settled principle, and often it is sardonically ambiguous. The beatific deaths of Philemon and Baucis are indistinguishable, in the horror of their actual detail, from those of Myrrha and the Heliades — a cancerous and strangling growth of leafy bark in each case. When Agamemnon threatens to abduct the daughters of Anius, their prayer for rescue is answered by transformation into doves, though oddly there is little to choose between the rescue and the rape: " 'Bring help, father Bacchus,' they said, and the author of their gift brought help — if miraculous destruction is called help" (13.669–671).

It is of course possible, at the cost of holding Ovid to be incoherent and fatuous, to take these celebrations of divine munificence without irony. Thus Hercules' deification "is represented as an act of justice." The idyll of Baucis and Philemon moves in a "world of crystal-clear theodicy" discontinuous with "the world of Medea or of Ceyx and Alcyone."[20] But then how does one explain the stylistic fact that the former idyll "has a coldness and formality that belie its message"?[21] It will not answer the difficulty to speak of the poet's "distaste for moralism," especially if one goes on (quite properly, in my view) to speak of Ovid's belief in "an essentially irreformable human nature" and of his "hankering for deities that are neither comic nor cruel, for love that is neither pathological nor perverse," for "conjugal love" as "the ethical apex of Ovid's amatory scale."[22] These are the hankerings of an inveterate if despairing moralist and of an embittered theologian for whom the heavens are empty only of compassion.

The same critic argues that the change of Ceyx and Alcyone to halcyon birds shows us "human tragedy converted into cosmic benevolence." The fantasy of transformation, on this view, "is the *deus ex machina* that softens the horrors of unrestrained sex and rewards the virtue of true love." For Ovid "the nonhuman or subhuman . . . shared the beneficence as well as the malice of man. This . . . is the deeper meaning of the *Ceyx and Alcyone*." "Beyond the usual anthropomorphism of mythology there lay a much more philosophic anthropomorphism by which nature as such . . . could be invested with human feeling and sympathy."[23] But the retrieval of disaster by a frankly decorative fantasy is a very strange way of expressing a cosmic hope, much less a seriously intended panpsychism; and the reduction of human beings to the mindless quintessence of their ruling passions is an equally strange way of softening the horror, much less of exalting the tenderness, of such passions. Whatever — if anything — the Ovidian gods symbolize, their spectacular fits of generosity are entirely consistent with what is classified in ancient political philosophy as the most efficient and durable form of tyranny. "It will promote the security of a tyrant's regime," Aristotle observes, "to make it more like a kingship, retaining one thing alone — the power to rule over the willing and the unwilling alike; for to surrender this is to surrender one's tyranny as well." The cautious tyrant must "appear not harsh but august in such sort that those who meet him do

not so much dread as revere him." Accordingly "he must so far
honor those who are good at anything that they believe they
would never be more lavishly honored by citizens under the rule
of their own laws." The scientific tyrant is thus both
hemichrestos and *hemiponeros* — semibountiful and semimalig-
nant. So long as he maintains his two dispensations, it will matter little if, as with Ovid's gods, the principle of dispensation is
pure caprice. Cicero favors us with the equivalent paradox that
"the tyrant is the worst kind of ruler and the nearest kin to the
best."[24]

It is clear enough that Ovidian theology is irreverent; but
Otis warns us against taking the irreverence to be theology. In
his view Ovid's gods are "quite ordinary men and women of his
own time." "Such 'gods' are, after all, only thinly disguised men
and women, especially such men and women as hold positions
of power and authority."[25] But this explanation of Ovid's divine
machinery makes his gods redundant; for if their stories are to
be mere generalizations about human tyranny, sexual
hypocrisy, and superciliousness, he can and does choose myths
about *human* roués and despots. Elsewhere in his study Otis
makes the quite different suggestion that Ovid's Olympus is a
"fantasy world" and "not the true reality." This is supposed to
come out in the fact that Olympians sometimes "act by intermediaries," and that in at least one episode "the plastically
conceived gods . . . are indifferent" to human affairs, whereas
the sympathetic gods "are but names for the forces of nature."[26]
But those gods who are identified with natural forces are by the
same token charter members of "reality," not "fantasy"; and if
action through intermediaries relegated a god to a "fantasy
world," many if not all ancient forms of theism would have to
be counted as atheism by implication. We cannot, in any event,
have it both ways; the Ovidian gods cannot very well belong to
the Augustan court and demimonde without belonging to a
part, however sorry a part, of the "true reality."

In fairness to Otis one must add that there are passages in
his exposition in which he seems to acknowledge that Ovid's
pantheon is neither a *roman à clef* nor a grotesquely illuminated
margin to the text of his human comedy: "The *Perseus* is not
about divine vengeance . . . it is in fact a heroic epic with a
human hero and an essentially human subject matter. It thus

provides both relief and effective demarcation to the Divine Vengeance episodes around it." In what Otis calls the third section (6.401–11.795), "Ovid is no longer dealing with the conventional mythology of divine comedy or divine vengeance but with the modernized and humanized mythology of neoteric and Alexandrian poetry." "The gods are never involved in passion to anything like the degree of the human characters." "The gods are different; neither human passion nor mortality is involved."[27] This view of the gods seems to me, as far as it goes, to be plainly right; their humanity is skin-deep, and often (if possible) even more superficial than that. These are beings who, if they grieve at all, may not weep (2.621–622).

Otis argues that in the shipwreck that kills Ceyx, Ovid reveals "cruel forces that recognize no justice and law," forces impelled by "the malicious intention of the sea-storm"; the poet thereby draws a "contrast between the real and the unreal, the demythologized storm and the mythologized Sleep."[28] But if Ovid's purpose is to demythologize, he has utterly defeated it by investing the storm with cruelty, malice, intention, and the refusal to recognize authority. There is, in fact, no such inevitable difference in kind as Otis assumes between the capricious Ovidian gods who are "plastically conceived" and those whose mythological names (when supplied) are "but names for the forces of nature." A poet in whose view there is no very plausible or hopeful way of conceiving ultimate causes can do worse than to conceive these "plastically" or, altering the metaphor when it suits, to conceive them less concretely, as wills or *numina.* In either case Ovidian gods are scarcely more than reified outcomes, like the medieval Umpire of the judgment of Mars: "God himself helps those who dare" (10.586).

A pantheon of morally random events, needless to say, is not very consolatory. "But Eurystheus is still hale and hardy," screams Hercules in his death agony; "are there people capable of believing in the existence of gods?" (8.200–201). A pantheon of amoral causes, which is what Ovid gives us in the main, is hardly less unsatisfactory, especially as the great anarch who presides over Olympian intrigue is a faceless Necessity. Hence Jupiter's apology: "I too am ruled by the fates" (9.434). The vyings of Olympian factions are very like those of the four winds in the middle air or of the contrary elements in Chaos, to which the doings of Cosmos bear an unedifying resemblance; the only rule of the game appears to be that the divine players "may never repeal the acts" of their fellows (14.784–785). The only discernible pattern of play is that "no pleasure is untainted; in every happiness is a dash of trouble" (7.453–454). "Humanity is roiled about by the inconstancy of things" (13.646).

The deeper irony of Ovidian theodicy, then, is that ultimately the denial of divine omnipotence becomes a plea of divine innocence: "The fortune of Hecuba had moved all the gods too — so unanimously that even Jupiter's sister-wife herself denied that Hecuba deserved what happened to her" (13.573ff.) — what (in the end) no god inflicted and no god may undo. Fortune, and no deity of narrower province, leads Glaucus to the herb that deifies him, and Dryope to the lotus whose plucking results in her suffering (in complete innocence) the horrible change of Myrrha, Baucis, and the rest: "I am undergoing the punishment without the crime" (9.372). And the gratuitous agony of Myrrha's thwarted birth labor, which no divine malice invented, is identical with the ordeal invented by Juno for the benefit of Alcmene. The Ovidian gods, or metaphors for causal principles, are neither a social class lampooned nor a superstition derided. Pictured or not, they are the carnival mirroring of a cosmic absurdity that, for the poet, is all too real.

It is no doubt true, then, as Walther Ludwig has insisted, that "Ovid's poetic intention was to achieve for poetry something of the function performed by the universal historian for historiography." But as Ludwig notes, "Ovid did not present even the 'historic' period in its factuality but, as poet, turned it into legend, thereby reversing the procedure of the historian, who tried to turn the legendary period into history."[29] Ludwig apparently fails to recognize, as we are now in a position to do, that Ovid's intellectual imperialism, here as elsewhere, is the purest of skeptical subversion; the art that transforms the domain of legend into that of history, or restores fact to its pristine state of myth, is an art of conjuration whose masters are the likes of Ulysses and Phantasos, Proteus, Vertumnus, and Circe. It is in the context of this Ovidian harlequinade that the wondrous translation of Romulus (14.820–851), the importation of Esculapius to Rome (15.622–744), and other jingo pageants of the final books acquire their meaning. In the same way Pythagoras recites Helenus' prophetic tribute to the future ascent of Rome only after entertaining us with a list of other Romes now contemptibly (and pointedly) defunct:

> Thus great she was in wealth and warriors, and capable of giving so much blood for a decade; now all that grovelling Troy has to show are antique ruins, and instead of her treasures her grandsires' tombs. For brightness, take Sparta that was. For energy great Mycenae was the place. And don't leave out the Athens Cecrops built, or the Thebes of Amphion. A cheap lot of real estate is the Sparta that is; the heights of Mycenae are the flats of Mycenae. What is Oedipus' Thebes but a legend? What is left of Pandion's Athens but the name? (15.422–439)[30]

Far from the manifest destiny of the empire or even the immortality of the soul, the obsessive theme of Ovid's Pythagoras is the oddly Heraclitean refrain that "all things flow" (15.178). "What existed earlier is left behind, and that comes to be which existed not at all, and the sum of things is renewed" (15.184–185). Ovidian time is a discrete series of sudden moments—*novae res* in the fullest Latin sense; and as time, so history. Revolution is the Ovidian transformation of the body politic, as grotesque and aimless and merciless as what Circe did to Scylla. The stories of the five ages and the flood, which like that of Chaos inaugurated the first book of the poem, put in a last appearance in the fifteenth to point the unedifying moral: "Both of you, world-eating Time, malign Antiquity, demolish everything, gnaw everything with age, and little by little, in a slow death, dissolve everything away" (15.234ff.). "Thus we watch the turning of the times, and those nations take on power, and these fall away" (15.420ff.). The consolation in all this, for Ovid's Pythagoras, is that though "all things change, nothing is destroyed" (15.165). What history lacks in continuity it more than supplies in vacuous repetition. In this it parallels the genealogy of the phoenix, which Pythagoras (it is well to remember) finds no more sacred or even diverting than the sexual versatility of the hyena, the fluid diet of the protean chameleon, or the effect of air on the urine of the lynx.

The wisdom of the phoenix' example is simply: *plus ça change;* and it is not very difficult to recognize its threatening parody in the tale of pious Aeneas' destruction of the Rutulian capital: "Ardea falls, famed for power as long as Turnus stayed alive. After he was despatched by the sword of the invader, and her roofs lay exposed as the embers cooled, from the midst of the wreckage, revealed to knowledge for the first time at that moment, a bird flew up and, smiting her vans together, beat away the ashes. Her cry, meagerness, pallor, all befitting the sacking of a city — even the city's name survived in her; and the ardea herself beats her breast with her own wings" (14.573–577). The transformation of the ardea is that of the phoenix without perfume but with the eternally recurrent cinders intact. The analogy between Rome and Ardea — or Sparta, Athens, and the rest — is not merely a piece of *samizdat*, of contraband dissent; it is the historical corollary of the view of things projected by the poem as a whole, and the butt of irony is as much the ironist as it is the Emperor.

Just how boastful in the end is the poet's final claim that in his better nature he will vault the stars (rather like the stellified Julius), kept alive forever by a Fame coextensive with the "power of Rome" (15.875–879)? We have just been hearing at eloquent length that imperial power, though not ephemeral, is sadly far from eternal. As for the other guarantor of the poet's immortality, it is a notorious truth of which the poet has already reminded us (12.54) that Fame is a compulsive equivocator. And what goes for the unbelieving poet goes more grimly still for his complacent master. How do we know that Augustus (despite his modest disclaimers) excels his uncle Julius? Our ultimate authority — our sole authority in fact — is again "free Fame" whose improvisations even emperors cannot suppress (15.852ff.). But still the poet finds a way of giving us some notion of the relative orders of magnitude of the two imperial stars. Among analogies that seem innocuous if not fulsome — like the superiority of Achilles and Theseus to their fathers — Ovid contrives to set a trap that is deadly enough: we are to understand that Augustus' honor excels that of Julius as much as Agamemnon's does that of Atreus (15.855) — of an Atreus who had the honor of serving a feast of his mangled nephews' remains to their credulous and doomed father.[31]

It would be tempting to see in Ovid's little joke a fervent protest against a particular man of power in favor of an ideal of power distributed in accord with republican liberty. But the poet of the Sisyphean phoenix or ardea is no more a man of political hope than of political despair, and it is to miss the epic sweep of his doubt to see a political caricature of Augustan self-aggrandizement, for example, in his anecdote of Cipus, who draws back in horror from the reign foretold by a nocturnal growth of horns. Those horns, suggests one critic, "signify that he [as precursor of Augustus] is to be king, and therefore he covers them up with a laurel crown. In the assembly he takes off the latter and the people now have the opportunity to accept him for what he is."[32] And what may that be? Not king of Rome, certainly, for by Ovid's account Cipus is fated to be king only if he is "accepted in the city" (15.584). But Cipus has no intention of meeting this requirement for the acquisition of a power he condemns: "He took a step back, turned a grim face from the city walls, and said: 'May the gods thrust such omens far, far off. As for me, it would be far juster for me to live out my life in exile than that the Capitol should see me a king'" (15.586-589).

What Cipus discloses to his countrymen with the dramatic removal of his garland is not kingship but the threat of kingship that to his grief, and theirs, he now poses to the city. "There is an individual here who, *if* you do not thrust him from the city, will be king" (15.594-595). "'If you do not thrust him from the city,'" according to our anti-Augustan critic, "either implies that Cipus actually is in the city or more subtly it betrays his desire to be there."[33] The "subtle" implication, I think, is genuine but not incriminating. The implication of fact is carefully excluded by the text. Cipus' convocation is held outside the walls immediately after he turns away from them (15.586-591). In his subsequent speech he warns his compatriots of what will happen "*if* he comes into Rome" (15.597), not what is happening now that he is there. He would hardly say "Keep the man from the city" (15.600) had the threshold already been crossed.

In our critic's unveiling of a *poète engagé* adept at caricaturing an infamous patron to his uncomprehending face, the whole point of the anecdote has disappeared from view, explicit though it is. Cipus' inverted coronation is the final confirmation of his claim to public honor for having saved Rome from "laws of serfdom" (15.597) at the cost of exclusion from his native city. It is also an admission that he will need the help of his countrymen in resisting the horror of exile and the temptation of power: though so far he has notably succeeded in repressing these impulses with no help at all ("I myself stood in the way," 15.599), the Romans will have to "thrust" him from Rome. That both he and his countrymen put liberty first is a contrast, not a parallel, to the Augustan polity. The Ovidian Cipus, in short, is no more a travesty of Augustus than is the Ovidian Pythagoras, who "in his hatred of tyranny was a voluntary exile" (15.61–62). Nostalgic idealizations like these cannot be construed as serious personal reproaches to the Emperor and his subjects because the target of reproach (if sardonic resignation can be so described) is far broader: the inevitabilities of human nature and history as Ovid has taken a whole poem to display them.

One of the republican Pythagoras' disciples at Croton is no less than Numa, the aspirant philospher-king (15.7–8, 479ff.). Can it be that Ovid's political intention is homiletic if not satirical? The emperor-to-be must learn, among other things, the difference between a monarch and a tyrant—and the lesson will succeed. "Philosophical doubts are resolved in faith," say critics of this more agreeable tendency—"faith in the Rome of Augustus and in his future. But with the commitment of a lofty ethic." "All this syncretism, pythagoreanizing as it is and in a degree Oriental, . . . is guiding us toward the idea of the individual apotheosis of Augustus . . . Numa is the prefiguration of Augustus"; "Far from shoring up an ethic that precisely finds its basis in the unforeseeable shiftings of reincarnation, the example of the phoenix symbolizes belief in an immortality that ensures the indefinite permanence of one and the same being."[34] I have already remarked that the endless snuffings and self-replications of a phoenix-form, uniquely exemplified, get little more attention from Pythagoras than the sexual or egestive accomplishments of other strange animals. The eternal recurrence of Numa-Augustus, the endless rarefaction and condensation of matter, the foreseeable succession of unforeseeable shapes, the variety that gives no spice to life—these are the materials with which the poet has built an edifice not of faith but of doubt. The *beau geste* of Cipus is no more paradigm than parody because in the sequel it proves to be utterly, and expectably, fruitless.

I have tried thus far to show how Ovid's cosmic poem, though it turns on a recurrent image of fabulous change far less obviously suited to synoptic vision than, say, the atomism of Lucretius, slowly builds up a claustrophobic portrait of the self: craving belief; dispossessed of criteria; fully at one neither with its mental nor with its physical aspect; apprehensible neither to itself nor to others; the principle of its unity a clueless riddle; its deliberate choices unmasked as the convulsions of a puppet; its moral standards the empty labels of fiat; its stable facts and objects at the mercy of the Ulyssean arts; its heroic ideals only another illusion among the many imposed on it by the gods of power and caprice; and its heritage of empire and culture and eloquence only the crowning illusion of all. In the final book of his poem Ovid seems to replace the central image in this vision with quite another. Instead of transformation, Pythagoras is brought on to celebrate metempsychosis.

A number of critics have energetically argued that the old showman is mugging up a semblance of philosophical coherence whose contemptible failure (as they think it) would neither have mattered to him in the least nor indeed should matter overmuch to us; for (says one critic) his "indifference to . . . unity . . . is not to be confused with indifference to the effect to be gained by creating an impression of unity," and in this latter effort the Pythagorean sermon largely succeeds. In this speech, another critic maintains, Ovid is merely saying "that the chain of mythologic metamorphoses . . . can also be described in the language of science and philosophy." The former critic finds in Pythagoras the same kind of superficially unifying perspective: "The introduction to his speech [15.67–71] is clearly grounded in Stoic physics, that is, in contemporary science." "There are," he adds, "obvious affinities between the phenomenon of transmigration and the phenomenon of transformation. If the soul can be housed in a new shape, why should not the body take a new shape also?" On the other hand, according to critics of the persuasion I am now considering, "while the epic is replete with mythological fables 'not to be believed,' the philosophical exposition stops short of the miracle. It is conceived throughout in a rationalizing spirit and thus it contradicts rather than clarifies the purport of the stories."[35]

Now the leading assumption of such criticism is that the shift from stories of transformation to discourse of transmigration is a shift from folklore to science despite the similarity between the two "phenomena." But the assumption is mistaken on various counts. Transmigration of souls is invisible; it is precisely *not* a phenomenon, and it forces no renovation at all in our notions of the regular course of phenomena. By contrast, transformation (granted for the moment that it occurs) *is* a phenomenon, indeed a variety of phenomena, all of them spectacular novelties. A scientist might conceivably wish to deny that transformation is possible, or to account for it. But what scientific interest could he find in the claims of Pythagoras? The *universality* of change and the transmigration of souls entail no explanation of any *particular* change in the physical order—to which in fact the truth or falsity of these claims makes not the slightest difference. Pythagoras' teaching fails altogether to involve the remotest approach to a scientific endeavor; it is the purest of metaphysics. The etiological myths of the earlier books, on the other hand (in the tradition of Boios and Nicander), do purport to lead us into the mysteries of paleontology—into the origin of living species and of some geological forms as well.

As for the list of Stoic *paradoxa* with which Pythagoras' harangue is crowded, Lafaye long ago demonstrated—what is clear enough on a reading of the list itself—that we are being offered the asides and anecdotes of savants, transcribed with an irresponsibility worthy of Sir John de Mandeville or Ripley's "Believe It or Not." In fact, as the corresponding texts in Strabo indicate, Pythagoras has a way of keeping the standard curiosities and leaving out the standard explanations.[36] The etiological myths on which Ovid plays his witty and sinister variations may once have been a primitive groping toward the goal of scientific hypothesis; to Ovid they are a mockery less of the groping than of the goal. And the bearing of Pythagoras' discourse on the poem it so oddly sums up is that despite the Stoic affirmation some scholars have found in it, the gospel of Ovid's Pythagoras is total and incorrigible doubt.

That gospel has sometimes been dismissed as a perfunctory versification of the doctrines of such eclectic Augustan philosophers as Sotion and his master Sextius. But Sotion's recorded teaching is "that souls are *allotted* to successive bodies . . . that nothing ceases to be in this world but changes its place, and that not only do heavenly objects turn through *fixed revolutions* but animate beings, too, go through a succession of states, and minds are led through a cycle."[37] As Ovid appropriates the curiosities of naturalists diligently stripped of the least suggestion of causal order, so he welcomes the neopythagorean vision only after methodically sterilizing it of its characteristic stress on a cosmic rule of *law*, and (we may add) of the cautious reservations of its authentic masters. Sextius, for example, had recommended metempsychosis merely as an edifying myth, on the ground that "cruelty becomes a habit when butchery is adopted as a means to pleasure"; Sotion pleaded what amounts to the equivalent of Pascal's wager: "If these suggestions are true, abstaining from meat is an avoidance of guilt; if they are false, it is a counsel of thrift."[38]

"Believe me," says Ovid's Pythagoras, "nothing ceases to be in this great world, but changes and takes a new face. 'Being born' is the name of beginning to be what one had not been before, and 'dying' of surrendering that identity" (15.254–257). These, says Lafaye, are "principles to which Stoics like Panetius had equally given their approval." But on the strength of a detailed review of Panetius' extant fragments, his modern editor van Straaten has made it quite clear that "Panetius expressly acknowledges the end of the human soul"; "Experience taught him, as well, that individual beings . . . are born only to perish." Certain scholars, notes van Straaten, "wish to give the impression that in Panetius' view *species* of individual beings had eternal existence . . . As far as the higher genera—plants, beasts, human beings—one could perhaps accept the suggestion; but conclusions of wider application seem to be unjustified." As for Posidonius, the afterlife he claims for the human soul is both spectral and finite.[39] Ovid owes nothing to these solemn schools but the petards with which they may be hoist. His fantasies of transformation are so many mockeries of the scientific enterprise; his fantasy of transmigration is a grand parody of the metaphysical enterprise, culminating in the celebration of immortality as perpetual durance in an awareness without criteria.

I think it is no accident that Ovid's tactics of philosophical iconoclasm are indistinguishable from those deployed by the Athenian Carneades in the notorious lecture on justice he gave at Rome during his diplomatic mission a century before. Carneades denies that there are natural criteria of justice; there is no way of knowing, for example, whether Pythagoras or Empedocles is mistaken in calling down "unatonable punishments" on those who, in the sages' view, violate the bill of rights inherent in all that is aware. The nature and existence of such a bill cannot be known. But if it exists then there is no more flagrant a collective offender against its articles than the Roman Empire, "which declares wars by a solemn priesthood thereto empowered, legitimates the perpetration of injustice, forever covets and confiscates the goods of others, and thereby acquires to itself the ownership of the whole world."[40] In Carneades and (I would suggest) in Ovid as well, Pythagoras is merely a polemical weapon against the Stoics, who insist on the absence of *logos* — of reason in whatever degree — from the beasts on whose flesh man must live. Its presence (as both Stoics and their adversaries agree) would entail that injustice is practically unavoidable, that moral perception is either meaningless or nonexistent.[41] The slightest gesture in a world of imponderables is liable to result in an atrocity.

"Even Pythagoras' vegetarianism," complains one critic, "is not far-reaching enough for the poem, since human beings are transformed into plants and trees as well as animals."[42] But this is a difficulty for Ovid's character and not for Ovid, who is not likely to have been unacquainted with the Horatian joke about "Pythagoras' relative the bean," or Empedocles' inclusion of the vegetable kingdom in the sphere of metempsychosis.[43] "It is interesting," notes the same critic, that just the themes . . . most open to [Roman] ridicule, namely metempsychosis and vegetarianism, are those which Ovid's Pythagoras chooses to expound at greatest length."[44] But it is a commonplace of Western thought that the clownish figure of a Silenus may conceal what is not clownish at all. It is not that the garrulous old vegetarian is other than comically wrong, but that, for all the mind in an Ovidian cosmos may know to the contrary, he may by the same token be disastrously right. The merchant at the oasis in the Arabian Nights had at least a wrathful genie to upbraid him for casually throwing the datestones of his lunch into the fountain: "I tell you, you have killed my son, for whilst you were throwing about the stones, my son passed by, and one of them struck him in the eye and killed him." But a genie, grim as he is, is an idol of certainty. And Pythagoras, with his drolleries and platitudes, is a harlequin figure of doubt.

THE GOLDEN ASS
Metamorphosis
as Satire
and Mystery

T HE SPHERE OF CAPRICIOUS CHANGE THAT INTERESTS OVID IS not merely the human body but human affairs in general; Circe shares the management of Ovidian transformation with History, and it is not at all clear who is the more potent witch. The central theme in Apuleius' romance of transformations has the same generous range. We shall be hearing, as the author promises, of "people's shapes and their fortunes turned into other images and again, by a bond of reciprocity [*mutuo nexu*], made back into themselves" (1.1).

The reciprocity Apuleius has in mind here, I think, is simply the one between shape and fortune: a radical change in shape will inevitably change one's other circumstances, but, *mutuo nexu*, a radical change in one's other circumstances will inevitably force a change in shape, as the mill slaves are shrunken and blinded by their servitude in a crucial episode of the romance:

Good gods, what kind of pygmies were those—skin bedaubed all over with black and blue welts, their lash-laden backs rather obscured than covered by a torn bit of rag, some having thrown a flimsy patch over their privates only, but the whole lot of them so shirted that through the tatters they had no secrets at all, foreheads branded and heads bestubbled and feet shackled; also disfigured by jaundice, with their eyelids corroded by the smoky darkness of a gaseous fog that had also damped the lights of their eyes, and (in the manner of prizefighters sprinkling themselves with fine dust as they skirmish) robed by cindery flour in a defiling white. (9.12)[1]

One drastic remedy for the transformations of poverty and enslavement is to take the pledge of banditry: "Not a few," reports a bandit recruiter, "reject a life of groveling and slavery and prefer to shift their way of life to a likeness of dictatorial power" (7.4). "The duress of poverty drove us to this way of life" (4.23), says another. But this antidote to monstrosity, unfortunately, turns out to be only monstrosity of another sort; everything about the revelry of the bandits is "like half-beast . . . Lapiths and Centaurs" (4.8), and their lives are indeed given over to the exercise of "dictatorial power," in the form of a devout and methodical cruelty. The pattern of one's transactions with the world, no less than the shape of one's body, is part of the figure one cuts in the world, and is equally a prey to disfigurement.

One might perhaps be tempted to prefer the disfigurements of poverty, painful as they are, to those of the criminal alternative if Apuleius made it easy to dismiss the bandit's appeal to the "duress of poverty." But he eventually introduces us to a destitute and gentle Greek vegetable farmer being accosted in Latin by a Roman legionary. The farmer, preoccupied by grief over the sudden death of a friend and ignorant of the imperial language, passes by in silence only to be rewarded for the apparent slight by a clubbing that knocks him off his donkey and (despite his plea of ignorance) by the announcement in Greek that the donkey on which his livelihood depends is to be commandeered immediately for heavy duty at the garrison.

The farmer, wiping his head clean of the blood from the gash of the earlier blow, once again pleaded with the soldier to treat him with more courtesy and forbearance and begged him besides with an oath on his [the soldier's] own hopes for good luck. "This little donkey," he went on, "is a slacker, and none the less mean-tempered for that, and what with the falling he does on account of his damned illness, he's usually hard put to carry even a few bushels of vegetables from the garden nearby, exhausted and gasping with faintness — let alone

resembling a pack animal fit for bigger jobs." But when the farmer
realized that, far from being mollified by any appeals, the soldier was
becoming even more of a brute [*efferari*] bent on his destruction, that
he had inverted his baton and was getting ready to split the farmer's
brains with the fatter knob, the farmer rushed to his last resort. Taking his cue from the situation he pretended that he wanted to touch the
soldier's knees to arouse his pity. The farmer stooped, bent over, and
grabbed the soldier by both feet, and lifting him way up sent him
crashing to the ground. The next moment — sometimes cuffing,
sometimes elbowing, sometimes biting, even using a rock snatched
from the road — he soundly battered the soldier's whole face, as well as
his hands and ribs.   (9.39–40)

The farmer's rage eventually drives him beyond self-defense and
retaliation; he will be content with nothing short of his enemy's
destruction, and the soldier saves himself only by feigning
death. It is plain enough where our sympathies are supposed to
lie, but the transformation in the farmer is equally plain; in the
space of a few minutes he has gone from deep grief to uncontrollable savagery. The oppressed has been driven to the *ef-
feratio* (see 5.1) — the emergence as wild beast — that comes so
much more easily to the oppressor. And the transformation, in
one respect at least, is irreversible: the farmer is now to be
hunted as a criminal and will end on the cross.

    These anecdotes of transformation concentrate on the vic-
tims rather than the wielders of power, but toward the beginning of his romance Apuleius shows us directly, in a wryly
satiric vignette, that good luck too can disfigure:

On my way to the baths, so as to get the makings of dinner first, I
visited the delicatessen mart, where I saw a luscious catch of fish.
Finding to my disgust that the price was a hundred sesterces I bar-
gained it down to eighty. Just as I was leaving the place, who should
fall in with my route but Pythias, my old schoolmate at Athens? After
taking rather a long time to place me, he strides up affably, favors me
with a hug and a chummy round of kisses, and says "Lucius, by
Pollux, it's years and years since I've laid eyes on you — why, by Hercules, not since we both took our leave of Professor Clytius. What
brings you on a trip to these parts?" "You'll know tomorrow," I reply,
"but what's this? I'm glad to find a wish granted. I look at you and see
attendants, fasces, outfit perfectly in keeping with the rank of
magistrate." "We inspect prices and keep the constabulary going. If

you're in the market for provisions, we're at your service." I was declining his offer, having already quite nicely provided fish for my dinner, when Pythias saw my market basket and shuffled the fish into plainer view. "How much did you pay for this garbage?" "It was all I could do to wangle the dealer into taking eighty sesterces." No sooner had he heard this than he seized my right hand and took me back to the delicatessen mart.

"From which one of those fellows did you buy these jokes?" I pointed out the little old man sitting in the corner. Pythias immediately adjusts his voice to a harshness befitting the power of his magistracy and berates the man in these terms: "Now has it reached the point where you don't even spare friends of ours — or any visitors at all, for that matter — that you ask such steep prices for a mockery of fish and reduce the flower of all Thessaly to the equivalent of a desert and a mountain crag by driving up the price of food? But you won't get away with it. Because now I'm going to give you an object lesson in how my administration makes the villains toe the mark." Emptying out the basket for all to see he orders his lieutenant to step up on the fish and stomp them all to pieces under his feet. Satisfied with this example of his uncompromising moral principles and urging me to make my departure, my dear Pythias tells me, "Lucius, this violent rebuke to the little fellow will do, I think."

Confounded and thoroughly stunned by these proceedings I go on to the baths deprived at one stroke by my prudent classmate's sound advice of both money and dinner.   (1.24–25)

In the process of rising in the world our student of Greek philosophy has become a self-important and scatterbrained bureaucrat, and the effect on Apuleius' hero is precisely the dizzy surprise with which he responds to manifestations of the occult.

This distinction, however, as we shall see, is rather misleading. For Apuleius, and eventually for Lucius, Fortuna is the manifestation of an occult cause. The breadth of the author's unfolding notion of the occult allows him to portray the extremes of familiar emotions as if they were so many prodigies of Thessalian witchcraft; hence the multiple forms of the son of Venus, from "the gentlest and sweetest of all wild beasts" (5.22) on whom Psyche is unluckily persuaded to spy, to the "savage and wild and viperish Evil One" (4.33) of whom she is warned by an oracle, and who is displayed in the character of a nightmare incubus as he possesses the heroine's soul in Apuleius'

variation on the story of Phaedra: "As long as Love was an in-
fant being nursed on his first elements that woman easily
repressed a barely perceptible flush and easily held her peace as
she stood up against his yet feeble attack. But at last when Love
flared up in abandoned Bacchanal, filling her breast brimful of
crazy fire, she lay down in submission [*succubuit*] beneath the
raging god" (10.2). The plague signs that now appear, no less
than the more uncanny spectacles I shall be considering in a
moment, assume the place reserved for them in the tableau of
bizarre "transformations" promised by Apuleius' foreword and
by the traditional title of his romance: "the face disfigured with
pallor, the eyes dim, the knees lax, the unquiet rest and sighs all
the wilder for the slowness of the torture" (10.2). When Psyche
is finally persuaded by her sisters to accept the possibility that
her unseen husband is a serpent waiting to devour her, we are
likewise invited to think of the whole process as a kind of
demonic possession: "Having reached their sister's mind . . .
they invade her thoughts" (5.19). "Driven by malign furies,
Psyche is not alone" (5.21) even when her sisters seem to have
left her; for despite appearances, as she has already been
warned, they are her Furies as well as her Sirens (5.12) and
Vampires (5.11). They too, in short, have been subjected to the
ordeal of transformation.

Apuleius leaves ample room in his romance for witchcraft
and vampirism in the technical sense as well. His principal setting is the Greek district of Thessaly, where an uncommonly tall
old man begging someone to rescue his grandson from a pit
reportedly becomes a vast reptile coiling over the half-eaten remains of his would-be benefactor (8.20–21); where gossip has it
that "the wise women bite off pieces here and there from the
faces of dead people to fill the prescriptions of their conjuring
art" (2.21), and few go to their graves intact because "the rotten
turnskins change their face into any animal you please and
creep up on the sly" (2.22). On the road to Larissa we should
beware of the innkeeper Meroe:

Because her lover had debauched another woman she changed him
with a single word into a beaver, because that beast, in his dread of
capture by pursuers, frees himself by cutting off his genitals . . . She
unshaped a neighboring (and hence rival) innkeeper into a frog, and

now the gaffer swims in a cask of his own wine and, sunk in the dregs, calls his old guests hoarsely with deferential croakings. Because another man, a pettifogger from the court, had spoken against her cause, she unshaped him into a ram, and now it is that argumentative beast that has taken over his practice. Because the wife of a lover of hers had been prattling scandal against her, Meroe blocked her womb up in a knapsack of pregnancy, suspended the birth, and condemned her to be pregnant in perpetuity. By everybody's account that poor woman is already ballooning with eight years' burden as if she's about to be delivered of an elephant.   (1.9)

In the town of Hypata, a hotbed of Thessalian magic, Lucius' hostess Pamphile has a similar reputation for jealousy and Circean arts of vengeance. And if hearsay is to be believed, both women are capable of mischief on a vastly grander scale than a menagerie of wayward lovers—the ability, for example, "to bring down the sky, hang up the earth, petrify fountains, liquefy mountains, put ghosts in heaven, put gods in hell, snuff out stars, and light up the very depths of the underworld" (1.8; see 2.5 and 3.15).

Rumors like these, in fact, are part of the reason for the hero's presence in Thessaly, and for his own magical transformation. Lucius' ostensible errand in Thessaly is business (1.2), but his reaction to a first morning walk through the streets of Hypata reveals clearly enough that his real errand is somewhere between a pilgrimage and a quest:

As soon as the new sun had scattered the night and made the day I escaped from both sleep and bed at once. I was excited in any case— and only too ambitious of becoming acquainted with oddities and wonders. I bethought myself that I was standing in the heart of Thessaly, that the spells of sorcery native to this place are hailed by the unanimous voice of the whole world . . . In a suspense generated at once by devout wish and by serious pursuit I studied things with minute curiosity. There was nothing I caught sight of in that city that I *believed* to be what it was; rather, that all things had been transformed by a funereal intoning to another shape. Thus I *believed* that even the cobbles I tripped against had each been congealed from a human being, that even the birds I was hearing had been fledged from the same source, that even the trees encircling the city wall within and without had come by their leaves in much the same way, that even the liquid of the springs was the distillation of human bodies.

Already the statues and effigies are on the point of walking, the façades of talking, cows and similar cattle of *uttering prophecy* —why, *from the heavens themselves and the sphere of daylight an oracle is on the point of sudden emergence.* (2.1; emphasis added)

Even apart from the increasingly liturgical cadence of the prose, it is clear that for Lucius Hypata is the shrine of a creed that interprets not only the city but the world overarching it as the mask of a kindred awareness. Lucius cannot yet name the creed, but he fully expects a divine illumination, and by the end of the romance he will have achieved one. The droll and crucial paradox of the romance is that to achieve his illumination —his divinely renewed humanity —the hero must first become an ass.

Perhaps it would be less misleading to talk of his *seeming* to become an ass, for as in Homer and Ovid, the nature of the transformation itself is a moot question. In fact, it is three moot questions: (1) Are the pristine Lucius, the magic beast, and Lucius restored one individual, two, or three? (2) Is the magic beast a person? (3) Is it in any sense human? Lucius anticipates the first of these when he tells us, for example, that in his amazement at Pamphile's emergence as a screechowl, "I thought I was anything else you please rather than Lucius" (3.22). Later, having persuaded the witch's maidservant Fotis to help him imitate Pamphile's transformation, Lucius asks for the recipe by which "I shall shed those owlfeathers again and go back to my Lucius" (3.23). Fotis answers with particularity only after her confusion between two jars of her mistress's magic ointment has trapped the hero in the shape of the wrong animal: "You have only to nibble roses to issue from the ass and go back to my Lucius" (3.25). The hero himself records that his state after transformation amounted to being "a beast of burden instead of Lucius" (3.26) and that on the first night of his ordeal he expected (falsely, as it turns out) that the next morning, "with rosarious assistance," he "would be Lucius again" (3.27). Later he implores divine mercy to "restore me to my Lucius" (11.2). It seems that by the idiomatic usage of these passages an individual has a name by virtue of meeting a criterion for the name's application.

In the ordinary idiom one's name is not a description one happens to satisfy. Lucius might conceivably not have been *named* "Lucius," but that he might conceivably not have *been* Lucius is absurd. In Apuleius' idiom the latter proposition is no more absurd and no less true than that the President once was not, one day will no longer be, and might conceivably never have been, the President. In Apuleius' grammar the first person pronoun has taken over by default from the proper name the job of unconditionally designating the persisting self of the speaker. It is the "I" of the text who ceases to be Lucius and whose successor in this capacity, if any, is whatever object contrives to fit the description abbreviated by the name "Lucius." Who then is this "I," this former Lucius, whose current body is indistinguishable from that of an ass? What is the essential ground of identity that we are forced to seek by the disappearance of such accidental grounds as determine the reference of a name?

Part of the answer seems to be that in the sequence consisting of Lucius I, the enchanted beast, and Lucius II each succeeding member recalls having had the experiences of his predecessors. As Lucius II, the memoirist, promises: "I shall both test my wit [*ingenium*] and at the same time give you an opportunity to determine with accuracy whether *I* was an ass in mind [*mente*] and feelings [*sensu*] as well as otherwise" (4.6; emphasis added). By appeal to identity of experience during the relevant period the memoirist already claims identity with the beast whether or not the latter enjoys *ingenium, mens,* and *sensus* of the appropriate kind; and that enjoyment is what will make good his claim that the beast is a *person*. Apuleius apparently found the issues of identity and personhood adumbrated in his model, a lost work by Lucius of Patras the gist of which survives in a Greek abridgment. In the abridgment the hero is engaged to his undoing in a conscious experiment: "I wished to learn by experience whether on being transformed from a human being I should be a bird in soul as well."[2] It is taken for granted here that if the worst came to the worst the "I" would survive, but not as a person — and not as a participant in humanity even in the figurative (honorific) sense of the term.

Is the honorific sense applicable even to a magic beast? Lucius' counterpart in the cognate Greek story takes this once again for granted: "As for me, in other respects I was an ass, but in *phrenes* and *noûs* a human being — old familiar Lucius minus the voice." "They were amazed at my performance, not knowing that a human being was stowed away in the ass.[3] In Apuleius the transformed hero's parallel claim to a measure of humanity is ironically subverted by his estimate of humanity itself; in his account of how he faced a contrite Fotis immediately after his entrapment by her blunder, Lucius II contrives to pay himself the following compliment:

Thus she lamented, but I, though a complete ass and a beast of burden instead of Lucius, continued nevertheless to have the feelings of a human being [*sensus humanus*]. It took me a long time, all in all, and much thought to decide whether I ought to dispatch that most worthless and wicked woman with a bombardment of kicks and a barrage of bites. But I was called back from this rash enterprise by my better judgment, which warned against a capital punishment for Fotis that would snuff out altogether the chance of a rescue for me.   (3.26)

It seems that in the hero's opinion the forbearance dictated by the *sensus humanus* is not fairness or compassion but self-interest. As moral philosophy this opinion is no doubt unedifying, but as an assessment of human nature it comes to us, at least, with the supporting testimony of its context, a romance in which human justice and compassion are so rare and transient as to seem freakish. We are allowed to view precisely the same irony from the opposite direction when the former Lucius upbraids himself with an "asinine thought" (6.26) and an "ass's judgment" (7.10) for which his current anatomy is far from obviously to blame. It is altogether consistent with Lucius' retention of his humanity in this unprepossessing descriptive sense that he should have the magic beast, and only the beast, to thank for the achievement of a fuller *humanitas* in the normative (and question-begging) sense made popular by Cicero.

I argued in the previous chapter that Ovidian transformation oddly fails to compensate its victims with the sympathetic insight one might expect to result from being put, in so radical a way, into the other fellow's shoes. What is notable in this connection about the response of Apuleius' hero to his entrapment is not his attempt to disown an awkward new body but his attempt to come to terms with that body's obstinate refusal to be disowned. When the "ass" is put out to cover mares, for example, Lucius acknowledges its lust — and species — as his own: "As for me, a free ass at last, joyful and capering and strutting along in a sensual canter, I was already picking out the mares that would suit me best as mistresses" (7.16). Later, falsely accused of atrocious attacks on women, he hears that the ass is too valuable to be put to death and will be gelded instead: "That sentence had withdrawn me from the spectral ranks of Hades, only to save me for the ultimate punishment; I grieved, in the mournful conviction that with the death of the last consequential part of *my body*, *all of me* would be perishing. In the end I resolved to snuff myself out by a protracted fast or by a headlong fall; granted, I should die just as surely, but I should die intact" (7.24; emphasis added). Lucius continues to be warmly solicitous for his body no matter how altered, but in its current state of alteration that body unites him in appearance and destiny with the members of a certain species; it is natural that he should come to think of himself as equally a member, and to identify powerfully with the sufferings of his adopted kindred.

Apuleius allows circumstance to give this process a healthy push in an episode in which his transformed hero, laboring under a merciless pack, is on the verge of feigning total exhaustion in order to induce a party of bandits to shift the pack and leave him behind:

But this magnificent strategy of mine was headed off by a dreadful coincidence. That *other* ass had foreseen and adopted my train of thought and immediately began playing the hopeless invalid: letting himself collapse pack and all, lying there for dead; not trying to rise even when cudgeled and goaded or raised up on all sides by the tail and the ears and the legs. This went on until the bandits were tired to the point of desperation; after persuading themselves that they could not afford to put off their escape so long in abject service to a dead — or rather a petrified — ass, they divided his load between me and the horse and, drawing a sword, cut through both his hamstrings. Then dragging him a little way off the road to the edge of a very high cliff, they upended him and sent him headfirst and still breathing into the neighboring valley. As for me, at that point I thought over the fate of my poor *comrade in arms* and decided to give up my tricks and ruses and acquit myself to my masters as an ass of good character. (4.5; emphasis added)

The "otherness" Lucius is forced to acknowledge in "the other ass," in his "comrade in arms," is not so much the denial that they are one in number as the affirmation that they are one in kind.

Lucius' ordeal has extended the range of his imaginative kinship to "other" suffering awarenesses than the biologically human. We have already considered his account of how a mill brutalizes the men who serve it; his account of how it brutalizes the brutes that serve it is no less full of pity and terror:

> Now as for my comrades in arms under the yoke [de meo iumentario contubernio], what am I to report of them, or how? What ancient mules those were, what feeble geldings! Around the manger with their heads lowered they were lopping piles of chaff, raw-necked with the decaying rot of their wounds, agape with nostrils going like bellows under the relentless thrust of their coughing, their breasts covered with sores from the incessant rubbing of the broom harness, their ribs stripped naked to the bone by constant scourging, their hoofs distended into gigantic soles by frequent running round in their own tracks, their emaciated hides roughened all over with ingrained filth and mange. Fearing the deadly augury to *myself* of such a household of bondage [talis familiae], and recalling the comfortable existence of *the former Lucius*—driven to the finishing line of all well-being—I bowed down my head and mourned.   (9.13; emphasis added)

By idiomatic usage a *contubernium* is literally the fellowship of eleven soldiers assigned to a single tent (*taberna*), and figuratively either the marriage of slaves or the dwelling together of animals—but ordinarily not (by amalgamation) a community of animals, slaves, and masters. By a parallel idiom *familia* is literally the fellowship of slaves assigned to a single household, and figuratively either the set of human beings related by blood to the master (that is, to the *paterfamilias*) or the household as a whole—but ordinarily not the membership of that household as united by a bond more comprehensive than kinship, status, or species. The being that was and is no longer Lucius has joined a *contubernium* of animals that belong in turn to a wider community: the *familia* of beasts and men linked with each other, as with their masters, by the capacity to suffer.[4]

This recognition marks a radical difference between Apuleius' and Ovid's use of their common motif; it is true that like Actaeon the erstwhile Lucius has lost his passport in the realm of matter, but unlike Actaeon he is compensated for this loss by finding his citizenship in the community of spirit typically affirmed by the Neoplatonism of Apuleius' age. Mind, in such an outlook, is ubiquitous, and the myth of Love "transforming the unclouded face [of Jupiter] into snakes, into fires, into wild beasts, into birds, into cattle" (6.22) is itself a bizarre transformation of a metaphysical truth.

This truth gives a piquant irony to Lucius' fantasies about a city of transformations, and our knowledge of Lucius' own transformation makes us privy to similar ironies elsewhere. The young bride Charite mounted on the ass tries to escape from her bandit abductors, and muses that "if it is true that Jupiter bellowed his way into a bull, then my donkey too may be hiding within it some divine or human face" (6.29). An auctioneer trying to get rid of the same animal, now much the worse for wear, impudently claims that it is "not a biter, not a kicker; it absolutely makes you believe that the ass's hide has a mild-mannered human being living in it" (8.25). By displaying just enough intelligence to provoke interest but not enough to run the risk of being killed as a bad omen, Lucius becomes the *contubernalis* (10.16) of a rich master who "chatted with me from time to time in the friendliest and most cordial way and, among many other things, used to confide that he could not be more delighted to have in me not only a mount but a table companion" (10.18). Only the ass, of course, is in a position to appreciate the literal truth of these remarks; for the ass, as I suggested earlier, marks a stage in the hero's progress toward a *humanitas* that, as far as the romance lets us judge, is neither peculiar not habitual to the species of the featherless biped.[5] It is in this sense that the ass, despite its shape, is divinely greeted by the name it has ostensibly lost (11.5) and is already capable of walking toward the place of its rebirth with "a perfectly human gait [*prorsus humano gradu*]" (11.12).

The disagreeable irony of the human affection the ass encounters is that it is nearly always abortive or perverse; Lucius' amiable master, for example, is really devoted to his own celebrity as an impresario: "the owner of a confidant and table companion ass, a wrestling ass, an ass that understands human utterances, an ass that communicates its meaning by gestures" (10.17). In the end the beloved confidant is booked by his master (10.23) for a public appearance in a pornographic travesty of marriage (10.28) with an accomplished murderess, an "illustrious wife" (10.24) convicted, among other things, of suborning a physician to poison her husband. The notion of such an exhibition is suggested to the master by a night of spying on his protégé's matrimonial intimacies with still another "illustrious wife" (10.23; *uxor egregia* in both cases), a "rich and influential lady" whose fascination with the animal's cleverness has grown somehow into authentic passion; she has rented it from its trainer and begins their night together by

kissing me with a kind of urgency—not such kisses as are familiarly bandied about in the stews, the money-demanding ones of the prostitutes or the money-refusing ones of the customers, but untainted and uncorrupted [*pura atque sincera*], and reinforced with the most beguiling speeches—"I love you," "I desire you," "You are my only love," "I cannot live without you any more," and all the others women use to encourage their partners and bear witness to their own ardor. (10.21)

Apuleius' insistence on the *sinceritas* of the lady's passion is, I think, worth emphasizing; it does not appear in the cognate Greek story, which has a gratuitously cynical denouement in which the lady rebuffs the hero, who has returned in human form to renew acquaintances: "You come to me after having been transformed from that noble and useful animal into a monkey?" I have already considered evidence elsewhere in the romance that Cupid is an enthusiast of perverse transformations. Lucius himself, in his eagerness to experience magic, had absurdly begged Fotis to help transform him into a lovelorn screechowl that would swoop down to Fotis as her "winged Cupid" (3.22). Now, from the amorous lady's point of view, as the hero observes, he is playing the bull to her Pasiphaë (10.19); that he is also burlesquing a hierogamy or sacred marriage—the masquerade of Europa's divine lover—is an irony (anticipated by the speculation of Charite) that only serves to emphasize the splendid perversity of the lady's misdirected love.

As it happens, the human vice that the ass most often has occasion to study at close quarters is precisely the misdirection of the impulse to self-transcendence. A bizarre case in point is the glory of bandit martyrdom reverently celebrated by a bandit laboring under the martyrs' grand illusion. One of the martyrs, Lamachus, has consented to the severing of his pinioned arm to make possible his escape from a foiled attempt at breaking and entering. But now

the man of lofty mind and matchless valor groaned and, with many appeals and many supplications, urged us by the right hand of Mars, by the bond of our military oath [per fidem sacramenti], to deliver a good comrade in arms at a single stroke from both torment and captivity; for why should the one hand fit for robbing and for throat-cutting be outlived by a bandit of courage? It was blessing enough for him that he should die of his own free will by a friendly hand. And when he failed to win any of us over with his plea for the deliberate slaughter of a kinsman, he took up his own sword in his remaining hand, kissed it long and repeatedly, and with a mighty blow at the middle of his breast, drove it clean through. Then, having paid homage to the hardihood of our noble-minded captain, we lovingly wrapped what was left of his body in a linen robe and entrusted its concealment to the sea. And now there lies our Lamachus with a whole element for his tomb.   (4.11)

Soon after, the bandits decide to use an elaborate bearskin disguise in the robbery of a wealthy breeder of wild animals: "We so arranged the solemn order for our current campaign [instanti militiae sacramentum] that one of our number, outstanding for strength not so much of body as of mind, and above all by his own free choice, should use the covering of that hide to put on the semblance of a bear, be brought into [the menagerie of] Democharis' house, and in the convenient stillness of the night give us an easy entry through the front gate" (4.14). Of the volunteers Thrasyleon is elected and dons the bearskin "with unclouded face," thereby "wholly becoming the beast" (4.15) and, as it turns out, dooming himself to an agonizing death. For the bandits, "reserving the moonless time of the night according to the lore of our calling [ex disciplina sectae]" (4.18), have carried off only half their booty when Thrasyleon, still in disguise and guarding the remainder until their return, is surprised by a servant who inevitably takes him for an escaped beast, a role he sustains in the ensuing general alarm to give his comrades time to get away undetected. Brought to bay at last by a panicky and merciless ring of hunters and dogs, Thrasyleon "betrayed the bond of his military oath [*fidem sacramenti*] neither by a shout nor even by a moan, but, already hacked and bitten to pieces by the swords and dogs of the hunters, kept up his stubborn roaring and feral growling, enduring his predicament with valiant hardihood, and thereby laying up glory for himself even as he surrendered his life to fate" (4.21).

Lamachus and Thrasyleon die in the cause ("robbing and throat-cutting") they have engaged their lives to uphold, and the emptiness of such life and death is turned to grisly comedy by the grandiloquent heroics favored by the bandit narrator, who speaks in a communal idiom patched together (with double-edged satiric effect) out of bits and pieces of borrowed finery. For example, the bandits not only talk as if they were imperial soldiers but reinforce the note of consecration in the term for the soldier's oath (*sacramentum*) by speaking of their orthodox way of life (*secta*; see 4.23, 6.31, 7.4), and the traditional body of teaching (*disciplina*) by which it is ordered, as if they were the initiates of a mystery cult or the adherents of a gnostic school of philosophy. It is, I think, no accident that the priesthood in which Lucius II is to find his fulfillment is also a "sacred army" bound together by a *sacramentum* (11.15). This theme of superstition, of half-articulate and distorted religious aspiration, is elaborated in the totemistic suggestion that by virtue of his costume Thrasyleon has "wholly become a beast [*prorsus bestiam factum*]" (4.15). Like the Jupiter of a later passage, Thrasyleon enters upon his transformation into a beast with a face like a clear sky (*serenus vultus*; 4.15, 6.22), but unlike the hierogamies of Apuleius' supreme being, or Lucius' regeneration, the purpose of Thrasyleon's ordeal is entirely corrupt, the last flourish of a *capomaffia*.

Apuleius offers us a final pathetic symbol of the cruel misdevotion of the bandit sect in the death of their superannuated and ill-used maid of all work, who has failed to prevent the escape of a prisoner being held for ransom; her masters find her on returning from a raid: "There, from the branch of a tall cypress, having donned a noose, was that old woman, hanging. Straightaway, trussed up, rope and all, as she was, they let her drop head first, and . . . ferociously charged into the dinner that the hapless little crone had prepared for them in a last piece of industry" (6.30). The old woman too has earned her place, invisible as it may be to her fellow communicants, in the calendar of bandit saints.

In the Graecoroman world through which Apuleius' hero makes his pilgrimage, "an oracle," as he puts it, "is on the point of sudden emergence" (2.1), but in the meantime the intensifying hunger for revelation is chiefly fed by charlatans whose unmasking by the romance is, in effect, an act of homage to what it will finally present as the true faith. The Chaldaean prophet Diophanes, for example, is interrupted during the sale of a forecast by an unexpected reunion that startles him into publicly discrediting himself; his trip from Euboea, he unguardedly tells his friend in the customer's hearing, was one long "Travels of Ulysses" (*Vlixea peregrinatio*), punctuated by shipwreck and the attacks of murderous bandits (2.14). Later on we are introduced to mountebanks of a religiosity far gaudier and more versatile than Diophanes': the *galli* (self-castrated priests of the Syrian Goddess) who buy Lucius to carry the shrine of the sacred image divide their time between male prostitution and various forms of religious confidence trickery, including the sale of oracles (9.8); but their *pièce de résistance* is a spectacular charade of ecstasy (put on for the edification of a pious magnate):

On first entering they immediately dashed forward as if divinely possessed, with a noisy chorus of dissonant whoops. For a long interval they kept their heads bowed; then they began moving their necks about in lithe contortions, wheeling their long tresses round in circles and sometimes ravaging their own muscles with snapping jaws. Finally, with the double-edged swords they were carrying, each slashed at his own arms. Meanwhile the holy fit was especially unruly in one of them, and panting convulsively from deep in his chest like one overbrimming with the divine spirit of a higher will he put on a show of wounded raving, for all the world as if the presence of the gods made human beings not better than themselves but helpless and diseased.

Now look at the reward he carried off from heavenly Providence. He began to prophesy at the top of his lungs with a lie he had concocted, reproachfully charging himself with a crime against the decree of holy religion and demanding a just retribution for the abominable deed from his own hands. Snatching up at last the standard equipment of those half-men, a whip densely fringed with bands of wool and tas-

sled with bunches of sheep's knuckles, he flogged himself soundly with
knotty strokes, brazened against the pain of the blows with an amazing obstinacy. What with the slicing of swords and the scourging of
whips you would have seen the ground become a pool of emasculate
and tainted blood. (8.27-28)

The charlatans have indeed offended against "holy
religion," and against a Providence whose divine artifice turns
their offense itself into a punishment. The same artifice will
make of the hero's transformation, as we shall see, a spiritual
version of Ulysses' divinely sponsored *nostos* or homeward return; the itinerant fortune teller Diophanes, by contrast, is a
Ulysses only in his itinerant ill fortune. The *galli* slander religious ecstasy by portraying it as a kind of epileptic seizure accompanied by self-abasement and self-mortification; their punishment is to earn their living by continual reenactment of their
slander.[6] Genuine prophecy transforms both the destiny and the
person of the prophet, but not as Diophanes or the *gallus*—or
Thrasyleon, for that matter—is transformed. In this respect at
least, Apuleius ultimately makes the same use of his dominant
symbol as do the scriptures of religions with which his own is in
strenuous competition: "And the spirit of the Lord will come
upon thee, and thou shalt prophesy . . . and shalt be changed
into another man" (1 Sam. 10:6); "And be not conformed to this
world, but be ye transformed by the renewing of your mind"
(Rom. 12:2); "But we all, with open face beholding as in a glass
the glory of the Lord, are changed into the same image from
glory to glory, even as by the spirit of the Lord" (2 Cor. 3:18).
The prevailing impression given by the charlatans, as with
the ass's ardent mistress or the bandit martyrs, is of authentic
energy perversely squandered. The same Diophanes who so in-
gloriously fails to foresee his own "travels" is gratuitously assigned a true prediction of Lucius' travels (2.12), and the "obstinacy" (*praesumptio*) with which the *gallus* has brazened
himself against pain is none the less "amazing" for being perverse. In the same way the "obstinate belief" (*praesumptio*) in
monotheism affected by the miller's wife is "sacrilegious" in part
because, unlike the true monotheism to be introduced later, it
fails to give polytheism its due, and in part because as literal belief it is pure hypocrisy (*mentita*, 9.14), but chiefly because a

genuine impulse has been perverted; the "uniquely divine being"
(9.14) she actually worships is her adulterous lover, whose arrival she anticipates as if it were "the advent of a particular god"
(9.22). Like the streets of Hypata as they present themselves to
Lucius on his first morning tour, the landscape through which
the magic beast moves on its way to a rendezvous with the true
faith is filled with mirages of that faith.

Even the hellish servitude of the mill, which Lucius mockingly calls a *disciplina* (9.12), is an ironic prefiguration of the
holy servitude he ends by celebrating. The oppressed mill
slaves, with their half-shaved heads and flour-coated bodies
"robed in a defiling white [*sordide candidati*]" (9.12), point toward the shorn priesthood of that other servitude with their
robes of pure white (*puro candore*, 11.10) and above all their
"voluntary yoke of service" (11.15). The magic beast resists the
disciplina (9.11) of the mill, only to enjoy a sudden "religious
conversion" (*sectae commutatio*) by grace of his trainers' whips
(9.11-12). Later the same magic beast baptizes itself in the Ae-
gean, praying to the supreme god "with tear-stained face" (11.1),
and still later the new Lucius will learn the ancient paradox that
the fuller enjoyment of his freedom will come when he enters actively on his service to that god (11.15).

What the mill is to the hero's destined service, the necromantic power of Thessalian witches is to the rebirth of body and
spirit he enjoys at the hands of his coreligionists. It is perhaps to
be expected that a magic that can make ghosts change places
with gods can also put the ghosts back in the bodies that gave
them up. What is more surprising, I think, is that even the hyperbolic superstition of Thessaly seems to be incapable of imagining such resurrections as other than pitiful caricatures—and
that the caricatures abound.

Meroe, for example, has used a sponge to seal the fatal
slash in Socrates' throat through which she siphoned off his
blood and drew out his heart: "You there, sponge, born as you
are of the sea, have a care that through a river you do not pass"
(1.13). The resuscitated victim, who is totally ignorant of his
condition, is furtively studied by his traveling companion Aristomenes, the teller of the tale: "I said to myself, 'Lunatic, you
entombed yourself in wine and had a nightmare. Look at Socrates here—whole, sound, without a scratch. Where's the wound?

The sponge? Where, last but not least, is a scar of the right depth and the right freshness?' " (1.18). As the travelers breakfast on the road, Socrates, who has begun to look more like the cadaver he is, kneels for a drink at the edge of a brook: "Hardly had he touched the outermost verge of his lips to the surface dew of the water when the wound in his gullet yawned deeply open and that sponge rolled from it accompanied by a tiny smear of gore" (1.19). A spurious life is brought to a close by a spurious death. In an even cruder burlesque of the dead arisen, Pamphile inadvertently lends a brief human reanimation to three inflated goatskins: "Immediately, by the irresistible potency of magic lore and the inscrutable violence of demons under compulsion, those bodies, the hairs from which were giving off a hissing vapor, borrow human spirit, feel, hear, walk, and come as directed by the aroma of their surrendered shearings" (3.18).

It is, as we shall see, no accident that magic power to grant a *postliminium mortis*, an authentic right of return from death, is attributed only to Zatchlas of Egypt, prophet of Isis, and is supposed to have been exercised in response to a desperate plea for justice:

The prophet, thus besought, lays a certain tiny herb against the mouth of the body and another against its breast. Then facing east he prayed in silence to the waxing of the mighty and dreadful sun and by this awesome setting of the stage riveted the onlookers in a rivalry of concentration on that great miracle . . . Already the breast swells and lifts, already the pulse beats in health, already the body is filled with spirit, the corpse rises up and the young man speaks forth.   (2.28-29)

But the young man's return to life is as brief as the reprieve of Socrates' sentient corpse, and as unwelcome as it is brief: "Why, I pray you, do you lead me who am already swimming in the marshes of the River of Loathing back to the duties of a momentary life? Relent now, I beg you; relent, and deliver me up to my rest" (2.29).

In addition to these disappointing approximations by Thessalian magic there are other occasions on which the romance, with an insidious casualness, gives us a conceptual glimpse of mystic death and resurrection. Lucius lifts a shroud and finds three punctured goatskins instead of the murderous brigands for whose dispatching he expects to be executed: "Good gods, what face was this my situation had taken on? What a miracle, what a sudden transformation of my fortunes. For even though already registered in the inventory of Proserpina and the liveried ranks [*familia*] of hell I was stunned into an opposite face of circumstance and fixed in suspense" (3.9). The spying Lucius watches Pamphile turn into a horned owl: "She willingly transformed herself by her craft of sorcery. But I, enchanted by no spell, stopped in my tracks only by the stunning impact of what had happened in front of me, thought I was anything else you please rather than Lucius" (3.22). In the former passage the hero's redemption from death is revealed suggestively by a change in the "face" of something, and his divine mistress as a member of the netherworld *familia* is later to be identified with his divine mistress as a member of the true priesthood (11.2). In the latter passage the hero temporarily suffers "mental banishment," as he goes on to explain; for the moment he is *exterminatus animi*. In both passages he undergoes a figurative death or transformation and a figurative renewal of life.

These necromantic scenes and metaphors, I think, are far from casual. The hero's own restoration to human form, again by herbal magic and at the hands of still another priest of the true faith, recalls him once more from a descent into the netherworld (*redux ab inferis*, 11.8) to a kind of rebirth (*renatus quodam modo*, 11.16), and the crowning reenactment of the same sacramental drama will be his passage as an initiate through a "voluntary death" that likewise leaves its participants "in a manner reborn [*quodam modo renatos*, 11.21]." The holy scriptures that the hero will eventually be shown "partly represent the abbreviated words of the ritual language by means of the shapes of every sort of animal, partly use intricate characters twisted round like wheels and crowded together with vinelike tendrils to bar their reading from the curiosity of the uninitiate" (11.22; see 3.17). The hero's experience as magic beast is a "discipline" of initiation (9.11-12, 32) written in just such an emblematic script.

If my analysis of Apuleius' romance is so far essentially right, we are to understand that magic is not alone in threatening human beings with disfigurements of shape and conduct; be-

ing well-to-do and being badly off can do similar damage without
spells and caldrons, and violent passion can leave its victim quite
unrecognizable. This universalizing of bizarre transformation
seems to reduce human life to absurdity, but the hero blunders
into a transformation that allows him to transcend its
absurdity by an act at once of criticism and compassion — by seeing that absurdity whole, and seeing through it to an unsuspected
ground of kinship among its victims; they — indeed every being in
its degree — are estranged members of a single "family" or "com-
pany," united by forgotten allegiance to a higher being. Their
endemic transformations are incurred largely in the course of an
inarticulate and panicky groping toward the reunion that Lucius
II achieves by joining the *contubernium* (11.18) of the true faith.

One might suppose that Lucius' blunder is quite as innocent
or even benign as the experience of transformation proves to be
despite its rigors, especially since the blunder was really Fotis'
rather than his own. But the verdict with which the priest greets
the restored Lucius is considerably harsher, and since I shall be
considering it at some length it will be convenient to begin by
quoting the speech in full:

You have gone through many divers labors, been driven by great
storms of Fortune and the greatest of whirlwinds, and have come at
last, Lucius, to the harbor of rest and mercy's altar. Nor at any point
was your lineage or even your high estate, or your flourishing erudi-
tion itself, of any avail to you, but from the treacherous footing of
your green years you slid down to slavish pleasures, and for your unlucky curiosity have carried off the unlucky reward.

But be that as it may, while your Fortune was racking you with
the worst of her trials, her blindness guided you along to this your estate of religion with unforeseeing spite. Now let her go and tyrannize
at the top of her rage and seek out other matter for her cruelty. For
against those whom the authority of our goddess has claimed for its
own, hostile Chance has no opportunity. What do bandits, what do
wild beasts, what does enslavement, what do the meanderings back
and forth of the rockiest roads, what does the fear of death day by day
avail the Fortune born to our curses? You have already been wel-
comed into the safe conduct of a Fortune — but of the sighted one who
by the brilliance of her light irradiates all the other gods as well.

Now put on a more joyful countenance to match the living white-

ness of the habit you wear, join the procession of your savior goddess
with the stride of the returning conqueror [who has shed no blood].
Let them see, the irreligious, let them see — and recognize their error:
"Look there: released from his former troubles, Lucius rejoices in great
Isis' foreseeing care and triumphs over his Fortune." But that you may
be the safer and the better fortified, add your name to this army of
holiness by whose sacred oath you will soon be sworn; now at last
dedicate yourself to the humble observance of our religion and
undergo the willing yoke of ministry. For when you begin your servitude to the goddess, then you will feel more keenly the fruit of your
liberty.   (11.15)

The priest's remarks are divided into an initial rebuke and a
long offering of congratulations to Lucius on his victory over
Fortune. But it seems to me that the two halves of the speech do
not fit very comfortably together; for however indispensable
the assistance of Isis proclaimed in the second half, the acknowl-
edgment of Lucius, not Isis, as victor implies an independent
contribution of merit on his part altogether discounted by the
first. It is odd, I think, that the moral of Lucius' experience as
summed up for the benefit of the unconverted in the second half
should fail to include, much less to emphasize, the redemption
of sin celebrated in the first. In fact, the moral eventually drawn
by the lay onlookers is, precisely as the priest anticipates, a matter of triumph assisted rather than of sin forgiven: "This is he
whom on this day the tremendous will of the almighty goddess
has shaped back to humanity — happy, by Hercules, and thrice
blessed; for by the innocence and faithfulness of his preceding
life he has earned so splendid a patronage from heaven as to be
in a manner reborn and straightway betrothed to the ministry of
holy rites" (11.16).

What the onlookers infer from Isis' unusual favor toward
Lucius is not his guilt but, on the contrary, his innocence and
merit; why should the goddess be making a public example of
Lucius the central point of which eludes the public so completely?
And it is not only the lesson Isis actually succeeds in teaching
that the priest's lesson misrepresents; it is also the whole
tenor of Isis' momentous personal interview with Lucius. For the
priest has mentioned misdeeds of lust and curiosity presumably

committed by Lucius in both his incarnations, but in a prayer for Isis' intercession that the goddess finds worthy of an answer Lucius goes no further than to speculate that he may have offended some god (11.2). Far from repenting of either alleged misdeed, he is at this climactic point aware of neither, and the goddess in the whole course of her epiphany registers not the slightest flicker of reproach.

I think, then, that we must discard the gratuitous assumption that the central point is indeed the one that the priest has been drawing. He is, after all, a fallible mortal as shaken as his fellows by events that only he has been prepared to witness (*miratus*, 11.13; *attonitus*, 11.14), and though we are told that he ends his speech gasping after "having prophesied in this way" (11.16), the text nowhere indicates that either the gasping or the prophecy characterizes the first (or retrospective) part of his speech. In what follows I shall try to show that, like the lay response, the priest's represents a partial view, one that is at least equally misleading.

In the priest's account the hero's arrival at his current "religious estate" coincides with the transference of his affairs from the control of "unforeseeing spite" (*inprovida malitia*) to that of "foreseeing care" (*providentia*). But it is highly unlikely that such a Manichaean division of cosmic labor should ever have recommended itself to a philosopher of Apuleius' antecedents. It is true that Middle Platonism of the kind he represents — the tradition of such writers as Albinus and Plutarch — refers evil to an irreducible principle of caprice personified as Typhon, the adversary of Isis — a hypothesis that serves to clear her divine benevolence of responsibility for human lapses into both ill luck and ill will.[7] By Plutarch's account, the rejection in such a hypothesis of the Stoic dogma that every event has an explanation makes up for the prejudice to rationalist faith by a definite provision for free will and moral responsibility. For Apuleius' contemporary colleague Albinus, the autonomy of *chance* is once more simply necessary to the autonomy of *choice* — to the possibility of the gratuitous act that lies, in his view, at the root of the notion of responsibility.[8]

The general position is duly summarized in the manual of Platonism that has come down to us under Apuleius' name: "All natural and hence rightly ordered events are controlled by the guardianship of providence, and no evil will be attributable to God. Accordingly all things in Plato's judgment are to be referred to the lot of fate . . . but something inheres in us, and something inheres in fortune."⁹ This concession to pure spontaneity, however, is distinctly un-Manichaean. In particular the limit on the scope of divine causation does not imply that providence is correspondingly limited or intermittent — for example, that sighted Fortune intervenes in Lucius' affairs only after blind Fortune has done her worst.

To understand Apuleius' accommodation of chance to divine omnipotence — of Typhon to Isis — it will be useful to bear in mind that as Apuleius portrays her Isis is indeed supreme — *summas dea* (11.1) — and that it is entirely proper for her priest to be invoked "by the stars of heaven, by the wills of hell, by the elements of nature, by the hush of night" (2.28), because his mistress "wields power by preeminent majesty; human affairs are absolutely regulated by her providence. Not only cattle and wild beasts but, by her light's and might's behest, inanimate things too are set in motion, and the very bodies in earth, sky, and sea now swell in accordance with her waxing, now shrink in compliance with her waning" (11.1). And her dispensation includes "the glowing peaks of the sky, the wholesome gusts of the sea, and the despondent hush of the underworld" (11.5). "The dwellers on high worship you, the dwellers below attend on you, you wheel round the world, light up the sun, rule the cosmos, trample the underworld. The stars obey you, the seasons return for you, the powers that be rejoice for you, the elements are in thrall to you" (11.25). The sovereignty of Isis, in short, is universal; she is, in her own words, "engendress of the scheme of things, mistress of all elements, initial scion of the generations, queen of the spirits of the dead, first of the dwellers in heaven, the gods' and goddesses' unitary face" (11.5).

That Apuleius goes so far as to identify the goddess with the Neoplatonic One is clear from the virtually equivalent terms and cadence in which he elsewhere describes the latter: "the cause and reason [that it, *logos*] and initial source of the whole scheme of things, highest engenderer of mind, timeless preserver of animate beings, tireless artisan of his cosmos."¹⁰ Since the gods emanate from Isis as their "unitary face" or essence (*facies uniformis*), as the Neoplatonic substances from the One, the jurisdiction of a god is simply a part of Isis' jurisdiction. Hence the royal style of Venus, in both terms and import, succinctly reproduces that of Isis: "ancient engendress of the scheme of things, initial source of the elements, sustaining mistress of the whole world" (4.3). The province of Jupiter likewise — "the laws of the elements and the vicissitudes of the stars" at his "bosom's" disposal (6.23) — is merely a sector of Isis' domain. The peculiarity and success of the monotheism entailed by her cult is its power to assimilate the pantheon rather than supersede it. As the sum of a set of numbers is not itself a set of numbers but a single number, so the sum of the pagan gods who is Isis is not a divine senate but a single god, indeed the only god. She is, however, in her capacity as sum, the *dea multinominis* (11.22) who is invoked variously as Ceres, Venus, Proserpina, Diana, Cybela, Minerva, Bellona, Hecate, and Nemesis, goddess of retributive justice (11.2, 5).

This multiplicity of names reflects not only an irenic reconciliation of all cults but the infinitesimal detail of divine influence on the course of events in the material universe. In the standard aretalogy or praise of Isis she claims that all things yield to her;[11] and this totality presumably includes events as well as objects. The inscription on the seated statue of Athena-Isis at Sais in Lower Egypt, as reported by Plutarch, makes history itself the god's incarnation: "I am all that has been and is and will be"; and Plutarch repeatedly insists that Isis foils Typhon's sabotage as continuously as he attempts it.[12] The characterization of divine Providence traditionally ascribed to Apuleius makes it equally exhaustive: "since the supreme divinity not only meditates on all these things in the accounting of its thoughts but traverses first things and middle and last and, having found them out, most inwardly rules them by the universality and constancy of its provident ordering."[13]

The narrator of the romance clearly subscribes to this theologized view of history, nearly though not quite equating Fortune and Providence: "Certainly nothing turns out right for anybody born human without Fortune's consent; one cannot, by wise precaution or judicious cure, overturn or transform the fateful ordering of divine Providence" (9.1). "Nor did the travail of [Psyche's] blameless soul elude the pondering gaze of good Providence" (6.15). "Human affairs are absolutely regulated by

Providence" (11.1). Lucius' hymn to Isis in effect simply rings devout changes on the theme of Isis' immediate deflection of her cosmic opponent's every gambit:

You are holy and the perpetual savior of humanity, always bounteous in the fostering of mortals. To the accidents of the wretched you mete out the sweet compassion of a mother. *No day, no rest, not the tiniest instant* passes free of your good offices but that on land and sea you shelter human beings, thrust down the whirlwind of life and stretch the saving right hand out by which you retouch even the fatal webs that are not to be unwoven, make mild the storms of Fortune and check the malignant courses of the stars. (11.25; emphasis added)

On such a view of divine influence, the ordeal of the hero as magic beast may result from Typhon's hatred, but from first to last it expresses Isis' love; it is not, as the priest supposes, a work of chance interrupted at length by Providence, but the work of Providence on the mere stuff of chance. As such it is far less likely to be a gross affliction than a subtle blessing.

But if the priest is to be believed, Lucius' ordeal is neither a blessing nor simply an affliction but a punishment (*sinistrum praemium*), and Isis' explicit and special favor (11.4–5) is not only distinct from the transformation to which it is only the sequel, but entirely unmerited. This, however, is another point of disagreement between the priest's views on Providence and the tradition of Platonic theology to which Apuleius is an heir and by which (once again in words that have come down to us under his name) divine favor has to be earned "in proportion to the *merit* of a life passed more purely and chastely [than the common run]";[14] the whole point of limiting Isis' providence so as to accommodate free will is to lay the ground for a theory of divine reward and punishment and not of unmerited grace.

One modern critic has claimed that "we are taught [by the romance] to expect very little of other men, or of ourselves, so that we may expect all the more of Isis";[15] but the denouement of the story, at least, makes it quite clear that one thing we can expect of Isis is a bountiful reply to a free act of petition: "Behold, Lucius, I am at hand, *moved* by thy prayers" (11.5). Such acts, being free and not necessitated, are of course not to be "expected" for the very reason that they are not to be despaired of: when their moment comes deeds are what you do, not what you wait for to happen to you. The crucial point is that they are grounds of merit that move the goddess to requite them. Her parting words to Lucius, in fact, are a promise of more abundant rewards contingent on more abundant merit (11.5). We are given no evidence at all that the goddess's favor is ever simply gratuitous; her cult, on the contrary, typically assigns an essential role — even a duty — to acts of faith. Thus her ministry is "a voluntary yoke" (*iugum uoluntarium*, 11.15), and the induction into her ultimate mystery is "in the form of a voluntary death and of a salvation by prayer [*ad instar uoluntariae mortis et precariae salutis*]" (11.21). The onlookers at Lucius' restoration, as we already noticed, take it for granted that divine favor argues the recipient's merit. Is it possible that what the priest has taken for acts of unchastity and profanation are, in eternal eyes, either indifferent or praiseworthy? In view of the merit Isis requires of her favorites, as well as Lucius' utter failure to act, or to be divinely received, as a prodigal son returned, this alternative possibility seems to me to be well worth exploring.

There are, it is true, details in the narrative that have persuaded modern critics to identify the priest with the author and consider that they are being invited to charge the hero with a "sin" of "obsession with sexual lust."[16] For example, Lucius' affair with Fotis has been cited to show his reckless dismissal of his aunt Byrrhaena's warning against the sexual advances of the witch Pamphile (2.5);[17] but Fotis is not Pamphile, and Byrrhaena says nothing about sexual abstinence or even about the need to break off his stay at Pamphile's house. Again, Lucius ends his vehement appeal to Fotis to help him steal a glimpse of the sorceress at work by pleading his amorous passion for Fotis; he is the willing slave of her charms, desiring no homeward return (3.19). But the context makes it only too obvious that the passion Lucius has yielded to in these protestings is not amorous, and that they are hardly to be construed as a genuine "admission of enslavement to the charms of Fotis," much less as a "preference for Fotis against the claims of friends and kin" — and still less as a "rejection of his kinsfolk."[18] The decisive impulse operating here is Lucius' fervent longing for firsthand knowledge of magic — he is "coram magiae noscendae ardentissimus cupitor" (3.19) — and fond as he is of Fotis, she figures in these serious plans chiefly as a means; his decision to carry on an affair with her in fact coincides with a decision to "refrain from an amorousliaison" with Pamphile (2.6) — in effect a decision to follow the gist of his aunt's advice.

As for Fotis, far from her being victimized or corrupted by the relationship, Apuleius takes pains to inform us that, as she herself boasts, she is as accomplished "a seasoner of beds as of bowls" (2.7), and hence amply qualified to conduct a sexual initiation of the hero quite as innocent as its counterparts in ancient New Comedy or the romance of Daphnis and Chloe. She is, moreover, well aware that as a self-proclaimed slave of love her new partner is being somewhat "foxy" (3.22), and it is worth noting that the allusive description of their lovemaking is entirely free of the clinical pornography routinely served up in the cognate Greek narrative. If Apuleius is playfully frank about what is going on, we should do well to consider his claim, in the Apology, that such frankness is entirely in keeping with the dignity of the philosophical calling and is formidably endorsed by the erotic verse not only of Solon, but of Plato himself. "To disguise and conceal such things is the part of a sinner; to acknowledge and publish is the part of someone at play."[19] If Ulysses' dalliance with Calypso and Circe does not inhibit Apuleius from setting him up as a model of the "highest virtues" to be acquired by extensive experience (9.13), it is not easy to picture the author succumbing to an attack of belated and selective moralism in the treatment of his own hero.

It is true that Isis requires absolute sexual abstinence of her initiates; but the hero before and during his enchantment is not an initiate, and beyond this it is dangerous to generalize about the code associated with the cult of a goddess of sexual love identified with Venus (11.5), a goddess who "engendered love and joined together the diversity of the sexes" (11.2), who is identified by Eudoxus (in the citation of Plutarch) as "the Umpire of matters erotic," and repeatedly by Plutarch as presiding over phallic celebrations of her own tragic love.[20]

If there is little to bear out the priest's complaint that Lucius has been the slave of his sexual appetite, there is more than a little substance to the twin charge of curiosity, which is repeatedly, even programmatically, substantiated by the romance. But here we need to be aware of certain commonplace distinctions that the priest, in his prosecutorial zeal, neglects to draw. In strictness it is not curiosity *tout court* that is the sin but malicious curiosity — "a kind of fondness," as Plutarch defines it, "for learning of the evils of other people."[21] And here Apuleius provides two crucial foils to the curiosity of his hero, whose worst impulse (from which he immediately draws back in any case) is to "plunge into the abyss" by retaining a mistress of the black arts as his tutor in magic (2.6).

The plunge that tempts Lucius is motivated by a disinterested if reckless desire for knowledge. This is a motive in vivid and, I think, pointed contrast with the envy and malice that embolden Psyche's sisters to leap from the same high cliff on three separate occasions (5.14, 17, 27), the last time to their deaths. But there is an even more obvious and carefully studied contrast between the moral precipices associated respectively with Lucius and with Psyche, who allows herself to forget her husband's urgent warning against throwing herself down "from so great a height of fortune" (5.6), and who thereby "plunged into the deep" (5.18) by giving easy credence to her sister's envious libel that her unseen lover is a gigantic viper (5.17). Here we are explicitly prevented by the narrative from excusing Psyche's disloyalty by pleading her ignorance; Cupid may be invisible, but the partner of his caresses (5.5) can hardly fail to know very well that he is not a serpent: "by these luxurious tresses of yours with the smell of cinnamon on them, by these cheeks as tender and smooth as mine, by your breast heated with I know not what passion" (5.13).

Psyche is willing to think the worst of her husband despite her better knowledge; Apuleius finally gives us in her a schematic portrait like Ovid's Medea of lost integrity or (what comes to the same thing) moral disintegration: "She hurries, delays, dares, quails, falters, rages, and, at the furthest extreme, in the same body hates a beast and loves a husband" (5.21). Her curiosity about Cupid is a breach of faith, and she later trifles with her atonement for that misdeed by succumbing to curiosity about a jar (6.19ff.) — like Lucius' fateful jar, a pyxis — whose contents she has been gravely warned against examining. The motive of this second access of curiosity is personal vanity redeemed in a degree by a wish to please her husband (she thinks she will find a divinely potent cosmetic), but it is worth noting that the passage equivocates — pointedly — on the operative word: Psyche offends "meddlingly" (*temeraria curiositate*) but immediately thereafter she is saved when Cupid revives her *curiose*—"with loving concern" (6.20–21).

Clearly not all curiosity is evil. Psyche's qualifies as such, by Plutarch's definition at least, because in the first instance she seeks and expects to find evil in an object of love and commitment. Lucius looks for no such thing as he blunders into transformation; his ambition is rather to be "a voyager throughout the heaven and the supreme Jupiter's trusty herald" (3.23). But this is a transparent metaphor for precisely the benign curiosity Plutarch prescribes as an antidote to the curiosity that kills: "How, then, does one escape? By a deflection or diversion of curiosity, especially when one turns one's mind to better and sweeter things. Be curious about the contents of the heavens, of the earth, of the air, of the sea." "Let us recognize in curiosity an edge, as it were, and point of the love of learning and not blunt and waste it on frivolities."[22] Apuleius himself extols those philosophers "who trace the steps of Providence in the world with greater curiosity,"[23] and it seems to me that the curiosity with which he has equipped his hero is, if not quite the same, at least near kin to theirs. By his own admission Lucius is a "thirster after oddity" (1.2); but in the sense of mere meddling, or collecting oddities for their own sake, he protests categorically on one occasion that he is *"not curious* but rather so constituted that I wish to know either all or at least the greater part of what there is" (1.2; emphasis added). If one is sincere in this ambition, one does not pass up the chance to investigate any possibility, least of all on the paltry ground that one has never run across its like: "As for me, I hold that nothing is impossible, but that all things come to mortals in whatever way the fates have ordained; for you and I—everybody has had staggering things aplenty, things well nigh impossible, actually happen to him and yet lose credit all the same when they get reported to the uninformed" (1.20).

But though Lucius' thirst for oddity is whetted by the urge to believe, what quenches it is explanation; to know all things is to know how they happen and can be made to happen again, and Lucius has a callow faith in the readiness of oddities, however baffling, to yield their secrets. "You have not the penetration to see," he lectures a skeptic,

that the things reputed lies by corrupt opinion are the very things that
seem odd to the ear or outlandish to the eye or at any rate high above
the reach of thought — things that, if you should use a little more care
to ferret them out, you will find not only simple to understand but
easy to do.

Take me for example. Last evening, trying to hold my own with
my fellow trenchermen, I got a bit careless and overeagerly lopped off
too generous a morsel of cheese cake; what with the softness of the
gluey confection sticking in my throat and stuffing my windpipe I all
but perished. And yet the day before in Athens, in front of the
Gallery, with these two eyes I watched a circus performer swallow a
cavalry broadsword sharpened to a wicked point and soon after, with
the incentive of a paltry fee, bury a hunting spear by the business end
in the depth of his bowels.   (1.3–4)

The wonders that fascinate, Lucius, then, are by his account
sword-swallowing writ large: mystifying only to the uninitiate
and accessible to a determined inquiry. His response to one such
offer of enlightenment is entirely characteristic: "For my part I
was reminded of my native curiosity and all agog that the hidden cause of the affair be stripped naked" (3.14). Lucius' enthusiasm has perhaps some warrant by the standards of his
culture. "Blessed is he," says Virgil in a celebrated passage, "who
has been able to acquaint himself with the causes of things and
has cast down at his feet all fears, and relentless fate, and the
crashing of Acheron."[24]

The narrator himself sometimes recalls his curiosity in the
favorable terms I have thus far been recommending — indeed,
even more favorable, for he twice applies to its effect (9.13, 15)
the same term of praise he elsewhere uses to describe the effect
of the revelations of Isis (11.22) — a *recreatio* or revivifying. One
of the relevant passages is crucial enough to quote in full:

And there was no consolation anywhere for the tormenting life
[of the mill], except that I was revivified by my own innate curiosity
as people indifferent to my presence did and said whatever they wished
without constraint. And it was far from unreasonable for the godlike
founder of the ancient art of poetry among the Greeks, wishing to
show a man of the highest prudence, to sing of one who by traversing
many cities and acquainting himself with divers peoples achieves the
highest virtues. For I myself am intensely grateful to my donkey for
having trained [*exercitatum*] me, in the secrecy of his own

covering, to a wide array of fortunes, and thereby rendered me, even if not prudent, at least a knower of many things [*multiscium*].   (9.13)

Being *multiscius*, by the way, is no mean praise in Apuleius, who in his Apology makes it an epithet of Homer himself.[25] As for the hero's Homeric interpretation of his travels in the shape of an ass, clearly none could be in sharper conflict with the views of the priest. Here that alien shape is a means to the hero's *exercitatio* (to his development of skill by practice) in the knowing of many things; and the skill is further specified by allusion to the proem of the *Odyssey*, for what the hero of that poem comes to know above all by visiting "the cities of many men" are the minds of the citizens. He does so very often, like Apuleius' hero, as a spy in disguise; and if in the ass's case the disguise forestalls hostile suspicion only at the price of obscuring the traveler's status as a person, he may once again plead the example of the strategist of the Trojan horse, and above all the hero whose most ironically effective alias is "No One." In fact he may plead the pregnant ambiguity of the Greek name itself, which in one of the forms played on by Homer (*Métis*)[26] is nearly a twin to the word for wisdom or skill.

Above all, Apuleius' hero has in common with Homer's the virtue of curiosity. In a celebrated instance, Odysseus has Circe's permission, which later he represents to his crew as a command, to enjoy the song of the Sirens. The curiosity he thereby indulges, we are assured by no less a commentator than Cicero, is far from idle:

Don't we see that those who delight in noble pursuits and skills take no account of health or material interest? that they endure anything when lured by the opportunity for finding out and knowing things? that they buy at the price of the greatest anxieties and pains the pleasure they get from learning? I personally believe that Homer saw something of this kind in what he imagined of the Sirens' songs. For their habit is apparently to use neither the sweetness of their voices nor some novelty or variation in the singing to call back men who were sailing by: rather they would claim to know many things, so that hunger for learning might fix men to their rocks.[27]

Their offer to the listener, in short, is to make him *multiscius*, and the offer supplies Homer with a measure of the strength of his hero's curiosity; a single set of ropes is not enough to restrain Odysseus from trying to take the Sirens up on their invitation. But the ropes are also Circe's way of partially gratifying a legitimate desire. The way of Isis, I suggest, if rather more bizarre, is also more effective.

"People indifferent to my presence did and said what they wished without constraint." This interesting fact, it seems to me, puts an intolerable burden on the priest's theory of Lucius' curiosity, a burden the Odyssean theory does not have to carry. On the former view we have a retribution that not only lets the sinner compound his sin but tempts us — indeed forces us on pain of refusing to read on — to join him in his guilty pleasures. On the latter view, the transformation is a divine artifice for promoting the virtue of knowing people's minds. It is of course possible to adopt neither view, or a distortion of both, by the bold expedient of disparaging the author's performance: "There is in fact a central ambivalence in the romance, a tension between Milesian ribaldry and Platonist mysticism, which reflects the complexity of the author's personality . . . The book lacks the homogeneity of a closely articulated work of art."[28] But the tension at issue here, it seems to me, is a critical illusion that comes of underestimating the complexity of the author's Platonic mysticism and altogether slighting his theory of curiosity.

I have already considered Apuleius' defense of Plato's erotic verse and, by implication, of his own erotic writing; of Platonism itself I shall have something more to say at a later stage. What concerns me at the moment is the thematically central question of the hero's curiosity and the transformation that gratifies it, which he thanks for his having become *multiscius* about people's minds. If this accomplishment amounts to a virtue endorsed by Isis, as I have suggested, which of the standard virtues is it, and why should it matter to Isis in particular?

The answer lies, I think, in another running theme of the romance, the ubiquitous danger of unfair or corrupted judgment. This, for example, is the moral of an elaborate masque of the Bribery of Paris that reminds the magic beast, among other things, that his favorite hero has an extra-Homeric vice quite as imposing and instructive in its own way as his Homeric virtues:

Why does it surprise you if the sheep of the court — no, the vultures in robes—if the whole guild of judges nowadays bargains away its decisions at a price, when at the inception of human affairs favoritism tainted a judgment at issue between gods and men, and a judge chosen at the great Jupiter's discretion, a man of the fields, a shepherd, sold his primordial decision along with the destruction of his whole race, for a profit in lust? For the same kind of thing, by Hercules, take another later judgment exercised among the famous Achaean generals: Palamedes, preeminent in cultivation and learning, condemned to death for treason by false accusations; Ulysses modestly endowed with military valor, preferred to mighty Ajax, whose endowment was outstanding. (10.33)

The list concludes with a lengthy comment on the death to which Socrates was condemned by the judges of no less a city than the schoolmistress-to-the-world of every science, including jurisprudence. In each item the abuse is the same: the corruption of judgment to which Ulysses, for example, prostitutes his forensic talents by pleading against Palamedes and Ajax. And Apuleius has frequent opportunities to reflect that one need not be bribed to arrive at unfair judgments of one's fellows.

"No doubtful proofs but probable reasons" persuade the people of Hypata to convict Lucius *in absentia* of robbing his host (7.1–2). The ass's panicky flight from an overheard plot to butcher him is construed, again on good circumstantial evidence, as an infallible sign of rabies (9.2). A party of refugees is taken by harried farmers for a bandit gang and unmercifully stoned and gored (8.17). A glib and malicious groom manages to persuade some shepherds that the ass has repeatedly attempted to rape women and should be either killed or gelded (7.21). The hero himself is misled by appearances into suspecting a young bride of sluttish disloyalty and into treating his suspicion as grounds for the moral condemnation of all women; the credit of the sex, he tells us in a self-mocking aside, "depended at that moment on the judgment of an ass" (7.10)—though this comment itself is an illustration of the theme of unfairness, for the misguided judgment in question is all too human. Finally, we are reminded at least twice that obligation is as equivocal as character; there is a misplaced reverence or compassion, an *illicita pietas*, that Psyche and the magic beast are both well advised to dismiss (6.18, 28).

The virtue that on the showing of these passages is in gravely short supply, and of which the essential ingredient is wide knowledge of other minds, is the judicial virtue of fairness or equity; and in her incarnations as Demeter Thesmophoros and as Nemesis, the goddess of equity par excellence is Isis, one of whose hieratic emblems is "the effigy of a left hand, palm outstretched. For by reason of its natural sloth and want of any crafty slyness the left hand rather than the right seemed especially proper to equity" (11.10). There is, then, a special irony and fitness in the circumstance that the loss of his crafty right hand forces the bandit Lamachus to do justice on himself by the effort of his slothful and uncrafty left. These requirements for a symbol of equity are of course also proverbially met by the animal chosen by the providence of Isis to be both the hero's disguise and the spy-hole through which he will contrive to take the measure of human nature in spite of human pretenses. In an ironic and benign sense not contemplated by the priest, that animal disguise is indeed a "left-handed reward" (*sinistrum praemium*) for the hero's curiosity.

I have been arguing that in Apuleius' moral lexicon, as in Plutarch's, "curiosity" names a virtue as well as a vice; the subject of inquiry makes the difference. It is possible to object, however, that the medium of inquiry also makes a difference, and that Lucius' offense is to indulge his curiosity by magic. But it is not clear what form of magic would be intrinsically offensive to a writer of Apuleius' persuasions. There is nothing evil, for example, in the Neoplatonic demons that dispense prophecy and "the multifarious wonders of magicians." The monistic and hierarchical scheme in which they figure makes them simply intermediaries between the human and the divine, "the carriers of prayers from the one quarter and gifts from the other."[29] A conceivable demonic accomplice in the abuse of such gifts is the notorious Hecate; but for Apuleius Hecate is simply the benign Isis by another name (11.5). It is true that Fotis has been taught by her mistress to believe that magicians coerce the divine will (3.15, 18); but on the monotheistic principles of the denouement, at least, there is no more an offense of coercing gods than there is one of squaring the circle. No doubt as a piece of blasphemy the belief in such coercion is itself an offense. But Lucius commits no such blasphemy; where Fotis talks of compulsion he talks of invocation (3.19; see 11.2). There is nothing in any of this to offend Isis.

In fact, the benign uses of magic are illustrated in the romance chiefly, if not exclusively, by Isis' priests — by the necromancer Zatchlas, an agent of "divine providence" (2.27), and by the hierophant Mithras, who at the goddess's direction finally restores Lucius (11.13). Nor is the offensiveness of magic traceable to its pharmacopoeia, which largely consists in fact of the common products of a nature whose ultimate patroness is Isis, the goddess of nature — anise, bay leaves, honey, aromatic plants of various kinds (3.18, 24; 2.28); it is entirely fitting that the roses Mithras uses to undo the transformation should discharge precisely the same function in the magic of Pamphile, and that only chance — or Isis — prevents Lucius from being restored by Fotis' roses on the morning after his accident (3.25).

As with curiosity, it is the use one's energies are put to that makes the moral difference — in this instance, the difference between black magic and white. In his extant defense against the charge of sorcery, Apuleius replies in part, a little disingenuously perhaps, by dignifying the art itself, associating with the unimpeachable statesman and savant Nigidius Figulus the practice of inducing prophetic trance in children by incantation (a practice, as one might expect, identified by a late Hellenistic text with the Memphitic rites of Apis-Epaphus, the son of Isis). It apparently goes without saying that such a feat would be innocent; for Apuleius the only interesting question is which innocent forces in particular could account for its success. The likeliest explanation, in the speaker's tentative opinion, is the operation either of demons or of the human soul in its original simplicity, which is demonic.[30] This no doubt illuminates the reverence for personhood that informs Apuleius' romance, but by the same token it gives no clue to what the author of that romance could find offensive in the magical ambitions of his hero. On the contrary: the charge Apuleius easily repels in the Apology is that he has resorted to *magica maleficia*. Though he is thereby relieved of the need to *assert* the possibility of *magica beneficia*, he does find an opportunity, in his categorical remark that "nothing done for a wholesome end is criminal," to *imply* it.[31]

On the author's probable assumptions, then, Lucius' quest for the principles of magic, whether he knows it or not, is ultimately a quest for Isis. Indeed, however feckless and laughable Apuleius' hero proves to be, the onlookers at his restoration who find him wholly deserving of Isis' patronage are at least as credible as the censorious priest who thinks deserts had nothing to do with it.

There is, however, no need to accept either view without qualification, as we should need to if they exhausted the possibilities that a Middle Platonist like Apuleius would be prepared to entertain. It is the Stoics who deny that merit or demerit admits of degree, and their absolutism makes them a laughingstock to the Academy's sympathizers. It is all too easy, says Plutarch, for a Stoic lecturer to pretend that there is no real difference between the intellectual shortcomings of a Plato and those of some accuser of Socrates, or between the moral shortcomings of a statesman and those of a tyrant. But outside the classroom such unrealities have a mischievous way of making their presence noticeable even to a professor. Albinus is willing to allow an absolute use of "virtuous" for the point exactly equidistant between any given pair of opposite extremes of conduct or disposition, but he recognizes the awkwardness in a correlative use of "vicious" or "morally defective" for even slight deviations from the mean. "Not all men are either morally perfect or morally defective." To do justice to the moral facts we need, and in fact (thanks to common sense) have, relative and dynamic uses of "virtuous" to describe behavior or tendencies that approximate or are advancing toward the mean.[32]

Lucius, as the onlookers guess, is among the relatively virtuous, though even these, as the censorious priest is quick to observe, must be accounted vicious by the absolute standard. But in the failure to which this kind of virtue is thus reducible, there is a whiff of glory for which Lucius may justly claim a reward from the goddess — and no sinister reward at that. The Platonic sage portrayed, for example, in the epitome *Of Plato's Teaching* attributed to Apuleius is as theoretically unreal as the Stoic equivalent, an ascetic who practices death and is incapable of grief. The best of what the same treatise calls the "middlingly disposed" (*medie morati*), like the Solon and Plato of Apuleius' Apology, dwell in the moral space where comedy and tragedy are possible.[33]

It is fitting that the Isis of Egyptian myth, an inhabitant of the same space, should thereby force an eclectic theologian like Plutarch to adopt a theory of progress toward divinity.

Those authors do better who hold that the events reported of Typhon and Osiris and Isis are not the experiences of gods or of human beings but of great demons. Plato, Pythagoras, Xenocrates, and Chrysippus follow the ancient theologians in maintaining that such demons are naturally more powerful than we but possessed of an impure divinity sharing the nature of soul and a bodily sensitivity capable of pleasure and pain and all the concomitant agitations to which some are more susceptible, and some less. For distinctions in vice and virtue occur in demons as well as men.

But Plutarch is unwilling to concede that the Isis of the great religion — Isis as she is now — is merely one of the greater demons; the essence of her history is that it is an initiation into full divinity: "She and Osiris were changed by virtue from good demons into gods . . . It is altogether fitting that they get the mixed worship of both gods and demons."[34] There is, as we shall see, a trace of this developmental notion in the more thoroughgoing monotheism of Apuleius' romance, but the significance of the Isis tradition for that romance is, I think, important in any case. It is all very well to contemplate moral polarities such as that of the carnal and spiritual Venus; Apuleius himself is willing to dichotomize in this vein.[35] But in any adequate account of moral experience one must recognize *media species amoris*, a love that is both of the flesh and of the spirit, "gathered by nearness to the divine and coupled in an equal fellowship."[36] The religious and philosophic strains in Apuleius' romance unite in rejecting the undiscriminating severity that sees degradation in all that is not perfect.

The fact remains that in her epiphany Isis herself seems to see degradation in an animal form so imperfect that, after all, her protégé would rather die than continue to wear it (11.2); the ass is "a beast I have long abominated" (11.6). In the festivals of Isis, Plutarch informs us, the ass is ritually hurled from a cliff because like Typhon he is redhaired and unteachable, and because sacrificial or impure beasts are those animated by wicked men who have endured transformation.[37] Though Lucius in comfortable reminiscence claims warm gratitude to his donkey guide through the maze of the world, surely (one might object) this complacency may be dismissed; how can a season in so unsanctified a shape be other than a season in hell? But I think on the contrary that it would be a mistake to dismiss the testimony of the hero on the basis of popular cult beliefs, the more so as neither Apuleius nor Plutarch allows us to credit such belief as literally understood. We are graphically invited to pity Lucius' fellow ass—his "comrade in arms"—precisely for suffering the treatment recommended by the cult (4.5). The festival of Isis at which Lucius is reborn shows an ass genially adorned, and at the climactic moment an ass unhesitatingly fed on roses by none other than a hierophant of the cult.

What seems to me more fundamental to the religious meaning of the romance is that as the goddess of the First Matter or potentiality, Isis herself has assumed this form along with the rest. "Her usual epithet is 'she of the infinitely many names [*myrionymos*]' because in the course of her transformations by absolute reason [*logos*] she receives all forms and aspects."[38] We are evidently to understand that this divine omnipresence or immanence in the world of change is the inner meaning of the demonic incarnation and the progress toward godhead suggested by Egyptian myth. By withdrawing into her self (*in se recessit*, 11.7) after delivering the oracle of salvation that Lucius has been seeking ever since his morning walk through the streets of Hypata, Isis demonstrates her transcendence; by presenting him later with a morning view of Cenchreae even more clearly animated by her spontaneous life, she expresses her immanence— what Plutarch had described as her passage through all forms: "All things seemed to me to be pulsing with a joy beyond what was uniquely mine, a joy so great that I felt even cattle of all kinds and all the horses and the day itself exult with unclouded face" (11.7). The goddess has withdrawn into a self of cosmic inclusiveness; clearly there is nothing, even what is comical and mean, that a deity so conceived will disdain to touch.

Thus religious initiation, or mystic union with Isis, inevitably requires a ritual enactment of the divine passage through all states, beginning with a "voluntary death" (11.21): "I advanced to the border of death and having trodden the threshold of Proserpine and been borne through all the elements, made my return passage" (11.23). The ordeal of monstrous change by which one achieves divine union is a requirement met by Io, the Greek avatar of Isis, who is blessed by a visionary marriage with Zeus at the mouth of the Nile only after an agonizing passage through the world in the shape of a heifer; and the general notion is clearly reflected in the dream of Habrocomes, a protégé of Isis in the late Hellenistic *Romance of Ephesus*, who in imagination must escape imprisonment and undergo long wanderings in the shape of a horse before being reunited with his lost bride and restored to the shape of a man.[39] To be initiated, in short, is to be transformed; that initiation ends in the solemn ritual of Lucius' ordination, but I think we must recognize that it begins with the holy farce of his life as an ass.

Plutarch puts the local cult practice of tormenting that animal into perspective by associating it with the similarly inspired reviling of redheaded men and the obsolete sacrifice of human beings designated as Typhonic.[40] The scandal in the beast-baiting for Plutarch, as I think for Apuleius as well, is a philosophical conviction of the special dignity of all awareness:

And this too is true, that we must recognize in soul an organ of the all-governing god and admit in general that nothing inanimate excels what is animate, nothing insensate what is possessed of sensation, not even if one gathers into one heap all gold and emeralds whatsoever. For it is not in hues and figures and surfaces that the divine inheres, but a value lower than corpses is the portion of everything that does not and by nature cannot partake of life. But the nature gifted with the power of sight and spontaneous movement and discernment between what does and does not belong to it has attracted an outflowing of beauty, a portion from that caring mind by which, in the phrase of Heraclitus, "the universe is piloted."[41]

It is characteristic of such a view that its advocate should have written a dialogue in which his own father is assigned an eloquent argument to the effect that sense perception is radically inseparable from intelligence and that cruelty to animals is a form of injustice.[42] As for Apuleius, his supreme being is par excellence "the eternal preserver of animate beings," and I think the only consistent way of reading Isis' abomination of such a being in the last book of the romance is to follow Plutarch's general recipe for interpreting the bestiary symbolism of the cult: the animal always stands for some one of its properties.[43] Isis hates *unteachableness* in human beings; she would doubtless not be scandalized by *intelligence* in a beastly shape.

In a passage of considerable interest for the traditional symbolism of the ass in ancient philosophical literature, Plutarch takes to task philosophers who claim to be scandalized by such a prospect, and in doing so brings to bear an oddly familiar parable of Heraclitus:

The Stoics hold that bodily seemliness and vigor contribute nothing of use or benefit to happiness. But this does not prevent them from buying health at the price of intelligence. For even Heraclitus and Pherecydes think it would be fitting, if indeed they could, to give up virtue and intelligence in order to get rid of dropsy and fleas. Indeed, if Circe poured out two drugs, the one making fools out of wise men, the other [wise asses out of human beings], Odysseus should drink the drug of folly rather than change into the shape of a beast while retaining his wisdom — and with wisdom presumably the essence of happiness. This is tantamount to their claiming that the precept of Wisdom herself is: "Discard me, scorn me if I am destroyed and corrupted into the face of an ass." But what is asinine, one is bound to say, is the kind of wisdom that gives that kind of advice — if in fact being wise and happy is a good and carrying about the face [of an ass] is a thing indifferent.[44]

In my first chapter I argued in effect that Circe's drug, whatever its external effect, has precisely the inward effect described by Heraclitus: its victim or beneficiary becomes what Lucius calls himself at one point, an *asinus prudens* (7.12). The same mystical comedy, I suggest, is enacted, with a far richer sense of its religious implications, in Apuleius' romance. The Circe of this later enactment, however, is not merely an agent of the cosmic intelligence, but Isis herself.

The long prelude to the hero's initiation is a religious comedy, and the religious outlook thereby projected is characteristic not only of Isis' worship but of a romance that, in my view, is dedicated to her glory from first to last. Before the solemn procession that leads to Lucius' restoration there is another prelude of comic mummers on parade that reproduces in symbolic miniature what we have lived through with the hero. The mummers are dressed up as soldiers, hunters, magistrates, philosophers, fowlers, fishermen; and we are also entertained not only with an ordinary female impersonator but with a she-bear tricked out in the garb of a Roman matron. Finally we have an ape as Ganymede and a tottering old Bellerophon leading a donkey Pegasus — an improbable aeronaut, by the way, whose image has flashed before us twice earlier in the romance to mock the hero and perhaps to celebrate him as well (6.30, 8.16). The theme of the parade — that all the world's a stage — is a commonplace of ancient philosophy and romance; but the festive piece on this particular stage is dedicated not only to Isis but to the demonic Mediterranean laughter of *carnaval*, and the distinction is perhaps not so sharp as it may appear. We have been told that the names of all the gods are hers; if so, and if her name at the festival of Cenchreae is Isis, it is still worth noting that the name by which she passed at the festival of Hypata was laughter (*Risus*, 2.31), and that the public sacrifice to her godhead on that occasion, as here, was Lucius.

The laughter that rings out from time to time in this book is explosive and painfully visceral (*ad usque intestinorum dolorem*, 10.16), like the response of a master to the graphic discovery that his donkey is a gourmet (10.16); sometimes it is the laughter of cruel derision, like the drunken *cachinnus* that greets a confessor's account of how he was indiscreet enough to lose his nose (2.31); and sometimes it is mixed with naked panic. At a wayside inn in the dead of night a dozing Aristomenes is blown underneath his rickety and now inverted cot by the volcanic entrance of two homicidal witches: "At that moment I found at first hand that certain passions naturally blossom into their opposites. For as tears sometimes grow out of joy, so in that state of extreme fright I could not contain my laughter at being no longer Aristomenes but a turtle" (1.12).

The sacrifice of Lucius to the god of laughter at Hypata consists in making the victim believe he is on trial for murder, has been convicted, and is now facing public torture to force him to reveal his nonexistent accomplices; much to his horrified disgust his oration in his own defense produces nothing but a mass guffaw (3.7). The miscarriage of justice with which the romance is pervasively concerned has been parodied to the ritual accompaniment of fear and laughter. This is finally the message of the droll parade of human estates that ushers in the procession of ecstatic worshipers. To perceive life as farce, travesty, and transformation is to be confronted by the comic mask of Isis. The laughter of intense dread, like the sobbing of intense joy, is a mystical state that testifies to her reality. It is an essential step in the process of initiation, a sacramental hazing of which the major symbol in the romance is the plight of the man with the donkey's body.

That farcical plight has an instructive echo in the "translation" of Bottom's head, and the fascination of Titania with that unworthy object (Shakespeare's version of the *matrona*'s unmentionable obsession). It is indeed as ass's head that arouses the drugged goddess's longing to "kiss thy fair large ears"; but even "love in idleness," to the degree that it is love at all, expresses itself in an urge akin to that of Isis, to "translate" its object into a vastly different order of being — to "purge thy mortal grossness so / That thou shalt like an airy spirit go." And perhaps in the sequel there is a hint that Bottom is purged not only *of* that grossness but *by* it; for the cadence in which he is moved to interpret his incommunicable dream to himself, however garbled, is recognizably that of Paul's message to the Corinthians on the beatific vision: "The eye of man hath not heard, the ear of man hath not seen, man's hand is not able to taste, his tongue to conceive nor his heart to report what my dream was!" Unlike Lucius, Bottom is and remains a tongue-tied simpleton. But even the skeptical Theseus is later moved to insist that "love . . . and tongue-tied simplicity / In least speak most." A god of illusion — the nocturnal Oberon — has vouchsafed his fools a vision at which rationalism scoffs in Theseus' celebrated lampoon against the imagination, the stuff of lunatic, lover, and poet. But the retort of the scoffer's bride may stand as an epigraph of Apuleius' as of Shakespeare's homage to the divine laughter:

> But all the story of the night told over,
> And all their minds transfigur'd so together
> More witnesseth than fancy's images
> And grows to something of great constancy.

Oberon, like Isis, is a mocking god of illusion, but in contrast to their counterparts in Ovid, here the mockery is benign.

If Lucius' transformation is a comic artifice contrived by a god, it is equally true and, I think, important that the narrative as a whole is a comic artifice contrived by the god's human votary. The *Book of Transformations* is religious art in a peculiar sense, an imitation of the *trompe l'oeil* in which its muse delights. From time to time, the text archly reminds us of this theme and its ramifications. The coffered roofs of Love's palace are of citrus wood "curiously" worked, and the walls are covered with a silver inlay of various beasts leaping forward toward the visitor: "A miraculous human being it was without a doubt — no, a demigod or god — who by the fineness of his great art had turned so much silver into wild beasts" (5.1). In the gallery of his aunt's mansion the hero finds a sculptural group of Diana's revenge that dominates the room, with the menacing goddess precisely at the center gratifying not only Actaeon's "curious gaze" but our own. The irony of the contrast between the theodicies of divine revenge and of divine providence is incidental to the impression of uncanny illusionary mastery, a mastery whose "most exalted evidence" (*summum specimen operae fabrilis*) is the rearing of the marble dogs: "Steeply raised breast up, their hind feet are braced backward; their front feet are running" (2.4).

But the artifice of the goddess, we find elsewhere, can reverse the process. Psyche's lovers "wonder at her (no doubt) as the image of a god — but as an image polished by the sculptor's art they wonder at her one and all" (4.32). Finding that his alleged murder victims are punctured goatskins, Lucius stands "cold and fixed in stone, just like any one of the *other* statues or pillars in the theater" (3.10; emphasis added). It is to be expected that a goddess who is an artist of transformation should require a corresponding performance of her celebrants.

It is perhaps more surprising, but equally appropriate, that a romance in her honor should itself be such a performance. We are forewarned of the trap being laid for us by Lucius' prefatory apology for his "exotic" prose in what is, after all, a second language painfully self-taught. "This change of voice itself, at any rate, matches the style I have affected, a style informed by the science of the *desultor*" — that is, of the circus rider who leaps without break from horse to horse (1.1). Lucius proceeds to inform us that he is a Thessalian Greek, a descendant in fact of the illustrious Plutarch. It is not until the close of the book that an incidental phrase lets us know, without any break in the tenor of the narrative, that he is an African from Madaura — that he is, in other words, Lucius Apuleius Platonicus Madaurensis, the famous rhetor and philosophical kinsman of Plutarch. Some critics have found in this detail a deplorable oversight; the author has forgotten to eliminate the telltale evidence that his concluding pages are a sacred memoir defensively patched onto the end of a narrative that is scandalously profane. It will be clear by this time that in my judgment they have subjected the book to a thoroughgoing misinterpretation. But what concerns us at the moment is that they have missed the inevitability of this crowning feat of the *desultoria scientia*. A fictitious character becomes his creator; a fable of conversion is converted into an autobiography on the same theme. And the *Book of Transformations*, to the greater glory of Isis, is itself transformed.

THE WEREWOLF OF MARIE de FRANCE:
Metamorphosis
Alienation
and Grace

LIKE HER PREDECESSORS IN THIS STUDY MARIE DE FRANCE confronts us in the *Lai de Bisclavret* with a dual challenge: to
the clarity of our cherished notion of what it is to be a person, and (even if that clarity is conceded) to our confidence that
creatures like ourselves could ever use such a notion to
recognize each other as persons. The occasion of these doubts is
the chronic lycanthropy of the central figure: "Of old one could
hear tell, and it used often to happen, that divers men became
werewolves. The werewolf [Norman *garvalf*] is a wild beast
that, while in that madness [*en cele rage*], devours men and does
great evil as it dwells and roams in the great forest" (5-12).[1] "My
lady, I become a werewolf [Breton *bisclavret*]. I enter the great
forest yonder in the densest part of the wood and live on prey
and plunder" (63-66). Critics of a modernizing bent will be
tempted to purge the tale of superstition by finding in "cele rage"
the meaning of the transformation itself, which would then
symbolize some such cannibalistic derangement as the "feral"
syndrome described by Aristotle.[2] But the transformation the
poet actually describes will not sustain this interpretation; its
victim is capable, without regaining his human form, of an affectionate meekness briefly interrupted twice by a ferocity that
is as understandable as it is sudden. Lycanthropy is represented

by the poet less as a feral state than as a feral mask that need not distort its helpless wearer's human face and always misrepresents it.

In another of the *lais*, just such a mask of predacity becomes an instrument if not an expression of love:

> She noticed the shadow of a great bird through a narrow casement. Into her chamber it entered flying; it had jesses at its feet, it seemed a hawk of five or six moultings. It alighted before the lady. When it had stood there a while and she had studied it well it became a fair and goodly knight. The lady holds him for a wonder, her wit wavers and trembles, in her great fear she covered her head. "Lady," quoth he, "do not fear. A noble bird there is within the hawk."[3]

Spitzer's attempt to allegorize away the uncanny is more elaborate than the appeal to derangement but in the end, I think, not much more persuasive:

> For Marie de France the beast in and of itself is something infinitely remote from humanity that precisely by acting and being treated "like a human being" becomes more mysterious and symbolically potent. It is just the suggestion of humanity in the beast that is the eeriness in the werewolf Bisclavret; indeed, Bisclavret is nothing but the beast-human in the so-called human being. Nothing is so exciting as intellect and volition in the wolf.[4]

This is misleading on two counts. The faculties of the werewolf, if not his appearance or species, are human and not merely suggestive of humanity; by contrast, his affliction is far from an ordinary concomitant of "so-called" humanity and hence unacceptable as a symbol of any such concomitant.

It is true and strange, on the other hand, that the unfortunate *baron*[5] is relegated by the poet's language, at least, to the status of a type. We are told at the outset that we are now to hear of the species *bisclavret*; and throughout the rest of the *lai* the Breton term oscillates at random between naming the species and naming a member whose uniqueness is thereby dissolved in abstraction.[6] The reduction is taken a step further when, as royal mascot, the hero is routinely designated, apparently by default, as "the beast";[7] now he is stripped of a species and identified by genus alone. The generality into which the baron is thus banished by nomenclature is not that of symbolic power but, on the contrary, of a featurelessness that defies interpretation: such is the exile of radical unintelligibility in which the monster — the being for which no place is reserved in the roll of creatures — is forced to languish. In his misgivings about letting his wife into the secret of his periodic absences, the baron too shows himself well aware that the natural response to monstrosity is alienation: " 'Lady,' quoth he, 'for the grace of God! Evil will come thereof if I tell it to you, for from the love of me shall I part you, and myself thereby shall I lose' " (53–56). And in the same spirit, near the end of the poem, the baron forgoes an opportunity to free himself from his monstrosity in the presence of onlookers to his shame (284–288). For the hero as for his betrayers, the *bisclavret*, or *Bisclavret*, or *la beste*, is in essence an object of loathing and terror. The victim of transformation is unrecognizable even to himself.[8]

Transformation, however, is not the only obstacle to knowledge of the Other; his (or her) pristine form, we find, is obstacle enough. The lady rightly observes that the secretive baron has no cause to suspect her loyalty. Up to the moment of the baron's confession, we have been pointedly told, she has steadfastly rebuffed "a knight of the country who long had loved her, and much had said and much besought, and in her service suffered much" (107–108). "I love you more than all the world," she protests to the baron; "you should not . . . doubt me for anything; it would not be like friendship. Wherein have I trespassed? By what sin do you doubt me for anything?" (80, 85). It is the baron's failure in "friendship," not his lady's, that is brought out by his hesitation in this interview. In the same way it is not at all clear that the obvious biblical parallel reflects exclusively on importunate wives.[9] To be sure, both of Samson's wives anticipate the lady in their favorite method of probing for the key to their husband's vulnerability: "You hate me and do not love; that is why you do not expound . . . the riddle" (Judg. 14:16); "how do you say you love me when your mind is not with me?" (Judg. 16:15). But the fact remains that in both Samson's case and the baron's the lady's inquiry is a test of love and her lord's hesitation a failure. For the baron in particular it is also a test of knowledge. If love presupposes a knowledge of its object, the lady is right to conclude that the baron does not love.

Indeed, a test that might unequivocally ground the missing insight is hard if not impossible to come by in Marie's *lais*. The bird-knight's proposal in the *Yonec*, for example, virtually reduces the enterprise to absurdity: "If you believe me not in this [my confession of Christian faith], send for your chaplain, say that illness has come over you and you wish to have the service that God has ordained to the world for sinners' cure. Your likeness [*semblance*] shall I take, the body of our lord receive, and all my creed shall I say to you; then hereof you will not doubt."[10] The possibility of fraud is — unpromisingly — to be excluded by dint of an exercise in fraud, the assuming of a false "semblance." Whatever primitive justice there is in the disfigurement with which the baron punishes his wife's treachery depends on the disastrous ease with which *semblance* may be abused: the lady and her issue will be deprived, by the permanent transformation she designed for her lord, of the means of beguiling anyone else. The impulse to betray that she will bequeath (presumably like original sin) will itself be betrayed — "easily recognizable . . . by *semblant*" (310–311). No longer, as at the outset, will she or her issue be able to "make a fair *semblant*" (21–22) — that is (as the sequel allows us to gloss this equivocal expression) to deceive.[11] But the equity of the poet's fundamentally tragic vision shows us that if her love was imperfect so was the baron's; in the same attenuated sense, "he loved her and she loved him" (23). Nor, in that vision, can it well be otherwise, for the imperfection of love is virtually guaranteed by its essential secrecy: "Love is a wound inside the body, and so appears no wise without. It is an ill that holds us long because its origin is nature. Many hold it in derision, like those ungentle gentlemen (*cil vilain curteis*) who frolic on through all the world and later boast of what they do. It is not love but foolishness, and viciousness and lechery."[12]

It is a rare gift indeed to be able to exhibit an essentially private disposition — a *talent* — to another, as Guigemar, for example, learns to do; and Guigemar's ability to love at all is notably far from a gift of nature.[13] On the contrary, "so much had nature injured him that never troubled he for love. Lady nor lass beneath the sky there was so noble or so fair, did he but sue her for her love, but she would hold him willingly. Many had thereto sued him oft, but *talent* for it had he none; no one was able to remark any desire to love in him. So strangers and his friends alike regard him as a creature lost [*peri*]."[14] To be lost in this sense, however, is difficult to avoid in a scheme of things in which *talent* is communicated only by *semblant*.

Two ironic touches at least underscore the fact that the lady has never been so truly a *privee* or intimate of her lord as he, for example, has been of the king ("de sun seinur esteit privez," 19): "By my knowledge you love [another woman], and if it is so, you have gone astray" (51–52) — the ground of this "knowledge" being no more than the baron's behavior (one might just as well call it his *semblant*) on returning from one of his unexplained absences. "But I dread your wrath so much, no other terror is so great" (35–36). If the human incarnation is so threatening, how can the horror of the bestial incarnation fail to be unbearable? Even before the lady hears the worst, she shows herself ready to think the worst: her husband's mind if not his body presents itself to her imagination exclusively under what from antiquity on are its two radically animal aspects, lust and anger. She is, in short, already self-exposed as hopelessly ill-equipped to meet the challenge to sympathy that awaits her. But for that matter so are we; *de te fabula*. She is living with something not fully human and therefore, in the strict sense, not human at all, an anomalous being that for half its life (if it runs true to the form described in the poem) ravages the species it counterfeits for the other half. The baron's forebodings at the outset and his shame at the end, in this context, are an eloquent if unwitting plea of extenuation on behalf of his lady. Her notion of personhood, no less than his, is a matter of *semblant* and not *talent*, and in this case is doubly strained by her lord's confession of moral as well as physical monstrosity — of a life of "prey" and "plunder" (60). With that confession her sense of a common bond is instantly dissolved: "In many ways she bethought herself how she might from him depart. She wished to lie by him no more" (100ff.).[15]

By the poet's account the empathic self-transcendence that the lady so disastrously and expectably fails to achieve is eminently possible for all its rarity; it is exercised, in fact, in the poet's own enterprise of interpreting Breton *lais*: "It was a custom of the ancients, as Priscian testifies, that in the books they made of old they spoke with some obscurity for their sake who were still to come and should serve as their expositors, that [these] therein might gloss the letter and use what more they had of wit [sen]."[16] Marie's sen will help her to divine the sen, or talent, of the ancients and hence the meaning they have deliberately reserved in obscurity for just such an encounter with kindred; the king's sen helps him likewise to identify the corresponding faculty hidden in the quarry that, on being brought to bay by the royal hunt, runs as suppliant to the feet of his sovereign: "Behold this wonder, how this beast humbles itself. It has the sen of a man, it calls for mercy. Drive all these hounds back for me, and beware lest any wound it. This beast has understanding and sen" (152–157).[17] It is significant, I think, that the beast's manlike behavior is not conclusive enough at this point to inhibit the huntsmen without the king's warning; the truth of the matter is available not to observation and inference but only to an intuition that has thus far been granted to the king alone but will eventually be extended to the members of the court in general as they come to perceive the beast, incongruously, as "free and noble [francs e debonaire]" (179), that is, as a heraldic emblem of the knightly virtues.

When the beast, with unexpected savagery, repeatedly attacks the new lord of the baron's lady on the couple's visit to the court, the knights find it natural to argue anthropomorphically that the attacks were not "sanz reisun" (208). But this kind of anthropomorphism in itself implies no very keen sense of the beast as a person; it is left to a particular royal councillor, a type of wisdom and valor (sages, 239; prozdum, 281), to intercede on behalf of the beast when the rest of the court is on the verge of dismembering it for having atrociously disfigured the former lady of the baron; the councillor comes very near, in fact, to putting two and two together: "This is the lady of that knight whom you were wont to hold so dear, who for a long while has been lost, nor knew you what became of him" (251–254).[18]

But the finest manifestation of the councillor's gift is not the imperfect detection of crime but a perfect and delicate act of compassion. The stolen clothes that alone can restore the baron's human shape are by order of the king offered to the beast, which refuses to take notice of them: "My lord, you do not well a jot; for no cause would this one endure to don his clothes in front of you or change his likeness [semblance] of a beast, and you know no jot of what this means. Sorely thereof has he great shame. Into your chamber have him led, and with him have the raiment borne. A great while let us leave him there. If he turn man we'll see it well" (283–292). And the subtle compassion of this advice is excelled by the king's want of horror or squeamishness, either of which would be venial under the circumstances, as he runs to embrace the old confidant whose reappearance unmasks him as a *bisclavret* (300). "Entire affection," Spenser remarks in a similar context, "hateth nicer hands."[19] The English poet is speaking of a rescue, both chivalric and priestly, from a physically and morally nauseous prison, and the virtue of "entire affection" required for this act is clearly just that *chierté* which Marie attributes to the king and his court.

Intuitive sympathy is possible, then, but clearly it is not to be had for the asking any more than a cubit is to be added to the stature by taking thought. It is as gratuitous in its own way as the periodic visitations to which the baron is subject and which prompt the poet to play repeatedly on the etymological meanings of the key words *devenir* and *aventure*:[20] monstrosity as something one "comes on" unawares and hence "becomes"; or as a freak of chance, a brute Happening to which the victim is helplessly exposed. As the condition of the *bisclavret* is gratuitous, so is the *chierté* by which it is tolerated and subdued—as gratuitous as grace. For it is, I would suggest, no natural capacity but the theological virtue of *caritas* that Marie is concerned to celebrate here by just that transfiguration of the chivalric ethos which Dante achieves in his tribute to Christ as *"sire de la cortesia,"* liegelord of courtesy.[21] By implication that ethos untransfigured—in the state of nature—is far from enough to keep us from the defection of the baron's lady. In this sense too, *de te fabula*.

THIEVES AND SUICIDES IN THE *INFERNO*
Metamorphosis
as the
State of Sin

IN THE FANTASY OF DISORIENTING CHANGE THAT UNDERLIES *The Divine Comedy*[1] we have once more the human body losing its form — not its spatial form this time but its fulfilling act or entelechy, the soul, an itinerant universal that between death and the day of judgment reincarnates itself by projecting on air a rainbow image disposed into organs of sense and expression.[2] Its ability to achieve separation from the body without loss of individuality is its tribute in spite of itself to the divine artifice; for unlike the angels, each of whom belongs to a species of his own, humanity is a single species. Why, then, do we not (as the Averroists might suppose) coalesce on separation from the body into the single form we share? By God's grace saint and sinner alike are marked out by an inalienable uniqueness that distinguishes the humanity of each: just as *Agnello's running* (which only one individual can possibly exemplify) essentially entails the universal form of running per se, so with the individual form of *Agnello's humanity* — though if indeed the individual soul is regarded as capable of disembodied existence it is hard to account for Dante's recourse to a posthumous body-substitute. Here, then, is another anxiety about personhood with which the fantasy of transformation is regularly led to engage itself, and on which a very different verdict is delivered in the ordeal of

Spenser's Malbecco: the individuality that (in Dante's account) not even a damned creature can wholly lose.

But not much more dignity remains in hell to the thing somehow enmeshed in a body of air. The being thus generated is only partly continuous with the earthly identity for whose career it is responsible; its status as a person is moot ("non omo, omo già fui," 1.67), and if it has mortally sinned it must confront an even more terrible challenge to its credentials: the nightmare transformations with which its aerial body is incessantly racked, in reenactment of its earthly sin and mockery of its heavenly loss. This process, in which the gaudy Ovidian chaos is huddled into an alcove of hell, will be the main concern of what follows.

In the pocket of the circle of fraud given over to the punishment of theft, Vanni Fucci, self-styled the Beast (24.126), is periodically transfixed at the base of the neck by a lunging serpent:

Never is "o" or "i" so quickly written as he took fire and burned and, as he must, turned in his tumbling down all into ashes; and having lain in such disintegration, the dust assembled of its own accord, and to that very man turned back abruptly. Thus, by the vouching of the great savants, the phoenix dies and then is born again, when it approaches the five-hundredth year. Lifelong it feeds on neither grass nor fodder, but only tears of incense and of balm, and its last bindings are of myrrh and spikenard. And even like him who falls and knows not how, pulled earthward by the violence of a demon or other blockages that tie one up, who at his rising up looks round about him, utterly baffled by the great ordeal he has endured, and in his looking sighs: such was the sinner when he rose thereafter. O how exacting is the power of God that in its vengeance showers down such scourges! (24.100–120)

The allusions in this passage are characteristically precise and telling. The moral analogue of the falling sickness, according to Aristotle, is the compulsiveness of the incontinent man, whose reason regains control only after the mischief is done.[3] The context of Ovid's description of the phoenix, invoked by a number of verbal reminiscences, is Pythagoras' dour meditation on the random rise and fall of nations, the universal gluttony of time, and the aimless transmigration of souls that "wander" from beast to man and back again.[4] The tradition has been made by Dante to yield, not a prefiguration, but a travesty of the resurrection. Again, as the phoenix (according to Lactantius) is its own creator,[5] so the delusion of self-sufficiency that inspires Vanni's obscene gesture toward God in the next canto (25.2–3) condemns him here to a bitter travesty of the continuous creation for which all creatures, including himself, are beholden to God; for "the being of all creatures so depends on God that they could not persist for a moment, but would [like Vanni] be driven back to nothing, were they not maintained in being by the work of the divine virtue."[6] And Vanni's egoism is unmasked as a delusion in still another way by the graphic reduction of the ego, or its visible expression, to a heap of particles without a trace of spiritual residue: the fact that unto dust thou returnest, in Vanni's case and in a newly spiritual sense, reveals that dust thou art.

Dante's analogy of demonic possession is here very much in point, for the soul without integrity might well hesitate between singular and plural as confusedly as the "man with an unclean spirit": "My name is Legion, for we are many" (Mark 5:9). The paradoxical difference, for Dante at least, is that to be self-possessed is in the end to have no self at all. The anagram of the first person pronoun "io" that introduces the transformation, its letters separated and reversed to spell out the first syllable of a cry of pain ("oimè"), is a sly emblem of this paradox of the egocentric impulse. Evil in the metaphysical tradition to which the poet is heir is always privation of being. In the sinner unto death this privation is represented by loss of identity. In Vanni what is in question is numerical identity — whether what we have to do with is an individual or an aggregate. His colleagues in theft, as we must now consider, suffer the privation of their specific identity; as we watch their anarchic transformations we shall be hard put to find a species — whether of personhood or of humanity — to which we can confidently assign them.

The transaction between Cianfa Donati and Agnolo Brunelleschi apparently illustrates a natural law of the eighth circle. Cianfa's three confederates have been wondering what has become of him when he overtakes them in the shape of a six-footed serpent and singles out the hapless Agnolo for his attentions:

With its middle feet it trammeled up his belly and with the ones in front shackled his arms, then fleshed its fangs in one cheek and the other; its hinderlegs it spread out to his thighs, and intermeddling its tail between them, stretched it behind him up along his loins. Never was ivy intricately rooted so to a tree as that abhorrent beast with the other's members intertwined its own. Then were they joined as though they had been fashioned of heated wax, and intermingled hues. Neither seemed what it had been any longer, as there proceeds before the burning part upward along the paper a brownish margin not yet of black although the white is dead. Each of the others cried out as they watched, "Agnello, woe is me, how you are altered! Already— see—you are neither two nor one." The two heads had combined in one already when there appeared to us two figures mixed in a single face, one face where two had perished. The arms were made up out of two strips each, the thighs and legs, the belly and the thorax, had grown to organs never seen before. There every former aspect had been voided. Neither and both appeared the effigy perverse; and walked its way with sluggish pace. (25.52–78)

The situation is that two souls mix their respective (moral and physical) properties of humanity and serpenthood, each soul coming to underlie the mixture. Even though they do not thereby lose their individuality, since according to the ordinary doctrine a soul is individuated not by the body itself but by an inherent fitness for it,[7] the fusion of shapes and bodies carries with it a penalty all the same: in the process humanity is stolen but only monstrosity enjoyed, so that the thieves are alternately punished by committing theft and by suffering it — and punished by a theft not of private property but (with a precise irony) of a property as public as common humanity. For in the *bolgia* of the thieves, whose presiding genius is the semihuman Cacus (25.17–33), there is not enough humanity to go around;[8] it is as if the air were subject to private ownership, and also to theft. And the crowning irony of this theft is that it coincides with a monstrously claustrophobic act of sharing; the partners in theft are now partners (like Ovid's two Narcissi) in ownership of the same aerial body with its anomalous species— "one face where two had perished."

This destructive mixture pointedly inverts the mystery of the Incarnation, for "a mixture is identical in species with none

of the things mixed . . . and thus Christ [were he such] would
not be of the same nature either with his Father or with his
mother." The two natures of the Word survive union because
they derive their unity not from fusion but from the singleness
of the divine person underlying them both; the transformation
of the two thieves thus manages to combine the theological fantasies of Eutyches and Nestorius into a single monstrosity too
ludicrous ever to have attracted its heresiarch; for "up to now
there has been no one so mad as to believe that there is in Christ
one nature but two persons." The snake-man, the *reductio ad
absurdum* of partnership in crime, is a walking idol of bizarre
misdevotion.[9]

And the virulent embrace of Cianfa and Agnolo is not only
profane but obscene; the mystery it burlesques, after all, is an
essential expression of the divine love, and to be complete the
pseudomystery must offer a perverted counterpart: the languid
and savage act of violation with its piquant allusions, once
more, to an Ovidian model, the suicidal craving of the nymph
Salmacis for Hermaphroditus.[10] Salmacis and Cianfa are driven
beyond the sexual impulse to a hyperbolic lust that is punished
by being allowed its total satisfaction: "Lovers would wish from
two to become one; but since this would result in the physical
destruction of one or both, they seek the union that befits
them."[11] But the thief, like the nymph, is not in the grip of love,
or at least of any love that is (like sexual love) compatible with
charity.

That sin is deadly which is contrary to charity according as charity is
the spiritual life of the soul. Now charity consists first in the love of
God, but second in a love of one's neighbor to which it pertains that
we wish and work our neighbor's good. By theft, however, one inflicts
damage on one's neighbor in his effects; and if people made a general
practice of stealing from each other, human society would perish.
Hence theft, as contrary to charity, is a deadly sin.[12]

By their violation of this categorical imperative the thieves of
the eighth circle are condemned to a lurid pantomime by which
they die eternally.

The pantomime is followed by another cyclic exchange in
which an aspect of love serves as a measure of the spiritual dis-

order in the soul of a thief. One of the shocked onlookers at the
earlier transformation (Buoso dei Donati) is suddenly pierced
through the navel by an angry little serpent, which

then fell down before him bloated. He who was pierced looked at it
but said nothing, instead remained implanted and agape, just as if
overcome by sleep or fever. He eyed the serpent and the serpent him.
One through his wound and through its mouth the other were smok-
ing mightily and the smoke was meeting . . . Such was the rule by
which they corresponded that as the snake's tail split into a fork his
victim forced his steps to come together. Leg joined to leg and thigh
joined so to thigh that in a little while the line of juncture betrayed
itself by no apparent sign. The snake's forked tail was taking on the
structure that was expiring yonder, and its skin was growing softer as
the other's hardened. I saw the arms recede into the armpits, and the
two feet of the brute, which had been short, assume the length the
other's had been losing. Then twisted in one skein the hinderlegs
became the member that a man keeps hidden, and of his own the victim stretched forth two. While the smoke veils the one being and the
other with unaccustomed hue, engendering hair on one part as it
leaves the other hairless, the one rose up, the other one fell down, but
not averting those ungodly lanterns under whose cover each was
trading snout. The upright one withdrew it to the temples, and of the
surplus matter passing there, the ears emerged from cheeks that had
been earless. Whatever ran not backward and remained of that excess
furnished the face a nose, and the lips grew to a convenient thickness.
He who was prone protrudes his snout in front, and lets his ears shrink
back into his head, just as the garden snail retracts its horns. And the
tongue, heretofore a single thing ready to speak, forks as the other's
tongue unforks itself again; and the smoke stops. (25.87–93,
103–135)

It is clear that the love being derisively mimicked on this
occasion is maternal, the *serpentello* being portrayed as a composite of fetus and suckling babe swelling contentedly with
what it sucks from "that part whence first we draw our
sustenance" (25.85–86); but once again there is a profane
embellishment: Buoso's maternity is as sacrificial as that of the
Christological pelican of the bestiaries whose pierced side pours
reviving blood and water on her brood.[13] However, the
newborn man in the present case (Francesco Cavalcanti) uses his
restored humanity to spit at a reluctant host whose loss of

humanity he relishes (25.138–141); the reflection of love in this distorting mirror is revenge. Indeed, the notion of mirroring seems to underlie the fascination with which the two celebrants fix each other's gazes throughout the demonic rite.

It is significant in this regard, I think, that the narrator's reason for finding this particular transformation more remarkable than any of Ovid's is that the latter poet "never so transmuted, face to face, a pair of natures that the form of either was ready to change matter with the other" (25.100ff.). Benvenuto glosses "face to face" in this context as "proportionally, so that part would correspond to part," and this seems to be correct;[14] the "rule" (25.103) that governs the transformation maps the features of each participant one to one onto those of the other. This rule is one of distortive reflection in which the vicious image is intelligible only by reference to its paradigm — intelligible, that is, only as a privation. Each partner in crime is condemned to view in the mirror of his counterpart's change the gradual emergence of an aspect of himself: the erstwhile snake, the depravity whose moral essence it can never shed; the erstwhile man, the decency whose moral essence he can never retrieve. But the dialogue of lovers too is, by pervasive tradition, a mirroring.[15] And this is especially true of the dialogue between the soul and its God: "But we all, with open face beholding as in a glass the glory of the Lord, are changed [*transformamur*] into the same image from glory to glory" (2 Cor. 3:18).

If the comradeship of thieves, in Dante's vision, is ultimately a profound estrangement from themselves and each other, the transformation of the suicides pushes the theme of estrangement to the point of obsession. By taking on the shapes of sterile and poisonous thornbushes the suicides have become not only paralytic but deaf, blind, and mute, a triple deprivation relieved only when their branches are agonizingly broken off, as by the unwitting pilgrim. As the canto proceeds, the poet makes it clear to us that the grim dryad state of Piero della Vigna and his fellow suicides is reserved precisely for those who in life "have eyes to see and see not . . . ears to hear and hear not" (Ezek. 12:2), who "walk in the vanity of their mind [*sensus*] . . . being alienated from the life of God through the ignorance that is in them" (Eph. 4:17–18) — in short, that the heart of their offense is a failure of belief. The relevant verb *credere* itself recurs with monitory insistence when at the outset we learn that the pilgrim is at a loss to identify the source of the groans rising among the bushes, and that the narrator is confident in retrospect that his guide was already well aware of the difficulty: "I believe he believed that I believed [*Cred'io ch'ei credette ch'io credesse*] so many cries issued among those trunks from people we had driven into hiding" (13.25).

In view of the sequel it is, I think, worth considering that "cred'io," "ei credette," and "io credesse" introduce respectively three kinds of belief, each with its own bearing on the psychology of violent despair. The object of "credesse" is the pilgrim's false persuasion about the source of the voices: he could not, as his guide later explains (13.46–49), "believe" the mystic truth of Virgil's *rima* about the man-tree Polydorus, which the pilgrim had rejected as "cosa incredibile" (13.50). In short, Virgil's "discourse" (*sermone*) was too much for the pilgrim's "faith" (13.21), the vacuum in faith being supplied by the corresponding misbelief. This failure of belief, hammered home by repetition of word and idea, is a venial counterpart of Piero's mortal failure of belief — "believing [*credendo*] by my death to flee contempt" (13.71); for Piero has been unable to believe the divine *sermo* itself and not merely its Virgilian prefiguration.

By contrast, the narrator has undergone a change of form opposite to Piero's, the Pauline "transformation by the renewing of mind [*sensus*]" (Rom. 12:2). He has enjoyed in particular a renewal of faith typified by the "cred'io," his confidence in Virgil's clairvoyance, to which the pilgrim indeed will presently submit: "Ask *you* yet [of Piero] the thing that you believe [*credi*] will satisfy me" (13.82–83). Dante's assurance about his master, like faith in the counsels hidden in the mind of God, is an *argumentum non apparentium* (Heb. 11:1). For the minds of God and man (Isa. 45:15, Jer. 17:9) are the two supreme unknowables. In the strict sense of "comprehend," "God is incomprehensible to any creature," even in the beatific vision. Likewise for other minds in general: "That one person's thought is unknown to another is due to a double barrier — namely, to the grossness of the body and to the will, which shuts its secrets away . . . The latter impediment will remain after the resurrection and obtains now among the angels."[16] But Virgil's clair-voyance is belief raised to the level of an intuition reserved for God alone and mediated to saints. Virgil is not a saint; so he too, like his ward and for his ward's sake, is transformed, this time by the kind of grace that "is ordered to the end that one cooperate with another toward the other's return to God," a grace that includes the "discernment of spirits."[17] Far from being a satire on Piero's rhetorical frigidities as imperial protonotary, "cred'io ch'ei credette ch'io credesse" is designed to show the range of the power to entertain assertions whose abuse brought Piero to hell and still threatens the pilgrim's ascent.

That abuse has left its imprint, in what is now an invincible ignorance and impenitence, on most of what Piero has to say in the thirteenth canto; his sentiments are specious but (in Dante's ethical perspective) ultimately discredited by the fallacies that inspired his suicide. Piero's eternal failure to take God's point is detectable even in his protest against the rending of his branches: "Why are you tearing me? Is there in you no spirit of pity [*pietà*] at all? Men have we been, and now have turned to trunks. Well ought your hand to have been more pitying [*pia*], if we had come from being souls of snakes" (13.35–39). "But surely," objects Benvenuto, "the souls of these who have despaired were crueler than snakes, because snakes do not vent their rage on their own bodies."[18] This, I think, is the response favored by the ethos of Dante's poem. Piero's argument presupposes that serpents are more savage and hence less worthy of pity than even savage human beings. But it is an Aristotelian commonplace familiar to Dante, and no doubt to his primary audience, that no beast can match the atrocities of reason perverted.[19]

More fundamentally, the whole passage through the netherworld is designed to wean the pilgrim from a sentimental pity for the damned that is in the end an attitude of uncharity toward God, of whose justice hell is the expression; hence the play on an older meaning of *pietà* — piety — in the guide's later reproach to the pilgrim's sentimentality in this vein: "Here *pietà* lives when it is safely dead" (20.28). There is a compassion for God (piety) that is at odds with compassion for the damned (pity); the former lives, say Virgil, only when the latter is dead. This harsh if (given Dante's premises) cogent lesson is impossible for any but a saint to learn; both Virgil and his charge yield to the sentimentality in question, and the pilgrim will master the sterner response only at the summit of his climb (*Paradiso* 15.10–11). What is crucial here is that in pleading for *mano pia* Piero misses the irony that his suicide was a rejection of just such a plea; he himself has raised an impious hand against a creature of God. "He who kills himself is guilty of murder, and becomes the guiltier the more innocent he was in that cause for which he thought himself fit to be killed."[20]

Self-murder, in fact, is from the standpoint of moral theology murder of an especially heinous kind, and the poet nicely fixes its anomaly for us by establishing that the thornbush speaks only by bleeding (through the gash in its trunk) — "parole e sangue" (13.44); Piero's voice, like the slain Abel's, is a *vox sanguinis* (Gen. 4:10). Having played Cain to his own Abel, he has committed a crime more unnatural than fratricide. On the day of judgment, when each suicidal spirit becomes an eternal gibbet for a resurrected body it will never reanimate (13.103–108), the punishment for a kind of murder that eludes human justice is carried out by divine justice.

Piero's way of explaining this punishment has the tortuousness one would expect of a chancellor, but characteristically evades the central issue of guilt: he considers it "unjust to have what one takes from oneself" — that is, the use of his body (13.105). As Benvenuto glosses, "One cannot lawfully recover as one's own that whereof one has voluntarily deprived oneself."[21] But this is pettifoggery; there is nothing in the relevant provisions of the civil law to keep a proprietor from succeeding himself simply by being the next to take possession, and Proculus at least ruled that in the interim such an owner retains ownership of what he has discarded in any case.[22] If there is a rule of jurisprudence that applies by analogy to the incompleteness of the suicide's resurrection, it is *proprietas deducto usu fructu legari potest;*[23] by his act of irrevocable despair Piero has made himself legatee of a body he will continue to own but not to enjoy. He himself has set this grim restriction on his inheritance by the suicide that is in effect his last will and testament.

In summarizing the course of his final despair Piero betrays an obtuseness that is once again the essence and the punishment of his sin: "My mind, because of the disdain I cherished believing by my death to flee disdain, caused me to be unjust to my just self" (13.70ff.). The injustice Piero thinks he did to his defense against a charge of treason, as his subsequent appeal for the pilgrim's advocacy makes clear, consisted in encouraging disdain when he thought he was avoiding it, for his suicide could be construed as a gesture of remorse. For Piero, in short, the injustice of suicide is that it incurs human disdain. He is not, from Dante's point of view, wrong to think this consideration highly important; but he is damned for thinking it paramount. The paramount consideration, of which he continues oblivious, is God's disdain for an act of cowardice — *fuggire* (13.71) — cowardice and, by an association that survives in Italian (*ignavia, poltroneria*), sloth or spiritual inertia. These are the grounds on which even the venerable Judean Razias (2 Mach. 14:42) is to be condemned for his suicidal disdain: "It is not really courage but rather as it were the softness of a mind without the strength to endure the evils of punishment."[24]

It is a softness that Piero and his fellow suicides are forever debarred from indulging, unlike the wastrels who dodge among the thornbushes to elude the dogs that eventually dismember them. "The destruction of the wealth by which one lives is in a sense a destruction of existence itself";[25] so that as the first runner hurtles by he screams for rescue by death (13.118). As despair is a misdirection of a sorrow that rightly used "worketh repentance to salvation" (2 Cor. 7:10), the mad squanderings of the wastrels are a misdirection of the voluntary poverty by which some devout persons "dismiss from their mind all concern for temporal things."[26] Trying to overtake his partner, the second wastrel "thought himself too slow" (13.119), anticipating in so many words the thought later ascribed to Bernardo di Quintavalle as he ran in the footsteps of St. Francis, poverty's "bridegroom" (*Paradiso* 11:81).

For an indirect form of self-destruction the wastrels are condemned to flight; for a direct, the suicides are eternally at bay, exposed to the mutilations of "Jove's dogs" the Harpies, who by traditional association with the Furies "engender grief, and unto grief a window" (13.102):[27] their periodic assaults are the Pauline "sorrow of the world," which makes an idol of temporal success and disappointment and now eternally "worketh death" (2 Cor. 7:10). As the cowardice inherent in despair is punished by a *cul de sac*, the uncharity of despair toward both man and God is punished by the solitary confinement of the suicide in hell — "spirito incarcerato" (13.87). For the obverse of the suicide's ignominious retreat is his refusal to honor his social bond. "Any man is a part of the community; hence in killing oneself one wrongs the community."[28] This is why the terrain of the wood of suicides, like that of the thieves' *bolgia*, reminds the narrator of the marshy forest of the Maremma (13.7ff., 25.19–20); here, as Benvenuto well observes, "the author shows the harsh imprisonment of those souls . . . and wishes to say tersely that no wild beasts that shun the acquaintance and companionship of men have for their dwelling so wild a region as have the savage souls of these despairing persons . . . Here have they bitter gaols wherein against nature they are enveloped."[29]

Against this background the intense pathos of Piero's delight at having visitors, with its hysterical overtone of entrapment, is offset by the irony of his failure to acknowledge the reason why he is not to be visited again: "Your sweet speech is such *bait* to me that I cannot be silent. Bear with me, that to a little talk I *snare* myself" (13.56–57; emphasis added). Piero's uncharity toward God is expressed in turn, not as with Vanni Fucci by overt hostility, but by an irony of which Piero is unaware: "I swear to you that I have never broken faith with my lord, who was so worthy of honor" (13.74–75). Benvenuto's incredulity is once again a useful index: "But on the contrary, Frederick . . . was a heretic, an Epicurean, an excommunicate; how then was he worthy of honor when honor is shown in witness of virtue?"[30] True enough; but that is precisely the point: with respect to a Lord preeminently worthy of honor Piero's reputation for infidelity is true and irreparable. "Life is a kind of gift granted man by God, who causes death and life. And consequently he who deprives himself of life sins against God even as he who kills another's bondsman kills that bondsman's lord."[31] The true master, in short, of the bondsman Piero killed is not Frederick II but God.

Piero swears his loyalty to Frederick by the "new roots" of a human thornbush whose symbolic associations made its choice almost inevitable. The roots, first of all, discredit the oath that names them; they are consecrated to the realm in whose soil

they are sunk: "Because the root of all evils is lust and the root
of all goods is love and both cannot coexist, if the one has not
been entirely torn out it will be impossible to plant the other."[32]
As a new member of the vegetable kingdom, moreover, Piero
belatedly enjoys an ironic immunity: "Do we then . . . when we
hear 'Thou shalt not kill' regard it as wicked to uproot a bush,
crazily assenting to the error of the Manicheans? . . . We do not
accept that this is meant of plants because they are wanting in
sensation, or of irrational animals . . . because they are not our
fellows in rationality."[33] Piero has reduced himself to a category
of being from whose killing the last moral constraint has been
removed.

The randomness with which the seed of the thornbush was
sown broadcast on a field of hell mockingly reproduces the vision of history projected by the despairing mind, a history
without Providence in which events, like the seed, are in-
discriminately "catapulted" by fortune (13.98) into occurrence.
The seed sprouts like a grain of spelt into a stunted bush that
feeds the nesting birds of hell with bloody leaves (13.79–102;
compare 10–15); it is the spiritual inverse of the heavenly
kingdom — the "grain of mustard seed, which a man took and
sowed in his field; which indeed is the least of all seeds; but
when it is grown it is the greatest among herbs and becometh a
tree, so that the birds of the air come and lodge in the branches
thereof" (Matt. 13:31–32).

But these ironies merely embellish the central comment on
the sin of despair embodied in the metaphor of the human plant.
For "despair comes of a man's not hoping to partake of God's
bounty . . . Isidore says, to commit some crime is a death of the
soul, but to despair is the soul's going down to hell." The source
of this premature surrender to futility is *acedia*, "a kind of
burdening sadness . . . that weighs down the mind so that one
prefers not to act at all . . . For this reason *acedia* means a
weariness of acting."[34] Piero's suicide — his escape from the
rigors of active defiance — is simply the ultimate expression of
this desire to be without will or motion. To live after death
without these faculties is (in terms of the prevailing
psychological categories) to be divested of one's rational and
animal souls and to be left with one's vegetable soul alone.

In his picture of the agonized man-tree Dante owes an obvious debt to Virgil's Polydorus and perhaps a little to the Ovidian Myrrha. The decorative horrors of the thieves' transformations are frankly Ovidian. One may wonder whether awareness of these connections is to be a part of the literary experience of these passages, and if so what part. We have a better recourse than guesswork in seeking an answer: Dante explicitly invites us to notice, in connection with the thieves' transformations, that the exchange of forms he presents between man and snake is more elaborate than any change invented by Lucan or Ovid (25.94–102). Is the poet ungratefully bragging about his technical superiority to his benefactors? Is that what we are being invited to notice? I think not; he has, after all, admitted (25.46ff.) that the reader will be justified in finding the description unconvincing, and later (25.143ff.) he apologizes for crudities in his style by pleading the oddity of his subject matter. The contrast Dante has in mind is rather between orders of significance, between what the masters feigned (*poetando*, 25.99) and what Dante witnessed—in the latter case, a symbolic revelation of the tortuousness of sin and the power and exactitude of its divine vengeance. It is the importance of what Dante has to say that in his view requires and redeems the *bizarrerie* he uses to say it; but the credit for this decisive advantage goes to faith and not merely to poetic mastery.

Some critics have supposed that the poet is unwittingly yielding here to what, as he himself would have had to confess, is the sin of pride.[35] But the notion of pride implicit in this judgment would have made little sense to Dante. "One is called proud because one wishes to seem superior to what one is." "That someone is aware of the good he has and approves it is not a sin . . . Likewise is it also no sin that one wishes one's good works to be approved by others." "Greatness of mind [*magnanimitas*] therefore causes one to deem oneself greatly worthy in respect of the gifts one has received from God." "And for this reason 'appetite for glory,' of itself, does not name anything vicious."[36] And the bearing of Dante's literary *magnanimitas* on his immediate concerns is apt to be missed by those who are pleased to imagine that they have caught him out in a weakness.

In his choice of imagery for portraying theft he shows us one way of taking another's goods that leaves no one impoverished and many enriched. The possibility of benignly alienating property demonstrates that the distinctive feature of theft is desecration of charity rather than failure to comply with a prescription for external behavior. More generally, in both sequences Dante avails himself of the Ovidian vocabulary to express a kindred but significantly qualified view of the problematic relation of minds and bodies: what Ovid presents as the human condition — discontinuity, depersonalization, estrangement — is for Dante simply the *malum damni*, the evil of loss, the existential rift suffered by the soul in its voluntary exile from grace. As with his pagan models, Dante saves the fantasy of transformation from phantasmagoric triviality by exposing the philosophical nerve of the unease it generates.

SPENSER'S MALBECCO
Metamorphosis
Monomania
and Abstraction

I T IS POSSIBLE TO ARGUE THAT HELL, AS WITH DANTE'S SUICIDES
and thieves, is the scene of Malbecco's transformation
in Spenser's *Legend of Britomartis* (*The Faerie Queene*, 3.10);
but if so it is a very odd Hell indeed, situated in quite another
corner of the scheme of things than the Inferno. In what follows
I shall try to specify its longitude and latitude. Malbecco—old,
miserly, and morbidly jealous—has been searching the forest
for his amoral young wife, who has run off with a kindred soul,
been jilted, and taken up residence as the "housewife" (36) and
"maylady" (44) of the satyrs: "And every one as commune good
her handeled" (36).[1] The cuckold, having sneaked into their
camp at nightfall,

> crept full light,
> And like a Gote amongst the Gotes did rush,
> That through the helpe of his faire hornes on hight,
> And misty dampe of misconceiving night,
> And eke through likenesse of his gotish beard,
> He did the better counterfeite aright.
>
> (47)

Appealing surreptitiously to his wife after having tormented
himself with the spectacle of her strenuous nightlong engage-

129

ment with "a Satyre rough and rude" (48), he tries in vain to persuade her to

> leave that lewd
> And loathsome life, of God and man abhord,
> And home returne.
>
> (51)

In the morning he rejoins the herd, which

> butted him with hornes on euery syde,
> And trode downe in the durt, where his hore beard
> Was fowly dight, and he of death afeared.
>
> (52)

The coup de grace to Malbecco's sanity is the discovery, after his stealthy departure from the satyrs, that his treasure has been stolen: "With extreme fury he became quite mad, / And ran away, ran with himselfe away" (54), though the only enemy remaining to him is precisely the self with which he is running; for "he himselfe himselfe loath'd so forlorne, / So shamefully forlorne of womankind" (55). By the time he reaches a seacliff

> suspended dreadfully,
> That liuing creature it would terrify,
> To looke adowne, or vpward to the hight,
>
> (56)

he is no longer any such creature;

> From thence he threw himselfe dispiteously,
> All desperate of his fore-damned spright,
> That seem'd no helpe for him was left in liuing sight.
>
> (56)

The rest of Spenser's account is, I think, remarkable enough to quote in full:

> But through long anguish and selfe-murdring thought
> He was so wasted and forpined quight,
> That all his substance was consum'd to nought,

And nothing left, but like an aery Spright,
That on the rockes he fell so flit and light,
That he thereby receiu'd no hurt at all,
But chaunced on a craggy cliff to light;
Whence he with crooked clawes so long did crall,
That at the last he found a caue with entrance small.

Into the same he creepes, and thenceforth there
Resolu'd to build his balefull mansion,
In drery darkenesse, and continuall feare
Of that rockes fall, which euer and anon
Threates with huge ruine him to fall vpon,
That he dare neuer sleepe, but that one eye
Still ope he keepes for that occasion;
Ne euer rests he in tranquillity,
The roring billowes beat his bowre so boystrously.

Ne euer is he wont on ought to feed,
But toades and frogs, his pasture poysonous,
Which in his cold complexion do breed
A filthy bloud, or humour rancorous,
Matter of doubt and dread suspitious,
That doth with curelesse care consume the hart,
Corrupts the stomacke with gall vitious,
Croscuts the liuer with internall smart,
And doth transfixe the soule with deathes eternall dart.

Yet can he neuer dye, but dying liues,
And doth himselfe with sorrow new sustaine,
That death and life attonce vnto him giues.
And painefull pleasure turnes to pleasing paine.
There dwels he euer, miserable swaine,
Hatefull both to him selfe, and euery wight;
Where he through priuy griefe, and horrour vaine,
Is woxen so deform'd, that he has quight
Forgot he was a man, and *Gealosie* is hight.

(57–60)

Malbecco's odd transformation into an abstract entity is
evidently the working out of reprobation — of every jealous
miser's destiny; his spirit is "foredamned" (56), and his very
name — a *becco* is a he-goat and a cuckold — proclaims his function as a type. But then what are we to understand this typical

destiny to be? Individuals do not turn into universals. No doubt the point is that what happens to a *malbecco* is merely *analogous* to a process of abstraction. But this is a useless explanation if the second term of the analogy is absurd—if it turns out to be senseless to talk of a person's becoming abstract. The preliminary stages of Malbecco's damnation, it is true, are clearly and powerfully conveyed quite independently of this crux. By seeking an affirmation of himself in externals like treasure and the acceptance of "womankind," the would-be suicide has already consumed his substance to nought; there is no self—no morally developed individuality—left for him to kill, and Malbecco's attempt to do so is thus forestalled by a transformation akin to that of Ovid's lovelorn Aesacus, the diver bird that habitually mimes self-destruction.[2] Indeed, Malbecco is now momentarily birdlike—an "aery Spright"—in his "flit" descent and "crooked claws," though the next moment finds him an agonized reptile, his "cold complexion" poisoned by its natural food of suspicion and self-hatred. The point seems to be that the jealous man's private hell—his "privy griefe" (60)—is an endless masochistic orgy. He is morally dead, but it is a death he feeds on, and a death ironically compounded by the ignorance that prompts his obsessive fear of dying (58). So far, it seems that the state of jealousy is being implicitly compared with eternal damnation. But Spenser goes further and compares it with an exotic process of rarefaction; which process?

It is interesting that Spenser is not along among his contemporaries in this odd stretching of categories.[3] Ariosto has the Infernal Council determine that no torment could be more apt or severe for a particular tyrant's soul than the suspicion he endured in life.

> Thus once more did Suspicion come into
> This soul and of himself and it make one,
> Even as in wilder stock they do engraft
> Various fruit, and medlar upon thorn,
> Or as of many colors one remains
> Whenas a painter takes of each thereof
> To figure flesh.[4]

But this mystic union would leave the damned soul, like Malbecco in transit, simply an example par excellence of its ruling passion. Ariosto (like Spenser) goes further: "From being suspicious as he was whilere, / Now was he turn'd into Suspicion's self." In his adaptation George Gascoigne dilutes Ariosto's paradox by having the tyrant's soul "sent into the world and restored to the same body wherein he first had his resiance, so to remain for perpetuity, and never to depart nor to perish. Thus this body and soule being once again united, and now eftsones with the same pestilence infected, hee became of a suspicious man *Suspicion* it selfe."[5] But an incarnation or instance of a universal is not the universal itself; unlike Spenser, Gascoigne flinches a little at the extravagance of Ariosto's bizarre Platonism, though his hero too is abstract enough to be subject to exemplification: at night "he stalketh about the earth, enfecting, tormenting, and vexing all kinds of people with some part of his afflictions."

In all three cases there is a survival of two Ovidian patterns of transformation: individual into species (Picus into the woodpecker in general) and individual into paradigm (Erysichthon, by union with Famine, into the voracious being par excellence). Moreover, as with the vampirism of Gascoigne's Suspicion or Ovid's Famine, a vicious quality can be represented as a demon achieving universality by possessing its prospective instances; Spenser in particular can rely on the corresponding Biblical notion of *ruah qineʾâ*—the "spirit of jealousy" (Num. 5:14) with which Malbecco becomes first fascinated and finally identical. One further parallel is worth citing: the Alexandrian motif of the lover's wish to be transformed into an object close to his mistress. If the object is abstract, we get a benign version of the paradox of Malbecco's destiny: "Sleep dwell upon thine eyes, peace in thy breast! / Would I were sleep and peace, so sweet to rest!"[6]

I think the paradox is a little easier to understand once we recognize its basis in two presuppositions: that the essential person is the mind by preeminence, and that the mind is the form of a body—that is, the set of intellectual and emotional properties exemplified by something with physical properties as well.[7] Considered as that concrete something, Malbecco is (among other things) calculating, greedy, and jealous. Considered as a mind, a set of mental properties, he is (among other things) calculation, greed and jealousy. In the white heat of his final

monomania, that mind—Malbecco's Pauline "inner man" (2
Cor. 4:16)—shrivels down to jealousy alone. To be sure, in the
temporal domain of bodies, a mind changes; it is not strictly the
set of one's mental properties at any given moment but rather
the whole sequence of such momentary sets from birth to death;
but after death, the notion of sequence no longer applies.
Malbecco is then conceivable only under the aspect of eternity,
and in this way if in no other becomes more like God: "In things
not composed of matter and form, in which individuation is not
by individual matter . . . the forms individuate *themselves* . . .
And so, since God is not composed of matter and form, God
must be his own divinity."[8] By the same token, "his substance
. . . consum'd to nought," Malbecco's disembodied inner man is
his own jealousy, frozen into changelessness.

The theoretical context, then, in which the rich irony of
Malbecco's frustrated individuation becomes intelligible is the
familiar Renaissance Neoplatonism that registers itself, for example, in the sonneteer's insistence that the object of his love or
veneration is nothing so paltry as a mere concrete individual;
no, that beloved is a universal in whose radiance the radiant
nothings of this workaday world merely participate:

> What is your substance whereof you are made
> That millions of strange shadows on you tend?
> Since every one hath, every one, one shade,
> And you, but one, can every shadow lend.

But the precipice of abstraction to which Malbecco has as-
cended is far worse than the low nothings or shadows—the
jealous people—who contingently participate in him; not all
transcendence, not all unconditioned being is worth our envy or
aspiration—certainly not the arrested moment, the rapt gaze, of
obsession. By comparing the changelessness of the incorrigibly
jealous man with that of the universal he persists in exemplify-
ing, Spenser manages to achieve a *frisson* of rarefied
metaphysical horror. By invoking to this end a vision of the
perilous grandeur of the human mind he allows a cautionary
tale to touch the sublime.

DONNE'S "SULLEN WRIT"

Metamorphosis
as Satire
and Metaphysics

T RANSFORMATION AND TRANSMIGRATION (TO WHICH LATTER I
shall now turn) are not of course quite the same; but both,
as premises of the fictive imagination, allow the same
crucial role to the riddles surrounding the fact that some things
with bodies manage at the same time to be things with minds.
The essential difference seems to be that in transformation the
victim's former body or shape vanishes to make way at the same
place for a successor, while in transmigration the former body is
left behind as a corpse the instant a newborn body is acquired
elsewhere. Transmigration thus entails no disruption in the apparent course of nature. But in both cases the victim somehow
dies and is reborn, and in both he achieves a uniquely radical
change in the angle of his vision, though he pays dearly for it.

Transformation provides Apuleius' hero with a convenient
alias for his espionage on social evil, and it is tempting to suppose that the successive incarnations that chart "the progresse of
the soule" in Donne's *Metempsychosis* perform very much the
same service with respect to physical evil.[1] This latter sort of
evil has traditionally been a scandal to theodicy because it might
be thought by the untutored to reflect unfavorably on the good
"intentions" of Nature, and hence of Nature's God. The usual
defense has been to shift the blame to chance—to the unstable

materiality of any possible creation: "That seems to derive from
the specific intention of nature which holds always and perpetu-
ally. What holds only by reference to a particular time, on the
other hand, does not seem to accord absolutely with nature's intention but to be ordered as it were to some other end; otherwise its destruction would frustrate that intention." "That things
happen to be deformed and weak on account of a necessity inherent in matter, and that some things are killed by others, hin-
dered from fulfilling their accustomed order, from growing and
lasting out their time and from propagating others in turn by
their seed — all of that, I say, derives from no intention of nature."[2]

That intention, in the world of the *Metempsychosis*, is honored more in the breach than the observance; indeed, the migratory soul in Donne's poem finds no evidence of it, but rather a
multitude of conflicting intentions (her own included) that are
uniform only in being randomly vicious, and vicious in ways
drearily reminiscent of the human microcosm. If, as its title informs us, the *Metempsychosis* is a "poema satyricon," the scope
of the abuse it satirizes is no narrower than the scheme of
things.

In one tiny corner of the cosmic Sodom we find a dissipated
roué of a sparrow:

> Selfe-preserving it hath now forgot,
> And slackneth so the soules, and bodies knot,
> Which temperance streightens; freely on his she friends
> He blood and spirit, pith and marrow spends,
> Ill steward of himselfe, himselfe in three yeares ends.[3]

(206–210)

In the sea, we witness a gratuitous and successful "project," by
the thresher and the swordfish, to assassinate the tyrannical
whale: "How shall a Tyran wise strong projects breake, / If
wreches can on them the common anger wreake?" (349–350).

> Who will revenge his death? or who will call
> Those to account, that thought, and wrought his fall?
> The heires of slaine kings, wee see are often so
> Transported with the joy of what they get,
> That they, revenge and obsequies forget,
> Nor will against such men the people goe,

Because h'is now dead, to whom they should show
Love in that act; Some kings by vice being growne
So needy of subjects love, that of their own
   They think they lose, if love be to the dead Prince shown.
                                   (361–370)

And to facilitate the moral analogy that haunts the narrative, we are shown a menagerie of beasts capable of exercising "free" choice (200), of knowing (270), hesitating (273), deliberating (276), practicing gluttony (294), wantoning (324), playing the sluggard (354), hiding themselves for shame (355), scoffing (359), addressing themselves to gallant mischief (380), feigning chivalrous love (416–417), breaking faith (424).

Donne's tireless anthropomorphism does little to humanize the beasts; it is clearly designed, on the contrary, to help us to detect, with Jaques, in "that [which] they call compliment . . . the encounter of two dog apes," or in the ostracizing of a "poor and broken bankrupt" the primordial instinct of the herd. One of Donne's Holy Sonnets asks:

If lecherous goats, if serpents envious
Cannot be damn'd; Alas; why should I bee?
Why should intent or reason, borne in mee,
Make sinnes, else equall, in mee more heinous?[4]

In the *Metempsychosis* the question loses its point, for there is disturbingly little to choose, in the way of "intent or reason," between beasts and men.

The narrator takes a particular interest in beasts of prey, whose behavior can be counted on to evoke aphorisms that balance between cynicism and disgust: "Hee's short liv'd, that with his death can doe most good" (170):

He that can to none
Resistance make, nor complaint, sure is gone
  Weaknesse invites, but silence feasts oppression.
                              (248ff.)

Exalted she'is [this of a fish snatched up by a gull],
      but to the exalters good,

As are by great ones, men which lowly stood.
It's rais'd, to be the Raisers instrument and food.

(278ff.)

The traditional explanation of the role of predacity in the design of a benevolent creator had been that "one thing's good cannot occur without another's evil, as we see that the generation of one thing is not without another's destruction, nor the lion's nourishment without the slaughter of another animal. Were evil entirely excluded from the universe it would follow that many goods would also be removed."[5] But the narrator in his bitter rejoinder calls in doubt the assumption that all conceivable alternative orders are worse than the actual:

O might not states of more equality
Consist? and is it of necessity
That thousand guiltlesse smals, to make one great must die?

(328ff.)

Are there not possible creations in which begetting and survival occur without aggression and death, and possible creatures whose greatness is not deadly to "thousand guiltlesse smals"? Need "natures great master-peece" (the elephant) have been "the onely harmlesse great thing" (384-385)? But the Creator has chosen otherwise, it seems, for the sake of a kind of plenitude at which the Prophets darkly hint: "Out of the mouth of the most high proceedeth not evil and good?" (Lam. 3:38). "I form the light and create darkness; I make peace, and create evil; I the Lord do all these things" (Isa. 45:8). The *Metempsychosis* is inscribed *infinitati sacrum*—"consecrated to infinity"—and describes a Pythagorean regress to infinity of increasingly sordid incarnations; it is consequently of some interest that in the Pythagorean scheme the notion of infinity is identified with that of evil.[6]

I began by observing that the incarnations of Donne's protagonist furnish her with a privileged view of the natural order. But the privilege is far from absolute, and the mood of the cosmic satire is as interrogative and as ironic at its own expense as it is bitter. The narrator, after all, is merely the amanuensis of a soul that in more than one of her incarnations is reduced to an inert and unthinking recorder: "Though this soule could not move when it was a Melon, yet it may remember, and now tell mee, at what lascivious banquet it was served . . . Her memory hath ever been her owne, which makes me so seriously deliver you by her relation all her passages."[7]

In each of her incarnations, in fact, the soul has had to rely on the perceptual resources of a particular organism. Her predicament is rather as Erasmus describes it in a whimsical speculation on minds and bodies: "That a beetle's soul does something else or does it otherwise than a human being's is partly due to matter. The beetle does not sing, does not talk because it lacks organs fitted for such use." "From this [the experience of being struck on the head] you infer that within the skull there are organs of understanding, will, and memory, less coarse I grant you than the ears, but none the less material . . . It is not the nature of the rational soul that is itself destroyed, but when the organs deteriorate the power and activity of that mind are obstructed." "[Trees] too have been assigned by some a dim capacity for feeling. It is hard to detect the feeling in objects that cling; the feeling in the sponge is detected by those who pull it up. Woodcutters detect feeling in trees, if you believe them, for they claim that if you slap a tree you intend to chop down, as timberers are in the habit of doing, the tree is hard to cut, having braced itself in its fright."[8] The difference between the tree's awareness and the human, on this showing, is a difference not so much of souls as of perceptual organs.

We may suppose that in the *Metempsychosis*, as in Donne's later and more orthodox meditation on her "progresse," the poet conceives of the incarnate soul as doomed to "peepe through lattices of eyes . . . hear through labyrinths of ears," to look always through "spectacles" that make "small things seeme great" (*The Second Anniversary* 293-297). This is the flaw in the credit of the soul's testimony, for as the narrator gratuitously reminds us at one point, "better proofe the Law/ Of sense, then faith requires" (127-128): the judgment ("law") of empirical truth ("sense") requires evidence more conclusive than is required by faith, the judgment of religious truth.

But conclusive evidence, whatever the domain, is hard for a bespectacled awareness to come by. And the speaker compounds this uncertainty by being a little too good to be true. In his epistle to the reader he portrays himself as the owner of a mind without secrets — "plaine, and flat, and through light" — and proceeds to offer, as evidence of his candor, a qualified plea for intellectual toleration: "I forbid no reprehender, but him that like the Trent Council forbids not bookes, but Authors, damning what ever such a name hath or shall write. None writes so ill, that gives not something exemplary, to follow, or flie." A heterodox writer must presumably resign himself to having his books sometimes proscribed or removed from circulation, but mere authorship should not place his work under a prior restraint; indeed, perhaps even a fallacious argument can edify by providing an illustration of the fallacy to be avoided.

This is, for its time, a liberal position; but his own ensuing excursion into heterodoxy suggests that the speaker's mind is not so "through light" (translucent) as he pretends. We are, to be sure, convicted "prisoners" of original sin and hence disqualified from acting as judges in our own cause, but (argues the speaker) "Were prisoners Judges, 'twould seem rigorous, / She sinn'd, we beare" (98–99): we are arbitrarily implicated in Eve's offense, not our own. The appearance of "rigor" is aggravated by the fact that God's brief against us is open to certain objections (no doubt in themselves signs of our hereditary "corruption"):

Would God (disputes the curious Rebell) make
A law, and would not have it kept? Or can
His creatures will, crosse his? Of every man
For one, will God (and be just) vengeance take?
Who sinn'd? t'was not forbidden to the snake
Nor her, who was not then made; nor is't writ
That Adam cropt, or knew the apple; yet
   The worme and she, and he, and wee endure for it.
                               (103–110)

It is hard to resist the impression that the speaker is disingenuous in his disavowal of responsibility for objections he represents with polemical flair, and one of which he has just now raised as his own (105–106; see 98–99, with the deprecation of "rigor" doing euphemistic duty for the question of "justice"). The "curious Rebell," it seems, is a convenient scapegoat for the speaker's own "curiosity," and the "Rebell's" bill of particulars in turn deploys the notorious tactic of *occultatio*, converting the resolve to avoid discussion into the discussion to be avoided. But Donne's narrator is not only an accomplished master of deviousness; he is also, as it turns out, a zealous would-be persecutor of those who are more candid in expressing the same theological reservations: "Not liberties/ Of speech, but silence; hands, not tongues, end heresies" (119–120).

The lengths the speaker is prepared to go to in venting his obsessive hatred of women sustain our doubts about his good faith; despite his profession of orthodoxy, he is willing to repeat the canard that it was Eve alone who brought about the Fall: "Man all at once was there by woman slaine,/ And one by one we'are here slaine o'er againe/ By them" (91ff.). (The Apostle, of course, strictures on women notwithstanding, tells a different story: "By one man sin entered the world" [Rom. 5:12]; "In Adam all die" [1 Cor. 15:22].) There is, I think, a clear irony at the speaker's expense in his casual mention of Cain just after equating femininity with miscellaneous vice:

> keeping some quality
> Of every past shape, she knew treachery,
> Rapine, deceit, and lust, and ills enow
> To be a woman. *Themech* she is now,
> Sister and wife to *Caine*, *Caine* that first did plow.
>
> (506–512)

Cain figures in this passage, strategically, as the father not of fratricide but of agriculture. The point is not that Donne deplores expressions of misogyny (of which perhaps some of his intimate lyrics are not innocent), but that he has chosen to portray this particular misogynist as something of a rogue. Is the soul's amanuensis fit to be trusted? What are we to make of a surrogate poet who announces by way of preamble that we are reading "A worke t'outweare *Seth*'s pillar's, brick and stone,/ And (holy writt excepted) made to yield to none" (9–10)—a work, in short, second in dignity only to the Bible? We must, I think, come to terms with the fact that the vehicle of the author's serious themes is a voice he has not made it easy to take altogether seriously. If the indignation that hums through Donne's satire is "dark," "heavy," and "sullen" (55, 511), it is also beset with doubt.

And the core of its doubt is ethical:

> Let me arrest thy thoughts; wonder with mee,
> Why plowing, building, ruling and the rest,
> Or most of those arts, whence our lives are blest,
> By cursed *Cains* race invented be,
> And blest *Seth* vext us with Astronomie.
> Ther's nothing simply good, nor ill alone,
> Of every quality comparison,
>   The onely measure is, and judge, opinion.
>
> (513–520)

Here at last we have a position that runs counter to an important segment of orthodox Christian thought. A recent editor of
the *Metempsychosis* correctly glosses the final couplet and then
unhappily proceeds to miss the point: "Comparison is the only
means of measuring every quality, opinion the only basis of
judging it . . . This world is . . . relative in its nature, and one
cannot judge without doubting and hesitation; it is 'opinion,'
not 'knowledge,' on which judgment must rely . . . [Donne's]
discontent seems to be at once more orthodox and more mature
than some have thought it."[9]

This rather depends on which orthodox view one matches
it against. A central tradition, traceable from the *Nicomachean
Ethics* and Aquinas to Hooker, refers moral comparison to a criterion without which it would be arbitrary: "The natural measure whereby to judge our doings is the sentence of reason, determining and setting down what is good to be done." Even if
earthly options are only relatively good or evil one will want a
standard of relative good or evil to compare them in these respects. "We judge by principles that are naturally known to us
in their essence, regarding those things that we discover by inference . . . Hence we must be endowed by Nature not only
with the principles of things to be accounted for but also with
those of things to be done."[10] There is in this view nothing to
choose between saying that the only standard of moral comparison is comparison itself and saying that there is no such standard. In the central tradition Donne's speaker is flouting at the
close of the *Metempsychosis*, the faculty by which moral opinions or judgments are properly arrived at is not opinion but

practical or appetitive intellect — understanding as it informs appraisal: "We elect those things we know are especially good, we entertain opinions about things we do not know at all."[11] On this account, to say that the faculty of judgment by which we form opinions is opinion is not merely to deny that the faculty is reason but to deny that it exists.

This parting shot of Donne's speaker draws out unmistakably the implications for him of the remark that "ther's nothing simply good, nor ill alone." That moral value is relative rather than absolute would hardly tell against its rationality if what it is relative to were a clear standard. But as the example of the Sethites and Cainites suggests, there is in fact a multiplicity of irreconcilable standards. By the pragmatic test of skills that bless earthly life, one must prefer the latter; by the test of saving grace (applicable only by God, and determined by His inscrutable will), the former. Nor does nature save the day for rationality in the *Metempsychosis*: "Nature hath no gaole, though shee hath law" (480). Once again the same editor strains overmuch to acquit his poet of dabbling in heterodoxy:

Donne refers here to the "libertine" conception of the Law of Nature, interpreted to mean that to live under that Law was to be free of the restraints and punishments ("gaole") imposed by the Laws of God and Man . . . Donne is not here expressing any opinion for or against the notion; he is characteristically pointing to a paradox—that under that "Law" of nature even violations of this law (by "unnatural" conduct, e.g., "Sinnes against kinde" [468]) incur no penalty and suffer no restraint.[12]

But Donne's grammar will not accommodate this account. The speaker is not "referring" or "pointing" to any proposition in this line; he is expressing two: that there is a lawful distinction between the natural and the unnatural, and that the distinction does not consist of rewards and punishments — the latter being the reason why the ape attempting to seduce Adam's daughter

lifts subtly with his russet pawe
Her kidskinne apron without feare or awe
Of nature.

(478ff.)

On its face there is nothing particularly libertine or paradoxical about the doctrine that nature does not punish or restrain violations of her law; if she did, civil law need take no cognizance of such violations. Indeed, the celebrated libertine law of nature — "that's lawfull, which doth please" — would seem to threaten its violators with an obvious and immediate punishment: pain. The doctrine of Donne's speaker is disturbing only in the context of a poem that leaves us no other criterion than retributive sanction for disciminating between the natural and the unnatural. Failing this last recourse, the notion of a "sinne against kinde" collapses into absurdity. As the speaker remarks on incest (another such putative sin) in an earlier passage, "till now unlawfull, therefore ill, 'twas not" (203).

Nature — the essence of things — is morally neutral; so things are made "ill" not by nature but by fiat — by becoming unlawful. Indeed, the very enterprise of framing law, as it turns out, is absurd. The framer likes to think that he can specify a reliable criterion for every offense he treats of, so that any case that meets the criterion has to be a case of the given offense. But his criteria are so porous that one can always devise a case that cannot be decided even though it meets the criterion; and however fanciful, such hypothetical anomalies are enough to discredit the definition and to cast doubt on the decision of easier cases.

Take, for example, the mating of the wolf (another avatar of the migratory soul) with Abel's bitch; when Abel finally kills him, the soul passes into the embryo of the whelp with whom his mate is pregnant:

> Some have their wives, their sisters some begot,
> But in the lives of Emperors you shall not
> Reade of a lust the which may equall this;
> This wolfe begot himselfe, and finished
> What he began alive, when hee was dead;
> Sonne to himselfe, and father too, hee is
> A ridling lust, for which Schoolemen would misse
> A proper name.
>
> (431–438)

The defeat of the scholastic doctors of casuistry is our defeat, too; moral discourse depends on classification, on the possibility of deciding on the propriety of its names. The riddle of the wolf's lust — its proper name — needs to be solved if it is to be successfully condemned by reference to a legal rubric. The posthumous son of X (the incarnate soul), by reincarnation, is X, who has thus cohabited with his mother-to-be. Is X guilty of incest? If so, is the begetter guilty or the begotten? But the begetter dies before becoming the son of his mate, and the begotten did not perform the act that alone might qualify as incestuous. The speaker's riddle amounts to a *reductio ad absurdum* not only of ethical categories but of categories in general.

I have been arguing in effect that it is futile to search the sardonic idiom of the *Metempsychosis* for the accents of heresy.[13] Heresies are alternative gospels. Donne's challenge to Christian theodicy, if it can be called a challenge, arises from a consciousness for which there is no such alternative. Theodicy for that consciousness is too mannerly a response to the pseudoprophet or the "rebell"; worse, it is a failure. The advantages of rational discourse accrue to those who recognize that it is no more than a competitive sport, and sacred truth cannot afford the ignominy of taking a fall:

> Arguing is heretiques game, and Exercise
> As wrastlers, perfects them; Not liberties
>   Of speech, but silence; hands, not tongues, end heresies.
>
> (118ff.)

It is clear that the possibility of so "exercising" champions of the righteous cause is not worth discussing.

Our recent editor is rather too nonchalant, I think, when he remarks of the heresies in question that "these speculations about the justice of God in relation to Adam, Eve, the Serpent, and to mankind in general are traditional, descending mostly from rabbinical sources . . . The 'curious' (ingeniously argumentative) rebel who entertained them would not be very daring; even so, Donne says that these questionings are due to the 'corruption' of man, and are characteristic of 'heretiques' [1.118]."[14] Donne's speaker is surely better advised than his jaded commentator; these "speculations" and "questionings" are in fact challenges to the Christian belief in the justice of God and the authority of Scripture. As such, however familiar, they are daring enough, and the objection to original sin in particular well deserves its central place among the preoccupations of traditional Judeo-Christian theodicy. A heretic would have reason to believe that this objection at least is weighty indeed, if not unanswerable.

The key to the dramatic meaning of this passage is that the speaker begins by heaping scorn on these "vanities" and "toys" as virtually self-refuting (114–117), but ends by refraining from engaging them on the ground that they emanate from disputants made perfect by practice. The "toys" are so far from self-refuting, it turns out, that the recommended way of refuting them is to stop their authors' mouths. Indeed, on the showing of the speaker's hasty retreat, it is not merely the recommended but the only way. This announcement that heresies can be successfully answered only by violent repression is, I would submit, an utterance of the deepest irony and intellectual despair.

It is Donne's harlequinade of doubt and not the literary genre of his poem that may fairly be described as Ovidian.[15] Through an anarchic fantasy of the change or exchange of bodies, both poets unfold before us a universe unredeemed by Providence, a universe of moral caprice to which their speakers (Ovid's Pythagoras at some length) take sentimental exception. Both reproduce quite accurately the standard skeptical attack on the notion of an objective morality, while they take care to put the attack in the mouths of persons whose views are clearly not to be trusted.[16] For both poets, trust is a chimera; the embodied mind's predicament is to be compelled to a cruel suspension of belief. Far from a gnostic assurance, the vision we are invited by the *Metempsychosis* to share is an anguished agnosticism.

I have remarked that Donne's poem is in effect a rejoinder to that tradition of Christian philosophy which sees no conflict between faith in God and faith in reason. It is ironic, I think, that the root of his malaise is his allegiance (in the *Metempsychosis* at least) to still another tradition, of no less authority — the tradition of Christian voluntarism: "God's will is so much the highest rule of righteousness that whatever he wills, by the very fact that he wills it, must be considered righteous. When, therefore, one asks why God has so done, we must reply, because he willed it. But if you proceed further to ask why he so willed, you are seeking something greater and higher than God's will, which cannot be found." "Nothing is so evill but that it becomes good, if God command it."[17] To have a moral value, in short, is to be the subject of a divine command, expressing a divine will. That will, however, is substantially hidden, and with it the meaning of our own vocabulary of protest. This is the final intelligence vouchsafed to us by the soul that begins its abortive journey by resting dumbly in the poisoned fruit of the knowledge of good and evil.

LAMIA AND THE SOPHIST
Metamorphosis
as the
Inexplicable

IN THE FANTASIES OF TRANSFORMATION WE HAVE BEEN CONSIDER-ing, the alien body serves sometimes as a lens for the dubious edification of the victim, sometimes as a mirror in which the victim's fellow creatures may see, or fail to see, a distorted image of something akin to themselves. It is in this latter capacity that the transformations of Lamia serve Keats in a poem that warns us from its initial episode (well before Lamia's central importance emerges) not to judge until we understand.

Is Hermes the sexual predator hinted at by the equivocal details of his first appearance?

> The ever-smitten Hermes empty left
> His golden throne, bent warm on amorous theft:
> From high Olympus had he stolen light,
> On this side of Jove's clouds, to escape the sight
> Of his great summoner . . .[1]
>
> (1.7–11)

The impression conveyed by "theft" is reinforced by the later indication that Hermes plans to dispense with wooing in favor of ambush—that the specific object of his quest is the spot "where this sweet nymph prepar'd her secret bed" (1.30); and shortly thereafter we are allowed to catch him in a pose that is hardly auspicious, lying on his pinions "like a stoop'd falcon ere he takes his prey" (1.67). No doubt the ostensible meaning of Hermes' having "stolen light from high Olympus" is that he has sneaked softly away, but the vicinity of "theft" encourages the hovering illusion that "stolen" is to be parsed as transitive: is it possible that, as by another larcenous god, so now by the notorious god of thieves himself, light has been spirited away from the Olympian citadel? Lempriere tells us that Hermes "increased him fame by robbing . . . Jupiter of his scepter";[2] has he robbed his master again, this time of the sacred resource that allows him, as we are later informed, to break through the clouds "as morning breaks, / And swiftly as a bright Phoebean dart" (1.77–78)? If so, the Jovian "summoner" whose sight he is said to be escaping is to be imagined not as calling a courier to his duties, but (in the technical sense) as warning a malefactor to appear before the bar.

But Hermes is not merely the god of theft. He is also (among other things) the god of luck, of interpreters, of hieratic wisdom, above all the god whom the oracular Lamia recognizes as the "too gentle Hermes" (1.80), a fearful lover who is "too frail of heart" (1.93), "the only sad [Olympian]" (1.72), who approaches his lady at last "full of adoring tears" (1.135). His meeting with Lamia occurs when his "painful jealousies" (1.33) are interrupted by

> a mournful voice,
> Such as once heard, in gentle heart destroys
> All pain but pity.
>
> (1.35ff.)

and the obvious presumption is that his is such a heart; the whole passage resonates with the cadence and meaning of its Chaucerian model: "Pitee renneth sone in gentil herte, / Feelinge his similitude in peynes smerte."[3] Hermes has the ennobling gift of sympathetic intuition — or does he? Which version (if either) are we to choose? The characters in the main story confront us with parallel ambiguities, expressed in much the same terms. Is Lamia describing, or merely exhorting, when she invokes Lycius as "gentle" (1.168) and asks for the "pity" he seems so ready to show (1.246–247)? But then what of the cruelty he

indulges with such relish when the opportunity presents itself
(2.75)? And how are we to reconcile the menacing reptilian
shape in which Lamia iş introduced, or the merciless teasing to
which she treats Lycius at first, with the tender "compassion"
(1.106) that induces her to save the nymph Hermes covets from
the "love-glances of unlovely eyes" (1.102)? And how are we to
reconcile this compassion in turn with her casual willingness to
reveal the nymph to Hermes in return for the restoration of her
human form (1.110–111, 120ff.)?

There is another theme by which the story of Hermes and
the nymph anticipates that of Lamia and Lycius: the elusiveness
or invisibility of the object of love. In fact, Hermes' passion for
the nymph is at first purely notional; he measures her unseen
beauty by its transfiguration of the brutally carnal gods of earth
and water (1.14–20):

> Ah, what a world of love was at her feet!
> So Hermes thought, and a celestial heat
> Burnt from his winged heels to either ear.
>
> (1.21–23)

The nymph's gift of invisibility, Lamia insists, is also a gift of
freedom:

> Free as the air, invisibly, she strays
> About these thornless wilds; her pleasant days
> She tastes unseen; unseen her nimble feet
> Leave traces in the grass . . .
>
> (1.94–97)

"She plucks the fruit unseen, she bathes unseen" (1.99). "Her
loveliness invisible, yet free / To wander as she loves, in
liberty" (1.108–109). But if Hermes' ear-burning lust for an
abstraction is an obvious travesty, the solitude of the invisible
nymph (by the standard Lamia applies to herself) is a delusory
freedom; it is like Lamia's loveless concealment in a reptilian
body, or the aloofness she describes in the fictitious autobiography with which she regales Lycius —

> in Corinth, where, she said,
> She dwelt but half retired, and there had led

Days happy as the gold coin can invent
Without the aid of love;

(1.311–315)

or like the egocentric freedom from "human trammels" (2.210)
conferred by Lamia's wine on her fatuous wedding guests. And
eventually it gives way to another and more satisfactory kind of
invisibility — that of the green recesses into which Hermes and
the nymph finally withdraw (1.144), visible only to each other:
"Thou shalt behold her, Hermes, thou alone!" (1.110).

Just such a covert awaits Lamia and her paramour in the
main story, and in both cases it is crucial to mark the distinction
between the two invisibilities. For the lovers' privacy is precisely
not, as one critic has supposed, "a spiritual experience of the
isolated self";[4] its inwardness is not only mutual but frankly
erotic:

                          upon the nymph his eyes he bent
Full of adoring tears and languishment,
And towards her stepp'd: she, like a moon in wane,
Faded before him, cower'd, nor could restrain
Her fearful sobs, self-folding like a flower
That faints into itself at evening hour:
But the god fostering her chilled hand,
She felt the warmth, her eyelids open'd bland,
And, like new flowers at morning song of bees,
Bloom'd, and gave up her honey to the lees.
Into the green-recessed woods they flew;
Nor grew they pale, as mortal lovers do.

(134–145)

As Hermes advances from his comic ardor for an abstract
nymph to his rendezvous with the nymph herself, so Lycius will
later find it less agreeable to deify Lamia than to appreciate in
her "a real woman, lineal indeed / From Pyrrha's pebbles or old
Adam's seed" (1.332–333).

It is worth emphasizing two crucial points before proceeding from the prologue to the tale: that the culmination of
Hermes' quest has the effect of putting to shame the suspicions
inspired by his first appearance, and that the sphere of his and
his partner's success is continuous with the sphere of Lamia's

and Lycius' failure. We are witnessing neither a rape nor an idyll of disembodied essences. This is of course not to dismiss the inducements we have found to think otherwise, but to suggest that they are in the text precisely to be undermined. The poet has led us into temptations whose danger we shall be better able to grasp when, later on, we are allowed to witness the worst consequences of succumbing to them.

To take the two points in order, it is an error, I think — but a thematically instructive error — to maintain that "what happens is that a virgin is taken by Hermes with dispatch, assurance, and complete freedom from self-question."[5] In this reading Hermes' first appearance, augmented by his mythological familiarity as thief and roué, has deprived his affair with the nymph of an accurate appraisal on its own terms. Whatever Hermes steals in Keats's poem, he steals *with* the nymph and not *from* her. Her dread is momentary and well rewarded. "Nor grew they pale": in the end both partners are blithely unscathed by the diffidence or dread they both suffered at the start. It is scarcely nearer the mark to suppose that "Hermes' passion for [the nymph] is little more than mischievous (he steals from Jove's stern prospect and Olympian responsibility to indulge it); this may be love between immortals, but it is hardly idealized. To underscore this point Keats makes his god ridiculously impassioned."[6] What Olympian responsibility does Keats license us to imagine? His Jove, in fact, is so far from being an ascetic bureaucrat that (by clear implication) he personally sponsors the first encounter between Lamia and Lycius: "Jove heard his [Lycius'] vows, and better'd his desire" (1.229). As for the comic tonality of the episode, it is humorous rather than sardonic and is surely part of the idealization of sexual love: the element breathed by Keats's Olympians, as by Homer's, is a laughter that, being divine, cannot be quenched. The effect of Hermes' love on the nymph is not and cannot be "mischievous"; both are gods, and gods are beyond tragedy.

Despite its idealization, the situation in the prologue of *Lamia* is no more an idyll of essences than it is a rape. There is a temptation, once again, to argue that "the love of Hermes and the nymph exists only in the pastoral world, the age-old repository of human wish-fulfillment," and hence that it "suggests the impossibility of any such fulfillment in the human

METAMORPHOSIS AS THE INEXPLICABLE

world of process and mortality" and "can have little purpose otherwise."[7] But this is a tenable reading only if one is allowed by the text to assume that the prologue "has no necessary organic connection with the story that follows,"[8] and it happens that if the blithe Hermes' Crete is "the pastoral world," so is the agonized Lamia's, for Keats makes no distinction whatsoever between them. The necessary connection between prologue and sequel is simply that Lamia must be released from the serpent if there is to be a sequel; Hermes' career would not be causally continuous with that of Lycius if we were to think of them as occupying different worlds.

And here the chronology of Keats's imagination is as crucial as its geography. The events that are to concern us occur

> Upon a time, before the faery broods
> Drove Nymph and Satyr from the prosperous woods,
> Before King Oberon's bright diadem,
> Scepter, and mantle, clasp'd with dewy gem,
> Frighted away the Dryads and the Fauns
> From rushes green, and brakes, and cowslipp'd lawns.
>
> (1.1–6)

Keats is not, as some critics have insisted, dating events by epochs of polytheistic belief or mythological fashion. There is no suggestion in the text that either the "Wood-Gods" (1.34) or the "faery broods" that will depose them are "products of human imagination . . . as subject to change as are ideals of heroism." The revolution of demonic empires cannot plausibly be reduced to the claim "that the hierarchy of Olympians would fade (according to Milton's record on the morning of Christ's nativity) and that Nymph and Satyr would be . . . replaced by new folk-myths of the fairy broods and Oberon."[9] Milton's pantheon is driven out by Christ, not Oberon. There is in fact no society in which a cult of Zeus was displaced by one of Oberon. As mythological history, Keats's *mise-en-scène* would be a pointless distortion. As a myth in its own right, the statement it makes about the scheme of things is pointed enough: that a concept of the divine adequate to the facts of earthly experience is to be found in a modified paganism, in which "sweet sin" (2.31), when the term is used of Lamia's ménage with Lycius, can hardly express a churchman's disapproval of the pleasures so described.

The modification Keats introduces is that nature is a perpetual theater of demonic war or theomachy, each dynasty succeeding its predecessor and yielding to its successor by right of splendor and power; as the Titans were superseded by the Olympians, so these in turn are superseded, and so on world without end. Recalling the familiar model of polytheism, the narrative sketches the obscure outlines of a division of cosmic labor whereby, for example, Lamia "governs the visibility of the nymph and yet requires the aid of Hermes" to be restored to womanhood.[10] In this eclectic mythmaking, Keats has neglected to provide for a *metacosmion*, an alternative universe incommensurate with our own. If the gods dwell anywhere, they dwell within us and among us, in "haunted air and gnomed mine" (2.236), and "even the very trees" (1.34) of which (as of persons) Hermes is so painfully jealous. The point of the contrast between Hermes' success and Lycius' failure, then, cannot be (in Lamia's brazenly disingenuous phrase) that "finer spirits cannot breathe below / In human climes" (1.280–281); nor is it that Lycius — unlike Hermes — will sooner or later die, for the latter answer does not tell us what it is in mortals that poisons their imaginative life well before they die, and telling us just this (as I shall try to show) is the main business of the sequel. The complicated question posed in advance by the prologue of Keats's poem is why Lycius will fail where Hermes succeeds.

Lycius' failure essentially consists, I think, in the eventual loss of his ecstatic union with a being both demonic and archetypally feminine. We are offered an opportunity to choose among three ways of interpreting the circumstance that when first seen she is, very much against her will, animating a reptilian body: "She seem'd, at once, some penanc'd lady elf, / Some demon's mistress, or the demon's self" (1.55–56). If these descriptions were incompatible, then of course she could not satisfy them "at once" even in appearance. But in fact there is nothing to prevent her from being both elf and demon except the narrative premise we have already considered, that the epoch of cosmic history in which the action is set comes before the ascendancy of the fairies; Lamia would then be a harbinger of the approaching order of things, and indeed we are encouraged in this kind of speculation from time to time: she has "elfin blood" (1.147), she lingers by the wayside "faerily" (1.200), her mystic dwelling is surmounted by a "faery roof" (2.123). It is perhaps of some interest in this connection that fairies are commonly associated with the underworld; though Shakespeare's Oberon takes pains to assure us that his subjects "are spirits of another sort," we find him later responding briskly to the approach of dawn: "Then, my queen, in silence sad / Trip we after the night's shade." And Chaucer identifies the fairy king and queen with Pluto and Proserpine.[11] Keats's poem is drawing on such traditions, I think, when it informs us that the snake weeps "as Proserpine still weeps for her Sicilian air" (1.63). Keats's "lady elf" is "penanc'd," like Proserpine the elvish queen, by confinement in a "tomb" (1.38) or "prison-house" (1.203); the association has the added effect of allowing us to suppose that Lamia's penance is as undeserved as the queen's.

Lamia can be both an elf and a demon, then; but can she be both a demon's mistress and the demon's self? Can she be both the ominous agent and the pathetic object of demonic possession? Her "Circean head" (1.115) is more likely to be pathetic than ominous; the suggestion is surely not that "she lures and seduces men to their own destruction,"[12] for the head so described is the object, not the instrument, of transformation into that of a beast like those in the train of Circe. The context of the reference to Circe is a passage that begins with an account of Lamia's benevolence and ends with the spectacle of her being restored, like Circe's Homeric victims, by the intervention of Hermes. The Circean transformation, in fact, is grotesquely incomplete, for Lamia retains the teeth and eyes of a woman (1.60ff.), and this detail has prompted the view that the resulting effect is "mocking humor" at the victim's expense, "not far from caricature," the point of the mockery being that "her ultimate attractions [are] highly ambiguous."[13] This suggestion is unfortunate, I think. Monstrosity and self-loathing are immune from mockery, if from nothing else. Lamia' gaudy deformity is a penance in itself and, as she is only too well aware, has deprived her of a body "fit for life" (1.39). Part of the penance is the irony that, like her decorative markings, what remains to her of the body fit for life merely compounds her deformity. These tantalizing relics of a face, in short, are presented as anything but attractions, nor does Keats's text entitle us to claim that "ultimately" Lamia has no other attractions than these.

So far we have the victim of possession rather than the agent — the demon's mistress and not the demon's self. And as we shall see, there is a demonic streak in the characterization of her lover, who will expressly make it his business to possess her, "to entangle, trammel up, and snare" Lamia's soul in his own (2.52–53). But of course Lamia ensnares as well; Lycius' is "the life she had so tangled in her mesh" (1.295) — "blinded Lycius, so in her comprised" (1.347). When she wants to be, she is ironically adept in playing "the cruel lady, without any show / Of sorrow for her tender favorite's woe" (1.290–291) — a consummate mistress of the sheer surgical technique, the "science" (1.191), of ensnaring "in the lore / Of love deep learned to the red heart's core" (1.189–190). The poem seems to confirm that Lamia is (as she appears to be) both elf and demon, and both the victim and the wielder of demonic ensnarement. If such ensnarement were an evil it would not, of course, be excused by being repaid in kind. But by the lights of the poem it is, I think, far from an evil; the evil, on the contrary, is to find oneself at large again. What the lovers enjoy in the "purple-lined palace of sweet sin" (2.31) is Keats's unabashedly sensual version of the beatific vision.

Lamia is uniquely qualified to confer such beatitude, being

> Not one hour old, yet of sciential brain
> To unperplex bliss from its neighbor pain,
> Define their pettish limits, and estrange
> Their points of contact and swift counterchange;
> Intrigue with the specious chaos, and dispart
> Its most ambiguous atoms with sure art.
>
> (1.191–196)

For the mistress of the demonic *ars amatoria* the raw material of love is a "specious chaos" — Romeo's "misshapen chaos of well-seeming forms" — that achieves cosmos only when one "intrigues" with it — intricates or ensnares oneself in it — so as to separate its "pettish" or warring elements of bliss and pain. The distinctions between these are, at the limit, so subtle that it requires a "sciential brain" to "define" and hence to "unperplex" or disentangle them — to sort them out despite ambiguities into their constituent "atoms" of bliss and pain. The creation of this particular demiurge, then, is an "empery / Of joys" (2.36), of "unperplexed delight and pleasure known" (1.327). Lamia's psychological theory is oddly mechanistic, but it is redeemed by its aim and apparent result: a "bliss" of absolute purity to be shared with her "youth of Corinth" (1.119).

She is, in short, a presiding genius of *eros*, enjoying like Venus the advantages of a renewable virginity (1.188–189), of being at once "unshent" and a "graduate" of the "college" (1.197–198); and Lycius comes, in fact, to identify her with Venus herself: "my silver planet, both of eve and morn" (2.48). The mythological allusions that underlie her nature and the shape in which she first appears are in keeping with this theme of erotic sublime. The Cretan Lamia is not, like the "African monsters" of the same name, mute and cannibalistic, but rather a deity of regeneration worshiped as at the Eleusinian mysteries. And by a kind of homeopathic magic, Hermes conjures away Lamia's serpent shape with his "lithe Caducean charm" (1.133), encircled by two serpents (1.89) that "some suppose to be a symbol of Jupiter's amours with Rhea, when these two deities transformed themselves into snakes."[14] As we have already noticed, Lamia is an answer to Lycius' prayers by which "Jove heard his vows, and better'd his desire" (1.229). Elsewhere in the text we hear of her "compassion" (1.106) and her "wild and timid nature" (2.71), and when when has dispensed with coquetry

> she began to sing,
> Happy in beauty, life, and love, and everything,
> A song of love, too sweet for earthly lyres,
> While, like held breath, the stars drew in their panting fires.
>
> (1.297–300)

The impression systematically conveyed by these and other details is enough, I think, to remove any doubt about the personality of the central figure, which is both benign and tragic. Lamia is not only "rainbow-sided" but "touched with miseries" (1.54); far from making her lover "a serpent's prey" (2.298), as she will later be accused of doing, she responds to his transparent ennui simply by proceeding to "set herself, high-thoughted, how to dress / The misery in fit magnificence" (2.115–116). "She faded at self-will" (2.142). By forcing this self-abnegation Lycius elects, not to rid himself of a curse, but (as we are explicitly informed) to "flout the silent-blessing fate" (2.147–148) — to reject a providential gift. If a Romantic parallel to the serpent-victim is wanted, I should recommend the situation in a novella contemporary with Keats's poem, E. T. A. Hoffmann's *Der Goldne Topf*, in which the student Anselmus temporarily betrays his "childlike" faith in his beautiful snake-nurse Serpentina, a princess of the realm of Faerie, by committing himself to the "hostile principle" of a degenerate common sense.

The narrator of Keats's poem is willing to concede that "Love in a palace is perhaps at last/ More grievous torment than a hermit's fast" (2.3–4). But he brings up this possibility only to dismiss it as irrelevant to love in the purple-lined palace that immediately concerns us: "too short was their bliss/ To breed distrust and hate" (2.9–10). What we are to be shown is not love dying a natural death — decaying spontaneously into its opposite — but love at the mercy of rival allegiances. The "thrill/ Of trumpets" interrupts the lovers' repose, leaving a "buzzing" in Lycius' head (2.29). The result is that "His spirit pass'd beyond its golden bourn/ Into the noisy world almost forsworn" (2.32–33). The crisis of *Lamia* is an inchoate act of "forswearing," of betrayal; its object, not love itself but the special intensity — the passion — that these lovers have been able to achieve. For "but a moment's thought is passion's passing bell" (2.39).

If one passion is needed to drive out another, the intruder in this case is threefold, and triply unsavory. Lycius wishes, first of all, to display Lamia as a trophy:

> What mortal hath a prize, that other men
> May be confounded and abash'd withal,
> But lets it sometimes pace abroad majestical,
> And triumph, as in thee I should rejoice
> Amid the hoarse alarm of Corinth's voice.
> Let my foes choke, and my friends shout afar,
> While through the thronged streets your bridal car
> Wheels round its dazzling spokes.
>
> (2.57–64)

He wishes to express his mastery by subjecting Lamia to an act of "mitigated fury" (2.78), of refined and intimate violence:

> For all his love, in self-despite,
> Against his better self, he took delight
> Luxurious in her sorrows, soft and new.
> His passion, cruel grown, took on a hue
> Fierce and sanguineous as 'twas possible
> In one whose brow had no dark veins to swell.
>
> (2.72–77)

And he is no longer content with Lamia's anonymity; he feels the need of a domesticating label, a "mortal name, / Fit appellation for this dazzling frame" (2.88–89). It does not make Lycius' new "passion" (2.75) any the less "perverse" (2.70) that Lamia herself should be corrupted by it — "she burnt, she loved the tyranny" (2.81); it is, the narrator tells us, a kind of exhibitionism — a "mad pompousness" — emanating from a "foolish heart" (2.114). I find it hard to believe that the trumpet call (2.27–28) represents Lycius' opportunity to see "seclusion or retreat, and to some extent love, in contrast to the salutary challenge and enterprise of the public world."[15] The enterprise suggested to Lycius by the trumpet is not notably salutary; it is to use Lamia for his own aggrandizement. Nor will Lycius readily pass muster as a sensible bourgeois who prefers after all to "have [Lamia] take her place beside him together with other companions and interests";[16] his only interest at this point is in converting a person into a "prize." His interest in other companions, beyond "confounding" and "abashing" them while his foes "choke," is nil.

Keats's language is not ambiguous about the vulgarity and emptiness of Lycius' new impulse. To violate "warm cloister'd hours" (2.148) — that is, the measured time of a holy order — for the diversion of a "gossip rout" (2.146), to "show to common eyes these secret bowers" (2.149), is unmistakably to profane a mystery. The "gossip rout" of wedding guests in this instance is the notorious Corinthians, with their "temples lewd" (1.352), including a "temple of Venus where lascivious women resorted, and sold their pleasures so dear that many of their lovers were reduced to poverty."[17] Lycius has fallen in with the meretricious tastes of his townsmen by resolving to turn an end in itself into a squalid means. The morbid opulence of the "banquet chamber" designed by Lamia for this occasion reflects her intention "to dress/ The misery in fit magnificence" (2.115) — ironically fit, that is, to mock the sensibility at work in "the revels rude,/ When dreadful guests would come to spoil her solitude" (2.144–145) at the whim of a lover for whom she is now a bauble and a weapon, and who has chosen to establish her precincts as an authentically Corinthian "temple."

Of the three impulses that lead to this disaster perhaps the most insidious is Lycius' desire to name the mystery, the "silent-blessing fate," and hence (presumably) to make it comprehensible. In his insistence on scrutinizing it, on plucking out its heart rather than simply accepting it, he reenacts with a fatal difference the ironic gesture with which at the outset he obeys Lamia's request to "look back" (1.246): "He did; not with cold wonder fearingly,/ But Orpheus-like at an Eurydice" (1.247-248). Like Orpheus, or Psyche, Lycius forswears himself by a violation of his own secret life. The act of intellect involved in this violation is the act of a voyeur. In this sense especially, "but a moment's thought is passion's passing bell."

Enabling thought to toll the knell of passion, in fact, is an accomplishment in some request among the philosophical sects of antiquity. Lycius has the corresponding virtue of philosophical indifference or Apathy to thank for his ability to maintain a "calm uneager face" (1.218) even while "charioting foremost in the envious race" (1.217). It is this assiduously cultivated abstractedness that Lamia must wean Lycius from when she first approaches him:

> His phantasy was lost, where reason fades,
> In the calm'd twilight of Platonic shades.
> Lamia beheld him coming near, more near —
> Close to her passing, in indifference drear,
> His silent sandals swept the mossy green;
> So neighbor'd to him and yet so unseen
> She stood: he pass'd shut up in mysteries,
> His mind wrapp'd like his mantle.
>
> (1.235–242)

The ultimate purpose of reason or dialectic in the Platonic scheme is to transcend itself in the contemplation of the One, and it is quite misleading to infer from this account of his musings

that "Lycius' mind habitually strayed from the rigors of philosophical speculation."[18] Lycius is being presented to us here, on
the contrary, as an advanced disciple of his "trusty guide/ And
good instructor" Apollonius (1.375–376), happy in the achievement of "calm" or "indifference" and in the enjoyment of "mysteries" accessible to the ecstatic mind only when reason has
served its purpose and faded. In yielding to the temptations of
Corinth Lycius is not forsworn, but "almost forsworn" (2.33);
the final test of his loyalty will be his ability to resist the temptation of a much more powerful challenge to the erotic sublime
than the tawdry voluptuousness of his wedding guests: the cor-
rosive intellectuality of the "bald-head philosopher" (2.245).

Intellectuality as it is envisaged in Keats's poem consists in
the development of theories designed to reduce complex experience to a manageable simplicity. It is the experience of Lamia
that Apollonius so reduces, at least to his own satisfaction. For
him it is precisely the "gordian shape" (1.47) to which she is compared in her reptilian incarnation — a knot to be untied or cut, a
problem to be solved or dissolved. When Apollonius finally appears as an "uninvited guest" (2.165) at the wedding banquet,
the untying is virtually complete:

> something too he laughed,
> As though some knotty problem, that had daft
> His patient thought, had now begun to thaw,
> And solve and melt — 'twas just as he foresaw.
>
> (2.159–162)

The metaphoric vocabulary is Shakespearean: "Oh that this too
too solid flesh would melt,/ Thaw, and resolve itself into a
dew!" "Oh that I were a mockery king of snow/ Standing before
the sun of Bolingbroke/ To melt myself away in water drops!"
Apollonius' solution will be the claim that Lamia is nothing but
the set of principles into which he chooses to resolve or analyze
her; as a person she is to melt away like the Snow Queen in the
fairy tale, before the sun of Apollonius' rational explanation.

The narrator hardly predisposes us in favor of this ready
and easy method of eliminating mysteries when he twice agrees
with Lycius' description of his old teacher as a "sophist" (2.172,

299; see also 2.285). But the narrator goes further, by indulging in a bitter invective against the reductionist mentality:

> and, for the sage,
> Let spear-grass and the spiteful thistle wage
> War on his temples. Do not all charms fly
> At the mere touch of cold philosophy?
> There was an awful rainbow once in heaven:
> We know her woof, her texture; she is given
> In the dull catalogue of common things.
> Philosophy will clip an Angel's wings,
> Conquer all mysteries by rule and line,
> Empty the haunted air, and gnomed mine—
> Unweave a rainbow, as it erewhile made
> The tender-person'd Lamia melt into a shade.
>
> (2.227–238)

The urge to eliminate one fact of experience by identifying it with a correlated fact, on this showing, is a reflex of philistine spite, the unweaving of the rainbow. It seems to me that this bitter charge is a reliable guide to the meaning of Keats's poem. In other words, I hold it to be quite false that "to interpret the poem in these terms is to make the unwarranted assumption that, if a poem contains a passage of abstract statement, this passage necessarily summarizes the poem";[19] rather it is to make the warranted assumption that if a storyteller at the climax of his telling explicitly draws a moral that is consistent with his story, and does so without a hint of irony or reservation, then he has provided us, like it or not, with powerful evidence that his story has, among other morals, at least the one he draws—in this case, that Lamia is among the charms that fly at philosophy's touch.

The theoretical simplicity of the reductionist vision of Lamia—as she fades or sickens under the stare of Apollonius—is achieved at a terrible price:

> now no azure vein
> Wander'd on fair-spac'd temples; no soft bloom
> Misted the cheek; no passion to illume
> The deep-recessed vision—all was blight;
> Lamia, no longer fair, there sat a deadly white.
>
> (2.272–276)

METAMORPHOSIS AS THE INEXPLICABLE

Of course, once before we have watched Lamia survive the cruelly systematic unweaving of her rainbow:

> in moments few, she was undress'd
> Of all her sapphires, greens, and amethyst,
> And rubious-argent: of all these bereft,
> Nothing but pain and ugliness were left.
> Still shone her crown; that vanish'd, also she
> Melted and disappear'd as suddenly;
> And in the air, her new voice luting soft . . .

(1.161–167)

A person in the extremity of physical dissolution, pain, and ugliness (if we are to credit this alternative account) somehow will not bear out the claim that she is "nothing but" pain and ugliness.

The gist of Apollonius' theory of Lamia is that in some fundamental sense she is nothing but a serpent (2.298, 305). As Lycius had done in cruel play, so now Apollonius in cruel earnest affects his namesake Apollo's

> presence when in act to strike
> The serpent — Ha, the serpent! certes, she
> Was none.

(2.79ff.)

In fact, it is a theory that the poem as a whole refuses to sustain. "I was a woman, let me have once more/ A woman's shape" (1.117–118). The prayer has been granted; what she was, she is — "a lady bright" (1.171), "a maid" (1.185), "a virgin" (1.189). As for the serpent, it is simply her "wreathed tomb" (1.38), her "prison-house" (1.203). It is a measure of Apollonius' persuasiveness that some critics have embraced his interpretation despite the clear evidence that the text repudiates it, and despite the inconvenient fact that it rests on the genetic fallacy that the origins of a thing exhaust its nature. "The source of attraction, Lamia, is a serpent, or at least she is a serpent much of the time."[20] The narrative, however, does not allow us to be so noncommittal on this point. Being a serpent much of the time is compatible with *not* being a serpent much of the time, including the moment of Apollonius' accusation, and the latter condition is at least as true as the former of the Lamia we are shown. Indeed, Lamia occupies the reader for longer as a woman than as a serpent.

But this way of reckoning is beside the point. The hypothesis put to us by the poem is that Apollonius' charge would not have been true even if it had coincided with the moment of Lamia's "imprisonment" or "entombment" in the serpent, for on the showing of Keats's metaphors the serpent radically differs from Lamia in being, rather than being in, a body of a certain kind. It is true that Keats's attack on Apollonius is all too readily confused with a strain of obscurantism that sometimes characterized hostility to scientific endeavor later in the nineteenth century: "The Victorians, preoccupied with the struggle they themselves dramatized between science and poetry, saw *Lamia* as an allegorical attack the theme of which was the blighting effect of science and analytic philosophy on the poetry of either the sensuous or the visionary imagination."[21] It was, of course, a great blunder to suppose that the construction of explanatory theories is a blight to the visionary imagination; but the concomitant blunder was the failure to see that the blight caused by Apollonius is precisely due, in Keats's account, to a perverse exercise of the visionary imagination. For it requires a leap of that faculty in heroic defiance of common sense to hold that serpent turned lady is really serpent still, and (more generally) that in reality a mind just is the bodily conditions on which its existence depends.

"But the point," we have been told, "is that Lamia is not a woman; she only looks like one. Since her real nature is unknowable, any form she embodies is necessarily a mere appearance, a kind of mask. As Keats later remarks, Lamia is 'playing a woman's part' [1.337]. In short, she is an illusion, and the state of being she now personifies is simply unreal."[22] This categorical dismissal of Lamia's womanhood and reality is rather arbitrary, it seems to me. By Keats's hypothesis Lamia has at present just the body she seems to have; it is not a mask for another. In physical endowment if not in biological history she is "now a lady bright" (1.171). To be sure, the endowment misleads about the history, for in the historical sense the victim of transformation strictly belongs to none of her ostensible species. But to mislead us in this way, Lamia must exist. Even if Lamia's nature

were entirely unknown, it would follow neither that she is unreal nor that her nature cannot be known. But in fact, though
her biological species—if any—eludes us, we are reliably informed not only that she assumes bodies but that she thinks and
feels. The nature of Lamia, as it concerns us, is that she is a person. The gravamen of Keats's indictment of the professional ex-
orcist is precisely his righteous indifference to the personhood of
his victim, as he

> fix'd his eye, without a twinkle or stir,
> Full on the alarmed beauty of the bride,
> Brow-beating her fair form, and troubling her sweet pride.
>
> (2.246ff.)

It is important to note that the villain of the piece is not
Apollonius but the ideology to which he has committed himself,
and that if *Lamia* is a story of misdirected love at all, it is the
story of Apollonius' devotion to the student whom he so de-
structively tries to shield from destruction:

> "from every ill
> Of life have I preserv'd thee to this day,
> And shall I see thee made a serpent's prey?"
>
> (2.296ff.)

The tragedy of Apollonius is that he is capable only of a virulent
devotion that alienates and finally destroys its object:

> with a frightful scream she vanished:
> And Lycius' arms were empty of delight,
> As were his limbs of life.
>
> (2.306–308)

The contest over Lycius' allegiance is after all remarkably symmetrical. For Apollonius himself, as Lycius unavailingly recognizes, is driven in his love by a demonic vision:

> "Corinthians! look upon that gray-beard wretch!
> Mark how, possess'd, his lashless eyelids stretch
> Around his demon eyes! Corinthians, see!
> My sweet bride withers at their potency."
>
> (2.287–290)

Apollonius kills by fascination, by a perverse exercise of vision; it is, by an apt irony, the mode of destruction favored by an illustrious mythical serpent: the basilisk. As a means of illumination the reductionist vision in Keats's portrayal is as delusive as it is impoverishing. The clear and distinct ideas of the sophist, mirrored in the docile reverie of his disciple, are in the end a mere "twilight of Platonic shades" (1.236). Lycius must choose, then, between quite different visions of the way things are; on opening his eyes to the one, it is quite natural that his first instinct should be to blind himself to the other:

> "Lycius! wherefore did you blind
> Yourself from his quick eyes?" Lycius repli'd,
> "Tis Apollonius sage, my trusty guide
> And good instructor; but tonight he seems
> The ghost of folly haunting my sweet dreams."
>
> (1.373–377)

The word "dream" figures crucially in various contexts in the narrative, and it is useful to bear in mind that for the most part it is interchangeable with "perception"; thus the "dreams" of perfect beings never deceive: "Real are the dreams of Gods, and smoothly pass/ Their pleasures in a long immortal dream" (1.127–128). Even in this explicit statement there is perhaps a handle for the mistaken inference that "the dreams of Gods are of the same *fictive* stuff as their waking moments."[23] But the reality of Keats's gods is beside the point here; since there is nothing to keep a dreamer (in the literal sense) from being fooled by dreams even in the course of a *fiction*, the gods can hardly be spared this inconvenience by being fictitious (though in fact the poem implies the opposite view of them). What spares them is simply that all their perceptions are divine and hence infallible: "where she will'd, her spirit went" (1.205).

> And sometimes into cities she would send
> Her dream, with feast and rioting to blend;
> And once, while among mortals dreaming thus,
> She saw the young Corinthian Lycius.
>
> (1.213ff.)

"I dreamt I saw thee [this on greeting Hermes] . . . and here thou art" (1.76, 79)

The oddity of Keats's usage is especially conspicuous when it transpires that, for the ecstatic Lycius at any rate, the perceptions one wakes up *to* are no less "trances" than those one wakes up *from*: "as he from one trance was wakening/ Into another" (1.296–297). In this perspective the waking state of the bourgeois is only duller, but not a whit more solid, than that of the lunatic, the lover, and the poet; perceptions in the public domain answer the same surprising description as those in the private: "As men talk in a dream, so Corinth all / . . . Mutter'd" (1.350, 353). If Lycius elects to turn from Lamia's bower to the streets of Corinth, his choice can hardly be justified on the ground that the former alone is a dream. There is, in this account, no basis for the claim that "the contrast which Keats establishes between Lycius' vacuous mortal life and his pleasure-filled existence with Lamia is undermined by this *spurious* dying into life, into a life, that is, of illusion."[24] No order of consciousness has the metaphysical backing this argument requires; it is enough, however, for the purposes of Lycius' choice that some illusions — some dreams — are inherently better than others: richer, subtler, or more intense.

In *Lamia* there is no theory of physical appearances — Corinthian common sense least of all — that has pride of place by transcending the status of a dream. But Lamia herself is neither a theory nor an appearance. Indeed, her independence of Lycius' awareness is so firmly axiomatic that one of her most extraordinary feats is concealed from Lycius and reserved for the admiration of the reader alone. The ambiguity of its locus is itself a commentary on the elusiveness of physical reality:

> The way was short, for Lamia's eagerness
> Made, by a spell, the triple league decrease
> To a few paces; not at all surmis'd
> By blinded Lycius, so in her compris'd.
>
> (1.344–347)

It would seem that eagerness can work a spell because physical magnitudes are the furniture of dreams. Lamia too, like Lycius, is a dreamer, but a dreamer with sovereignty. If her house too is a dream, it is at no disadvantage to Corinth at large, in this regard, though critical opinion (by inattention, I think) has been variously inclined to think otherwise: "Insofar as Lamia represents a delusive world of bliss, such exposure [as Lycius inflicts on her] means certain death for the illusion." "[Lamia's] house represents a withdrawal into purely imaginative activity, for it is known only by Lycius. Other human beings cannot see it, and when subsequently the wedding guests arrive, they 'enter'd marveling . . . ne'er before had seen/ That royal porch' [2.152–155]."25 How does one enter a nonexistent porch?

These lines show, on the contrary, that other human beings can not only see but enter Lamia's precincts, and surely the narrator's talk of Lamia's secret longing, anguish, and resignation would be pointless if he intended us to dismiss her as a hallucination of her lover. In fact the place is known not only to Lycius but to "a few Persian mutes, who that same year/ Were seen about the markets" (1.390–391); and it shows no sign of disintegrating, though "a haunting music" is its "sole supportress" (2.122–123), until Apollonius' dissonance begins to drown it out. The ordinary guests simply accept it, just as Corinthians had casually accepted both Lamia and Lycius as real when they "watch'd to trace them to their house" (1.393). It is of course true that "with the 'wine at flow' [2.202] and the music of powerful instruments . . . the guests seem to enter and share Lycius' state of mind."26 But if these materials are needed to *generate* a state of mind like Lycius', it is hardly possible that they too, with the palace they furnish and its mistress, are simply the *contents* of that state of mind. Nor is it easy to see by what esoteric process she could gradually *become* such contents: "[Lamia's] existence increasingly depends on the complete subjective commitment of [Lycius'] eyes to her . . . Only when at the feast he takes his eyes from her to look at Apollonius does Lamia begin to vanish."27 Lycius, however, seems to be acquitted by the text. By the time he dispatches a cup of wine (2.241) and faces Apollonius, the philosopher already "*had* fixed his eye" on Lamia (2.246; emphasis added), and she is already alarmed, browbeaten, and troubled; these are the opening stages of her gradual death.

Criticism of the kind I am challenging succumbs to a temptation that tries Lycius as well. If the mere fact of the wedding reveals him as "almost forsworn," the forswearing is surely an accomplished fact when at the spectacle of the blight settling on his bride he cries: "Begone, foul dream!" (2.271). But if this is a betrayal, Lycius' atonement is immediate; he dies not in disillusionment but in grief, after a futile attempt to save Lamia by accusing Apollonius of "unlawful magic" (2.286). It is in the end, I think, a matter of one witness's credibility against another's. Apollonius charges that Lamia is a serpent about to prey on Lycius. The chief evidence, which seems hardly formidable, is that Lamia is pierced by his stare, withers under it, gestures to him not to repeat the charge, and, on his refusal and "echoing" of it (2.301–306), vanishes. It is not easy to attribute Lycius' subsequent death to irrational disregard of a just accusation, for the killing grief is at work before Apollonius makes his charge:

> a death-nighing moan
> From Lycius answered, as heart-struck and lost,
> He sank supine beside the aching ghost.
>
> (2.292ff.; see 2.298)

That grief is surely not a form of capitulation; Lycius is not forswearing himself for a third and last time. On the contrary, he is testifying against what for him are his master's "impious proud-heart sophistries" (2.285). It is not a body's serpenthood or want of solidity or substance but the loss of its owner that he is unable to survive.

In the end that owner is nothing but an "aching ghost" (2.294), and reductionist physicalism no doubt sees through aches as piercingly as through ghosts. But Lycius dies in the conviction that the aches of the Other—and the self they afflict—need not be seen, to exist. When Apollonius acts on the opposite view, it is not Lycius' opinion he disposes of, but Lycius. The latter now fulfills the promise he had made at the outset: "Even as thou vanishest so shall I die" (1.260). The assumption underlying that pledge is clearly not that to vanish one must first be a figment, but rather that eluding sight is also a talent of the highest realities.

For Keats these highest and indeed sole realities are minds, partly replicated worlds or monads of passionate intensity; and the highest intensity is the empathic moment when for two such worlds the overlapping of dreams becomes total. This romantic monadology will recur, shaded with skeptical reserve, in the transformations and epiphanies of Woolf's Orlando. And divested of romanticism and rapture, the vision of personhood it entails recurs as quotidian nightmare in the mutual imprisonment of Gregor and the rest of the family Samsa.

THE ORDEAL OF GREGOR SAMSA
Metamorphosis
as Alienation
without Grace

I T IS UNDERSTANDABLE THAT READERS HAVE OFTEN BEEN RELUC-
tant to take Gregor Samsa's predicament literally. Being
forced to seek a way of living with a human mind and an insectile body is undoubtedly an ordeal, but it is also an impossibility; how can one contrive to pity or fear it? How can one take
it seriously? One obvious remedy is to hold that by "the total
implication of the story" Gregor's transformation is to be construed as "a psychotic breakdown or other serious mental
regression." To quote a second medical opinion: "It is the
schizophrenics who are often truly and irrevocably transformed
into other people, historical personages, into animals or objects.
If Gregor Samsa had told his story it would be the sincere confession of a schizophrenic."[1]

Unfortunately, appropriate substitutions for troublesome
expressions in the text will not easily produce the desired result:
the account of a bourgeois household's response to the sudden
madness of one of its members. For one thing, the central
metaphor—if it is a metaphor—is a composite of body and
movement, the latter being a property of the former. But if the
figurative meaning of the insectile body is abnormal behavior,
then the figurative meaning of the insectile movement must
likewise be some property of abnormal behavior: which prop-

erty? Gregor's crawling, for example, is perfectly normal in an insect; is normality to stand for abnormality? It is only if we take the movement literally that we get a clear picture of possible human derangement, though crawling comes rather short of what might plausibly warrant the revulsion and terror that attend Gregor's first appearance; the victim might be having a stroke. On the other hand, if we take the movement literally, we shall need to find an ad hoc figurative treatment for Gregor's new habit of walking on the ceiling. And what are we to make of the embarrassing consequence of the current interpretation that Gregor's insanity—his insect body—survives its victim? What is posthumous insanity?

Even if we somehow allow Gregor's new body to stand for unspecified symptoms of derangement, we shall need to accommodate his state of mind to this interpretation. For he is evidently in agreement with the onlookers, and with the narrator for that matter, that he has acquired an insectile body. If the others' perceptions are the measure of sanity, then his perceptions are sane; but then what becomes of the insanity of which his new body is the figurative symptom? Or are we to take his warranted responses as the symbol of unwarranted responses? Nor can our exegetical program neglect the family's inability to recognize Gregor's affliction as a derangement, or their failure even to contemplate summoning professional assistance, or their acquiescence in the consignment of Gregor's corpse to some dust heap or other by a domestic; taken literally, these are not the responses of a bourgeois household to the madness of one of its members.

I do not doubt that these objections can be met by an assignment of meanings, literal or figurative as convenient, cobbled up to fit the "total implication" we are bent on finding. But it is hard to see how the story, in whole or part, can be said to imply the result of a procedure that, with a little ingenuity, will generate any implication we please. If Gregor's physical catastrophe refuses so stubbornly to be naturalized as a mental catastrophe in disguise, then I think we may conclude as well that it is wasted effort to coax it into expressing a mental disorder that is a good deal less catastrophic. When the theory of psychosis fails, it takes that of neurosis with it.

But the latter theory, as I shall presently try to show, is as crucially relevant to the interpretation of Kafka's story as it is untenable. The first thing worth remarking about its most elaborate version, I think, is that neurosis in this context suspiciously resembles vice; it would appear that Gregor has only himself to blame for his predicament: "The son took on himself the family's debt. In the beginning this led to 'fine times' of love, warmth, and harmony, but thereafter to the gradual usurpation of the father's role by the son, who now made his appearance as sole breadwinner and supporter of the family." The transformation, in short, is "an undoing of the inversion of the natural relationship between father and son. Through Gregor's transformation his father is restored to power and youthfulness, takes a post that permits him to wear a splendid uniform, and reasserts his position as head of the family." "With the transformation itself the alienating principle . . . or 'pure I' seizes possession of Gregor and automatically hurls the usurping son down from his position of power in the family while it helps his father once again to his old power and status."[2]

It is odd how little there is in the text to corroborate this account. Gregor is the mainstay of the family willy-nilly, by the bankruptcy and subsequent abdication of his father, who did nothing to relieve his son of the false impression that the family's resources had been reduced to "utter hopelessness" (101);[3] the only alternative to breadwinning would have been desertion. Perhaps the theoretical crime Gregor is somehow punishing in himself is rather his decision, which was to have been announced the following Christmas Eve, to send his sister to conservatory over his parents' objections (102, 130). "Right from the outset we see a function of this transformation. It is a judgment in advance, a forestalling of the son's usurpation of his father's authority."[4] But there is no crisis of paternal authority in the case. The parents' (not specifically the father's) objections will be no more than prudential, for Grete can hardly have been studying the violin without their approval. Nor is there anything in the text to indicate that the "natural" status of a father, either in fact or in Gregor's conception, is an absolute *patriapotestas*; or that the essential attraction of Gregor's plan, for him, is his father's discomfiture rather than his sister's best interests.

The corrective reversal of roles between father and son is as

questionable as the usurpation. It is true that Gregor has acquired "pitifully thin legs" and a "vaulted belly" (71), has lost his
teeth (85), and (after his father wounds him) walks "like an old
invalid" (119). But the prostrate son's impression of a contrary
change in his menacing father, who astonishes Gregor with his
bank messenger's livery and "the gigantic size of his bootsoles"
(116), turns out to be no more than a trick of foreshortening.
The splendid uniform is a mark of servitude, not command, and
the splendor fades at closer quarters: "While his dressing gown
hung useless on the clothes hook, the father would doze in his
seat fully clothed, as though he were ever ready for service and
even here waited on the voice of his superior. . . . Gregor often
looked whole evenings long at the completely stained garment,
bright with its continually polished gold buttons" (119–120).
"No sooner would the women grasp him [the father] under the
shoulders than he opened his eyes . . . and used to say, 'This is a
life. This is the repose of my declining days' " (120). "What the
world demanded of poor people, they fulfilled to the uttermost;
the father fetched breakfast for the officials of a bank"
(121–122).

As it happens, the throne from which Gregor is deposed by
his affliction is precisely that to which his father is thus elevated:
the humiliations of a lackey. As Gregor has cringed before the
hectoring of his Principal (73) and the Head Clerk (83), so now
his father, an elderly messenger boy, makes his daily obeisances
to his employers and boarders (127), deferring to the latter even
when they are cruelly uncivil to his daughter (129). The irony of
the lackey's uniform is at the expense of both breadwinners, for
both, in their harried wage slavery, are mocked by the photo-
graph of Lieutenant Gregor Samsa in a halcyon period before
duty imprisoned him in the role of breadwinner, "as hand on
sword, with an untroubled smile, he demanded respect for his
bearing and uniform" (87).

It is true that the elder Samsa is fastidious about his buttons, if not about the rest of his livery. But the point clearly is
not that their maintenance affirms his pride, but rather that
their tarnishing would simply aggravate the humiliation of his
having to wear them at all. The old man is hardly rejoicing in
the dignity of labor. He is, instead, making a virtue of the piti-
less necessity that keeps him hopping on the string. And he is

well aware of this. There is, then, an analogy between Gregor's status immediately before the transformation and his father's immediately after it, though not the analogy required by the thesis of Gregor's usurpation.

Between Gregor's lot as a beetle and the enforced retirement from which his father emerges, there is no significant analogy at all. Unlike Gregor's affliction, his father's five years of idleness have neither isolated nor tormented him. Although these years have seen him become fat, awkward, and diffident (104), they are at the same time "the first vacation of his laborious and yet unsuccessful life" (104). Unlike the desiccated beetle with the ominous rash—itchy and frigid—on its abdomen, the elder Samsa remains healthy (104), with a "mighty chest" (87) and the daily habit of late, sumptuously protracted breakfasts (87) that Gregor bitterly resents in his fellow commercial travelers, who "live like harem women" (72). If the sort of argument I am considering were genuinely psychoanalytic, of course, the pivotal question would be not whether Gregor has in fact been amassing power at his father's expense, but instead whether he thinks he has. (The question would be vacuous, for Kafka has neglected to supply the copious detail that alone might warrant a belief in the existence of an answer.) But the question put before us is Gregor's objective and not his subjective guilt; as I observed by way of introduction, what we are now studying is at bottom not a diagnosis but an indictment.

It is doubtful that Gregor's transformation has restored his father's power or confidence, the more so as it is far from clear that the elder Samsa ever had much of the one or the other. But it is clear enough that Gregor's transformation effectively excuses him from his duties as breadwinner. This is its result; can it not also be its purpose? If Gregor is innocent of usurpation, perhaps he is guilty of defection: "Gregor's interior monologue at the outset . . . discloses that he has for some time cherished feelings of reluctance and aversion toward his work . . . So regarded, the transformation is a refusal to obey dispensed from guilt [or debt—Schuld in both cases]; no open rebellion, but a flight into dereliction that must have even worse consequences for the family than open denial of service. At one stroke the family loses its breadwinner." This new suggestion, then, presupposes that by transforming himself Gregor evades the hardships of his post as well as blame for his evasion.[5] But this assumption is ruled out by the very monologue that is cited to confirm it: "Oh God . . . what kind of taxing employment have I chosen! Day in, day out en route. The business irritations are much greater than in the real business at headquarters, and in addition this plague of traveling is imposed on me, the worries about train connections, the irregular bad food, a human intercourse that always changes, never lasts, never becomes affectionate. The devil take it all!" (72). Gregor seems to itemize his grievances roughly in order of increasing importance, ending with a prolonged *cri du coeur* about the one that matters most. Fundamentally, they are anxiety, constraint, physical discomfort, and (above all) isolation. It is difficult to see how "imprisonment" (101) as a monstrous beetle — as a victim of loathing, of physical neglect, and on occasion of attack or the threat of attack — can be regarded as other than a horrifically magnified version of the torments from which (on the current theory) the insectile condition is to be the refuge.[6]

A bondage as severe as Gregor's in his new incarnation, it would seem, is not a plausible candidate for an excuse from bondage. But perhaps it is an excuse all the same — not for a forbidden inertia but for a forbidden activity; perhaps the effect of Gregor's debut as an insect is also its purpose: the terrorizing of his parents and of the pompous Head Clerk, who has just been subjecting him through his bedroom door to a humiliating lecture on malingering. Consider Gregor's hot pursuit of the fleeing Clerk, who "must be detained, appeased, persuaded, and finally won over; the future of Gregor and his family, after all, depended on it!" (90). Can we credit this ostensible motive? What actually happens? His mother recoils in horror, overturning a coffeepot that streams onto the rug; then: " 'Mother, mother,' Gregor said softly and looked up toward her. The Head Clerk had for a moment altogether slipped his mind; on the other hand, he could not deny himself, at the sight of the flowing coffee, a repeated snapping of the jaws in the void. At this his mother shrieked again, fled from the table, and fell into the arms of his father, who was rushing to meet her. But Gregor had no time now for his parents; the Head Clerk was already on the stair; chin on the railing, he was looking back for the last time. Gregor took a run so as to be as sure as possible of overtaking him; the Head Clerk must have had a premonition, for he made a leap down several steps and disappeared: but he was still shrieking 'Ugh!'; it sounded through the whole stairwell" (91).

Here if anywhere, our "psychoanalytic" exegete will say, a deeper stratum of the self is in full if inarticulate control: "This stratum, which stands in diametrical opposition to consciousness, is by far the stronger and more essential, for it controls the body and molds the shape . . . The idiom 'he could not deny himself' is pregnant, for in it are stripped bare the lawlessness, the contumacy, the indiscipline, the retreat into irresponsibility and license, the parasitism of the transformation . . . In his consciousness, in his intention, Gregor wishes to be, and is in fact, a petitioner. But he appears as a pursuer and acts as an assailant."[7] But all this rests, once more, on assuming what is to be proved, that Gregor has indeed transformed *himself*. Otherwise it is hard to see why his conscious intent must be discounted merely because it runs afoul of a body that its bewildered new owner has not yet learned to manage, a body whose members we have seen spontaneously "jerking" and "writhing" not in concert (malign or otherwise) but wholly at random (77). The jaw-snapping that Gregor cannot deny himself is explicitly presented as a reflex activated not by the sight of Gregor's mother but by that of the spilled coffee, and we have already been told that Gregor has been experiencing a "powerful hunger" (74). It is one thing for an author to veil his intention, and quite another for him to subvert it in this way. It seems to me more likely that the intention Kafka's text subverts, if any, is the exegete's.

As with the theory of Gregor's psychosis, that of his unconscious aggression obliges us to go to implausible lengths in extending the range of what is to be counted as figurative; in particular, if Gregor's shape answers metaphorically to a neurotic assault, then the Head Clerk's blithering panic and permanent disappearance can hardly be taken literally but will somehow have to do duty for all his expectable responses to such an assault — indignation, the summoning of a policeman, the threat of prosecution or cashiering. To what form of behavior, in any case, can Gregor's mere shape correspond (for the latter above all is what terrifies the others)? What kind of gesture will satisfy the requirements of the alleged symbol, by conforming both to

a conscious attempt at conciliation and to an unconscious attack? What behavioral disorder confers resources of perception
and locomotion that will plausibly answer to Gregor's feelers
and numerous legs? If the beetle shape is an assault, how (once
again) can an assault anticipate the presence of its object and
persist after the death of the assailant? Why the descriptive
stress on the fragility and defenselessness of the creature, in
whose carapace a crippling wound is produced by the mere toss
of an apple?

If we choose to concede that Gregor's new shape stands for
the expression of a neurotic (by which it appears we must understand a morally unacceptable) impulse, it is easy enough to
find expressions of still other such impulses, notably of a cruelly
selfish and incestuous design on his sister Grete:

Was he a beast, when music gripped him so? For him, it was as if the
way were being shown him [namely, by Grete's violin playing] to the
longed-for, unknown nourishment; he had decided to force his way
up to his sister, to pluck her by the skirt and thereby to signify to her
that she might come into his room with her violin, for nobody repaid
her as he wished to repay her. He would never let her out of his room,
at least as long as he lived; his bogey shape was to become useful to
him for the first time; he would be at all doors of his room simultaneously and mew and spit at attackers; his sister, however, should not
be forced but stay with him of her own free will; she was to sit next to
him on the settee, incline her ear to him, and then he would confide to
her that he had the firm intention of sending her to conservatory, and
that last Christmas — was Christmas already past? — if his misfortune
had not intervened he would have told them all, without troubling
about any opposition. At this declaration his sister would burst into
tears of affection, and Gregor would raise himself to her shoulder and
kiss her neck, which ever since she had gone to business she used to
leave free of ribbon or collar. (130)

The moral substance of this fantasy, on the "psychoanalytic" view, is as transparent as the cravings it betrays: "Were
this incestuous wish-dream to come true, it would operate as a
frightful rape of the sister. Under the pretext of tenderness
Gregor would keep her imprisoned forever, 'of her own free will'
she would have to renounce her life. Her fate would be ghastly."[8]
But the troublesome phrase cannot be so lightly dismissed: in

Gregor's idyll Grete figures as a willing and indeed grateful participant, and quite specifically not as the victim of coercion; the
significant point about the idyll, incestuous or not, is Gregor's
momentary but glaring delusion about Grete's probable response to his efforts on her behalf. For, as the current theory
conveniently overlooks, Gregor's efforts are indeed on Grete's
behalf; the emotional impetus of his fantasy, and attendant in-
vasion of the sitting room, is not self-indulgent whim but fierce
indignation at the boarders' flagrant insult to his sister:

> The family was totally claimed by the violin playing; the board-
> ers, on the contrary, who had at first, hands in pockets, taken up their
> positions behind the sister's music stand, so that they could all have
> seen the score (which must surely disturb the sister), soon drew back
> to the window conversing in undertones with bowed heads; where,
> anxiously observed by the father, they also remained. It was now
> really all too clearly evident that they were disappointed in their ex-
> pectation of hearing a beautiful or entertaining violin concert, had had
> enough of the whole performance, and were consenting to the con-
> tinued disturbance of their leisure only out of politeness. (129)

The demands in defiance of which Gregor will never let
Grete out of his room will not come from Grete but from a
world that (in Gregor's distraught imagination) has just proved
itself abysmally unworthy of her. In the face of this contempt,
and the elder Samsa's obsequious tolerance of it, Gregor's frustrated craving to give and receive love seems to operate at least
as powerfully as his frustrated sexuality. This, surely, is "the unknown nourishment" that is at last within reach: Gregor im-
agines that for once he is in a position to offer service—a "reward"—that a loved one cannot fail to appreciate.

This is a nourishment, we are aware, that Gregor has never
been permitted to enjoy. Trapped in his room before his first appearance to his family as a monster, and hence before the reality
of his transformation has been brought home to him, Gregor is
inspired by the promised arrival of a locksmith to feel himself
"once again drawn into the human circle" (85); the implication is
clear that his sense of exclusion from that circle is far older than
the monstrosity that makes it irrevocable. In his job he must put
up with "a human intercourse that always changes, never lasts,
never becomes affectionate" (72). And the eventual response of

his family to that sacrifice is that "his money was gratefully accepted, he provided it gladly, but a special warmth would no longer be shown" (102). In his monstrosity and confinement the hunger has risen to the pitch of starvation: "Gregor often snatched at [*erhaschte*] a remark [of Grete's] that was kindly meant or could be so interpreted . . . While Gregor could get no news [of his family's affairs] directly, he overheard [*erhorchte*] a good deal from the adjoining rooms, and when he could hear only voices he ran immediately to the relevant door and pressed himself against it with his whole body" (100). Something of the abject desperation of this hunger for human rapport is conveyed by the alliterative cadence of *erhaschte*, *erhorchte*, but far more by the emblematic attitude of the beetle straining against the closed door. The incestuous impulse is thus amply excused by the ordeal that induces it, and is not so much a decadent as a pathetic nuance in a complex emotion dominated by tenderness and indignation on Grete's behalf.

A cruel irony of that ordeal is that overwhelmingly it is indignation rather than tenderness that gives Gregor momentary access to his humanity, as when he rails to himself at the injustice of his job (78) or summons up the pluck to contradict the Head Clerk in a speech that (again by a cruel irony) is drowned out and mocked by the insect's "irrepressible, painful chirping . . . which left the words in their distinctness only in the first instant if at all, in order so to muffle them in vibrations that one didn't know whether one had heard correctly" (74): "Herr Prokurist [Head Clerk]! Spare my parents! All the reproaches you've just made to me are groundless" (83). The measure of this momentary triumph is the cringing and petty shrewdness into which it characteristically relapses when Gregor finally confronts the Clerk: "You, however, Herr Prokurist, you command a better general view of conditions than the other personnel, yes even — be it said entirely in confidence — a better view than the Head himself, who in his capacity as entrepreneur is easily misled in his judgment to the detriment of an employee" (89).

Gregor again affirms his dignity by anger when he protests his sister's neglect of his room by stationing himself in especially squalid corners (123); when "sheer fury filled him over the poor care [accorded him by his family]" (123); and when, overhearing a hysterical family quarrel, he "hissed with fury that it occurred to no one to shut the door and spare him this noise and spectacle" (125). Once again, and with the same pathetic abortiveness, his anger flares up at the jeering of the old charwoman:

> In the beginning she called him to her with words she probably took for endearments, like "Come over then, old dungbeetle," or "Now look at the old dungbeetle." To such greetings Gregor gave no reply, but remained motionless in his place, as if the door had not been opened at all. If only, instead of letting this charwoman uselessly disturb him at her pleasure, they had instructed her to clean his room every day!
>
> Early one morning — a turbulent rain, perhaps already a token of the coming spring, was drumming on the windowpanes — on the charwoman's resuming in her usual style Gregor was so exasperated that, as if bent on assault, though to be sure slowly and unsteadily, he turned against her. The charwoman, however, instead of taking fright, merely raised up high a chair in the vicinity of the door, and as she stood there with her mouth wide open her intention was obviously not to close her mouth until the seat in her hand had been smashed down on Gregor's back. "So, it doesn't go further?" she asked when Gregor had turned round again; and coldly replaced the seat in the corner.[9]   (124–125)

The most disastrous such episode is Gregor's response to the removal by his mother and sister of the furniture that is the only testimony to his otherwise obliterated humanity:

> They were clearing out his room, taking from him everything he was fond of; the chest in which lay his fretsaw and other tools they had already carried out; were now loosening the writing table, firmly trenched in the floor by this time, on which as a student in the commercial academy, in high school, yes even in elementary school he had written his lessons — then he really had no more time to appraise the good intentions of the two women, whose existence he had nearly forgotten in any case, for in their exhaustion they were already working silently, and the only thing audible was the heavy sound of their footfall. And so he broke forth (the women were leaning just next door on the writing table to catch their breath a little), changed the direction of his path four times; he really didn't know what he should save first; then he saw hanging conspicuously on the wall, which was otherwise already blank, the picture of the lady dressed all in furs, crept up hurriedly and pressed himself on the glass, which held him firmly and did

his hot belly good. This picture at least, which at this point Gregor entirely covered, no one, surely, would now take away. (112–113)

Much has been made of the elementally erotic imagery of the lady in the picture, with her forearm buried in a heavy fur muff and extending toward the viewer (71).[10] But this detail should not be taken out of context; it is the memorial of a human sexuality of which transformation has irrevocably deprived Gregor, leaving behind "an itchy region occupied by nothing but tiny white spots," a region that chills on contact (73). What the picture now offers Gregor in the way of consolation is not the titillating pose of the lady but the coolness of the glass that calms his rage and panic at being dispossessed. This latter process, in fact, is by now virtually complete. For the picture that claims Gregor's devotion is precisely not his most deeply cherished possession; it is virtually the only possession of his that has survived the casual removal of the things that matter. Of these, what apparently matters most is the writing table that Gregor construes as the chronicle of his life and that is now being discarded as rubbish. Hence his rage: "And so he broke forth."

   Like Gregor's attempt at self-defense, his attempt to defend Grete is predicated on three articles of faith: that his personhood and dignity transcend his body; that in devoting these to Grete he gives what is eminently worth receiving; that Grete will recognize these facts. The third of these convictions at least, as I observed, is a glaring delusion that, like others he has labored under, he will eventually surrender. For Gregor has a demonstrated talent for self-deception that allows him, for example, to delay the horror of confronting his change — "what has happened to me?" (71) — by distracting himself with the spurious worry that he will be late to work, and diagnosing his condition as "vertigo" (82), "silliness" (72), or "notions" (75) brought on by inadequate sleep (72) or by a cold (75). His assumption that he is capable of compensating Grete for the slight she has suffered is a still more ludicrous and pathetic flight of fancy; but it effectively rules out the view that Gregor's idyll is a dream of exploitation, for when he relinquishes that assumption, the idyll goes with it.

   We have not quite exhausted the wealth of corrupt egoism

that a resolutely selective reading can find in the characterization of Gregor Samsa. Two other charges are worth examining before we consider the current theory as a whole. They do not help to establish that Gregor transformed *himself*, much less that his new shape is to be taken figuratively; but they will, I think, instructively round out our picture of the general attitude that underlies the theory.

Here, then, is Gregor: "If only his sister had been here! She was clever, she had cried when Gregor was still calmly lying on his back. And surely the Head Clerk — that lady's man — would have consented to be led by her. She would have shut the door to the flat and, in the anteroom, talked him out of his fright" (90). The critic may now proceed as follows: "Woman is also a decoy, a means of bribery and influence to propitiate the powers that be. Thus Gregor would gladly have used his sister as an ally and as bait to influence the Head Clerk."[11] The context of the speech, however, is the nauseated and horrified retreat of the man on whose appeasement, as far as Gregor is aware, the livelihood of the Samsas absolutely depends. If his sister were present, her intercession (on Gregor's knowledge of the facts) would be a service to herself and her parents as well as to Gregor. There is no suggestion in the text that Gregor wishes his sister to play the coquette; that her femininity will give her an advantage over this particular gentleman is not such a suggestion.

The intercession Gregor describes would have been not only obligatory but, as we learn elsewhere, long overdue; for Grete's life to date has consisted exclusively in "wearing new clothes, sleeping late, helping keep house, taking part in a few modest pleasures, and above all playing the violin" (104). Gregor, in fact, has at times vaguely sensed that Grete has been exploiting *him*: "And why was she crying, then? Because he hadn't got up and let the Head Clerk in? because he was in danger of losing his job? and because the Head would pursue their parents with the old demands?" (81). There is some confirmation for this guess at Grete's attitude in the coincidence between her increasing indifference to feeding her brother or cleaning his room and her hysterical insistence on reserving these duties to herself (123–124): by monopolizing Gregor's care she monopolizes her parents' attention and dominates the family, even though the Samsas "had hitherto often fretted about the sister because she seemed to them a rather useless girl" (107). Yet on the current theory, of all the candidates for the title of exploiter or usurper of authority in Kafka's story, the most plausible is Gregor.

Finally, here is Gregor's fastidious reaction to the sound of the gentleman boarders at their dining: "To Gregor it seemed extraordinary that of all the manifold noises of eating, their chewing teeth were continually audible, as if it were thereby to be demonstrated to Gregor that one needs teeth to eat, and that even with the most beautiful toothless jaws one can accomplish nothing; 'I *do* have an appetite,' Gregor told himself apprehensively, 'but not for these things. How these boarders feed, and I perish!' " (128). "Here," declares the critic, "the hubris of the pure self comes to light. Gregor is puffed up with pride in his anomaly, makes of his misfortune a sign of Election and looks down haughtily on common men who use teeth to grind up earthly food."[12] But on the contrary, these particular men are specifically denatured and machinelike. The context of Gregor's remark is a satirical vignette of their rigidly concerted movements at table; they figure in Kafka's story as no more than a bureaucratic automaton in triplicate and a little later as callous prigs. Nor is Gregor exulting in his affliction; he is simply acknowledging a spiritual hunger that is by this time chronic with him — a hunger for the recognition of his kinship and the requital of his love. This is the "longed-for, unknown nourishment" whose mirage is sustained for him by his sister's violin; and he is stating no more than a fact when he suggests in the present passage that the object of his "appetite" transcends metabolism. As he listens to the violin, he asks: "Was he a beast, when music gripped him so?" The sentence is amply glossed by its association with the theme of "unknown nourishment": an insect is not tormented by spiritual appetites. Gregor is bearing mute witness, not that he is a person rendered elect by anomaly, but simply that despite anomaly he remains a person.

Granted the offenses (or morbidities) with which the current theory finds Gregor burdened, it is perhaps natural to interpret his acquiescence in his own death as an atonement; he is yielding as he should to the claims of life, in which he has, on this view, no part: "But faithfully heeding his summons, the inner meaning of his transformation, he can also 'go away,' that is, realize that he is destined to withdraw from the world, redeem the world from himself and only in this way be held 'in honor.' " "The Samsas are no more and no less 'common' than life itself, and it is just this 'commonness' that the death of the individual must serve."[13] Just as Gregor earlier approves the "rational grounds" on which his father and sister dissuade his mother from visiting him, so now he must and does approve, even more decidedly than his sister, her contention that he must (as he paraphrases) "disappear" (136). At this point, in fact, the current theory itself is a simplified paraphrase of Grete's sentiments on the fate of the monster:

We have to try to get rid of it. We've tried what is humanly possible, to care for it and tolerate it; I believe that no one can offer us the least reproach . . . You simply have to get rid of the idea that it is Gregor. That we have believed so this long is our real misfortune. But how, after all, can it be Gregor? If it were Gregor he would eventually have come to the insight that it is not possible for human beings to live together with such a beast, and would have gone away of his own free will. (133, 134).

Grete disposes here of any constraint derived from familial duty by adopting the reduced version of this duty on which the Samsas agreed much earlier:

Gregor's serious wound, from which he suffered for more than a month — the apple remained, since no one dared to remove it, stuck in his flesh as a visible souvenir — seemed to have reminded even his father that Gregor despite his present sad and repellent shape was a member of the family whom one must not treat as an enemy, but that on the contrary the precept of familial duty was to swallow aversion and be tolerant, nothing but tolerant. (118)

The parenthesis comments with transparent irony on this recipe for duty: tolerance of a disfigured relative, one therefore not to be treated as an enemy, is evidently compatible with the modest concession to one's sensibility of letting the relative's wounds go on festering indefinitely. For Grete this duty of "tolerance" has already expired, for two reasons: on the one hand, the impossible is not a duty, and it is impossible to live with such a beast;

on the other, it is not their relative anyhow, for if it were it would spare them the trouble of getting rid of it by getting rid of itself.

The interpretation we are considering agrees with Grete's on two points: the impoverished conceptions of human duty and human moral possibility. In one crucial respect it differs from Grete's views: Kafka deprives us explicitly of the luxury of "getting rid" of our burden by "getting rid" of our burdensome ideas about it; unlike Grete, we cannot claim uncertainty that the "beast" is Gregor, much less knowledge that it is not. And we are so much the less excusable if we adopt a cruel mysticism, or rather cant, of human sacrifice to the *élan vital*. With the appeal to this doctrine, the judicial or diagnostic mask is dropped; the crime Gregor can expiate only by "going away" is his affliction.

I began my discussion of the current theory by remarking that it is as crucially relevant to the interpretation of Kafka's story as it is untenable. I may now add that, if I am right, it is relevant *because* it is untenable — because it succumbs to clues that are as genuinely alluring as they are obviously false. The inclination to find offenses or morbidities in Gregor's dutifulness, discontent, shyness, or panic is not warranted but fostered by the loathsomeness of his deformity. We are being shrewdly tempted to surrender to a corruptness that, with vigilance, we may thereby be enabled to confront in ourselves: the impulse to "get rid" of the presence of offensive suffering by contriving to persuade ourselves that the offense is intentional. It is only this impulse that obscures the affinity of Kafka's story to the literature of imprisonment in which the valor of the central figure is measured by his maintenance of elementary dignity against crushing odds. It is only this impulse that puts us on the side of the jailers and induces us to identify them with "life." For in fact what saps the energy of the Samsas is not a querulous parasite but a person's right, as person, to the loyalty and compassion of his family. The parasite that drains the Samsas, in short, is duty; and it is their "commonness," their banality, with its unimagining righteousness and egoism, that transforms the duty into a curse. This is no reason to dismiss the curse as unreal; but it is a sound reason, I think, to withhold our congratulations when the curse is lifted. For it is clear that the Samsas' mourning at the end is for the presentable Gregor and not for the monstrous

METAMORPHOSIS AS ALIENATION WITHOUT GRACE

kinsman of whose moral claims the mourners are now so happily relieved. Kafka's hopeful ending, in the light of what leads up to it, is desolately ironic: a vision of souls so banal that their happiness is without a moral dimension.

It is tempting, but too hard on a much-maligned social class, to read the implicit indictment of the Samsas as a parable of the depersonalizing influence of bourgeois values and institutions. It is also too easy on ourselves by half. We succumb to the urge to blame the victim not as we are bourgeois but as we are (in a greater or lesser degree) Samsas ourselves. And it should not perhaps be forgotten that Gregor, too, is more or less a Samsa; we cannot be sure that, if another of his kinsmen had been afflicted in his place, he would have resisted the urge to which they succumb. To rationalize one's surrender to such urges, the bourgeois ethos is neither indispensable nor especially useful.

Of the Samsas, Grete is in one respect the least banal: her need forces her to invoke a theory of what it is to be a person, a theory that excludes not only Gregor but — if we share the bias of the narrative — the rest of us as well. There is nothing conceptually disturbing about a person's unconditional right, as person, to compassion; or about our corrupt urge to deny compassion to offensive sufferers, important as the latter concern is in Kafka's story. If these were the story's central preoccupations, it would be letting us off much more easily than I think it does, and indeed the fantastic premise would then be a trivial mystification; a physically possible disfigurement would have done as well or better. For reasons that I shall try to spell out at a later stage, the fantasy of transformation is necessary to testing the adequacy of such a theory of personhood as Grete builds on. At the same time, the emergence of that theory is indeed conceptually disturbing, and the concept of which it threatens to make an absurdity or a nonsense is precisely that of compassion. What, then, is the ground of Grete's claim that an animal whose body is evidently continuous in space and time with the body of her brother is nevertheless not her brother at all?

The thing, after all, is a "monstrous insect" (71). To be the same person as Gregor the monster must first be a person. But the latter proposition is absurd. In the first stages of the new life, to be sure, Grete and her new charge manage to develop

certain reciprocities: Gregor spares his sister the horror of seeing
him by stifling himself under the settee (98–99), and in return
Grete, noticing his chair twice pushed to the window, routinely
puts it there herself thereafter (105). Gregor spends four hours
maneuvering a linen sheet on the settee with his back so as to
cover the parts of his body that cannot quite be crammed underneath, for the sight of the least part of the monster is still evidently unbearable to Grete: "that it could not conduce to his
pleasure to barricade himself so completely was surely clear
enough"; in return he "believed he had even caught [erhascht] a
grateful look" (106–107) on his sister's face. On the other hand,
Grete's telltale reaction to the unexpected sight of the monster
motionlessly looking out of the window is not merely not to enter but to start back and lock the door. "There remained by this
time, surely, no reason for the sister to fall into astonishment at
the sight of Gregor's appearance. . . . A stranger could actually
have thought [on the strength of Grete's reaction] that Gregor
had lain in wait for her and wanted to bite her" (106). But it is
wishful thinking on Gregor's part that the stranger would have
been misreading Grete's fright; she herself is now a stranger casting about for an interpretation of her charge's behavior, which
like his attempts at speech is unambiguous only to himself. For a
monstrous insect a windowsill could be a ledge from which to
pounce.

Being thoroughly barricaded, by parity of reasoning, could
indeed "conduce to the pleasure" of an insect; we ourselves have
witnessed Gregor yielding to an uncontrollable reflex of agora-
phobia by taking refuge under the settee:

But the high-ceilinged vacant room in which he was forced to lie flat
on the floor made him anxious, from causes he was unable to
discover, for it was after all his room, the one he had occupied for five
years, and with a half-conscious turn, not without a touch of shame,
he hurried under the settee, where despite a little pressure on his back
and his inability to raise his head any longer, he immediately felt very
comfortable, and regretted only that his body was too broad to
accommodate quite underneath the settee.   (96)

Here we have an entirely adequate alternative to moral delicacy
as an explanation of Gregor's addition of a linen sheet. What

Grete sees is a scavenger of menacing proportions given to fits of aggression and withdrawal that are nerve-rackingly unpredictable. For Gregor, outraged at being dispossessed by his mother and sister, his attempt to salvage what remains is a "breaking out" of a degrading captivity ("so brach er dann hervor," 112). For Grete, reporting the same behavior to her father, it is a zoo animal's anarchic "breaking out" of its cage ("Gregor ist ausgebrochen," 115).

Even Gregor's new susceptibility to music, which he lacked in his human shape (102), is similarly ambiguous, and the protest he makes by appeal to it — "War er ein Tier, da ihn Musik so ergriff?" (130) — ironically partakes of the same ambiguity. For it may but for the context quite easily be taken to mean "Was he a beast, that music gripped him so?" Was his new responsiveness due (in one critic's paraphrase) to "the grounding in primitive emotion of his animal constitution"?[14] This at any rate is the connection suggested by our last glimpse of the violinist herself, as the "voluptuous girl" sensuously "stretched her young body" (145). There is a penumbral vagueness about the behavioral test for dispositions like "animalism" that comes out here and there in the text. It is a question, for example, whether the spastic toothlessness of the ascetic beetle is really more beastly than the noisy chewing of the gentlemen boarders. But it is not a question Grete herself is inclined to ask.

There is tact on both sides, it is true, in the evolving ritual of feeding performed by brother and sister, but Grete's tact does not go beyond consideration for Gregor's creature comforts. It is not merely that he shows (from her point of view) no sign of being more than a creature; it is rather that (from her point of view) he shows every sign of being a creature and no more. For the Samsas in general, in fact, a single sign of the latter is all but conclusive; unintelligibility is practically equivalent to unintelligence: "Since he was not understood, no one, not even his sister, entertained the possibility that he could understand the others" (109–110).

The notion of possibility here is crucial, I think. It has been suggested that Kafka's story is principally concerned with "futile efforts at communication," and that "the loss of humanly comprehensible speech, and with it the ability to communicate, is . . . only the one side of the existential catastrophe. There is no

less evil in the helplessness of [insectile] movement, whose vocabulary of gesture, strange and suggestive only of animality, is
forever being misconstrued."[15] But Gregor's difficulty, as Kafka
presents it, is far more fundamental. If the family — and Grete in
particular — had been able to conceive of the *possibility* of a sur-
viving intelligence, alternative gestures could have been developed in collaboration. There are no attempts to communicate
beyond Gregor's speeches at the outset, where such attempts are
shown to be vain without the commitment of the family. And
there is no such commitment; one can hardly commit oneself to
the realization of an impossibility.

The nature of this impossibility may perhaps be clarified by
Frau Samsa's reluctance to accept it. Dissuaded at first on "rational grounds" (*Vernunftgründe*) from visiting Gregor, his
mother must later be forcibly restrained from doing so: "Let me
go to Gregor, I tell you! he is my unhappy son! Don't you understand at all [*begreift ihr es denn nicht*] that I *have* to go to
him?" (107). Frau Samsa vaguely suspects that the difference between her and the others is conceptual, that the notion, the *Be-
griff*, of maternal duty in their view does not sensibly apply to
her relationship with the current occupant of Gregor's bedroom.
The issue between mother and daughter comes to a head, in
fact, in their debate about the propriety of cleaning that bedroom; Frau Samsa is "not at all certain that the removal of the
furniture will result in pleasure for Gregor. The contrary seemed
to her to be the case. For her, the sight of the blank wall was
nothing less than a weight on the heart. And why shouldn't
Gregor too have this feeling [*Empfindung*] when, after all, he
has been used to the furniture for a very long time and on that
account, with the room empty, would have a sense of being
abandoned?" (109). For Gregor's mother it is merely false, and
not at all absurd, that Gregor should *understand* what is being
said around him. He is in the appropriate category; such an as-
scription would be very different, say, from ascribing color to a
number.

On the separate question of how the monster would *behave*
in a featureless hole, Frau Samsa, we know, is mistaken: Gregor
has found an "almost happy distraction" in climbing in all directions over the walls and ceiling, and especially in hanging from
the latter with "a light oscillation" — a new "entertainment" that

his sister has rightly deduced from "traces of sticky secretion" (108). We also know that this diversion of Gregor's is a last resort of boredom to which he has been reduced by the "consideration for his parents" that inhibits him from showing himself at the window (108), where he could at least celebrate the memory of "the liberation that lay for him" in looking out (104). It is this interior life of personal feelings — of *Empfindung*, to use Frau Samsa's word — for which Grete can find no place in her theory of guardianship. Her ward represents, to be sure, a form of life, a disposition to behave that Grete has decided to indulge. But it is not her form of life, and that there could be a determinant of personhood other than shape and behavior to consider evidently does not occur to her. The *Vernunft*, the rational scheme by which Grete interprets her world, makes allowance exclusively for what is public or observable.

Kafka has been obliging enough, in his ironic way, to provide arbiters of this debate between mother and daughter. One is the elder Samsa, who turns out in this context to be notably indecisive and open to the suggestion of stronger minds; the scene is the aftermath of Gregor's disastrous effort to defend Grete from the boarders' contempt:

"Child," said the father sympathetically and with extraordinary understanding, "what should we do about it, though?" The sister only shrugged her shoulders to signify the helplessness that, in contrast to her earlier assurance, had now overcome her as she wept. "If he understood us," said the father half questioningly; the sister vehemently shook her head from the midst of her weeping to signify that this was unthinkable. "If he understood us," repeated the father, and by shutting his eyes assimilated the sister's conviction about the impossibility of this, "then perhaps an agreement with him would be possible. But as it is—" (134)

Another arbiter is Gregor himself, from whose addiction to mindless crawling "only the voice of the mother, which he had not heard for a long time, had jolted him awake" (110), and who had earlier remarked, in a similar vein, that Frau Samsa "understood everything much better than the sister, who despite all her courage was nevertheless only a child" (107).

Still another, if inadvertent, arbiter is Grete herself, in the scene in which the sight of Gregor defiantly clinging to his last possession frightens his mother into a dead faint; here Grete reverts from *Vernunft* to the anthropomorphism of which she will cure her father later on: " 'You, Gregor!' called the sister with raised fist and piercing glances. They were, since the transformation, the first words she had directly addressed to him" (114). The importance of this vocative to Gregor is profound; the main conclusion he had drawn from his mother's remarks on the furniture removal was that "the lack of every direct human address . . . must have deranged his understanding" (110). The only other such direct addresses are awarded to Gregor by a last, rather dubious arbiter of the debate on his personhood: the old charwoman who "credited him with every possible understanding" (137) but who is also capable of reporting his death as *krepieren*, the death of a beast (137). Innocent as she is of *Vernunft*, the old charwoman treats Gregor with an Aesopic fellowship that is not easily acquitted of superstition.

In the ancient tragic pattern a hero's homecoming culminates in his recognition by his kinsmen. Gregor is a tragic hero whose home is closed to him even though he is in it, and for whose recognition there is no "rational" basis. It is not simply that the Samsas can identify in the monster no behavioral criterion of mind, but that from the point of view adumbrated by Grete, to have a mind virtually *is* to exhibit some such criteria. Here is a mature philosophical expression of that view:

"Only of a living human being and what recalls (behaves like) a living human being can one say: it has sensations; it sees; is blind; hears; is deaf; is conscious or unconscious." The human body and human behavior are the paradigm to which third-person attributions of consciousness, sensations, feelings are related . . . It is by analogy with the human form and behavior that I attribute consciousness (or unconsciousness) to animals and fish; the more remote the analogy, the less sense in the attribution.

To experience a pain, on this view, is not to be contemplating an object or state immediately evident to no one but oneself; it is simply to be acting in a certain way. "We only say of a human being and what is like one that it thinks." Inner states are a myth generated by pseudo-naming words like "pain." Even in what is *recognizably* a person, the essence of its personhood and the object of our compassion amount to behavior and nothing more.[16] For a person, so conceived, to be *disfigured* is in a measure to disintegrate; to be transformed as Gregor is transformed is no longer to exist. The cogency of this position is that the only evidence of a private mental domain is introspection, and in Gregor's case it is sometimes too tenuous to convince even the claimant, who on one occasion regards his humanity as a thing of the past — "seine menschliche Vergangenheit" (110) — and on another defers for inclusion in "the human circle" to the good offices of the locksmith and the physician (85).[17]

The crucial fact remains that the reality of the monster's private domain is presupposed by the story; that domain is Gregor's reflective consciousness, the *Besinnung* that he "must not lose just now at any price" (77). However abject the hero is in his failure to be recognized by his kinsmen, his claim to the stature of a tragic figure is confirmed, I think, by the doomed stubbornness of his effort to recognize himself in his interior monologue. Consciousness is the essence of the value Gregor attaches even to his pathetic antennae (94), and of the "freedom" he begins to lose with the loss of his sight (104) — a freedom both endangered and burlesqued by the facilities of *das freie Zimmer* (his vacant room, 96); by his random crawl of "derangement," "entertainment," and forgetfulness (110); by the "pleasure" of the rubbish heap into which his room is converted by the charwoman (125–126). Gregor keeps at bay this freedom of spontaneous mindlessness partly by the remembrance that inspires his single attempt at escape (112–113), but above all by the *Rücksichtnahme*, the unrequited moral commitment, that is his pride (129) and that inspires his final resignation (136).

Toward the beginning of Gregor's ordeal, as he struggles to slide out of bed on his armored back, he contemplates the possibility of calling for help only to dismiss it: "Despite all his trouble he could not suppress a smile at the thought of this" (78). The smile on the beetle's face, the smile it could not resist, is a piece of whimsical nonsense, an impossible event reminiscent of Lewis Carroll. Gregor's interior "sayings" ("sagte Gregor sorgenvoll," 128) have, for the metaphysical behaviorist, exactly the absurdity of that evanescent gesture; but it is an absurdity indulged only to be transcended.[18] It is true that, in Kafka's despairing vision, the grace by which Bisclavret's lord is enabled to penetrate his vassal's bestial disguise is denied to *us* as well as to the Samsas; but where the grace of God has failed us, the grace of art succeeds, and the justice we cannot do to one another, the fictive imagination teaches us to do to its creature.

VIRGINIA WOOLF'S *ORLANDO*
Metamorphosis
as the Quest
for Freedom

UNLIKE GREGOR SAMSA'S ABRUPT DESCENT INTO THE BONDAGE of the carapace, Orlando's transformation into a woman is the initial stage of a gradual unfolding of comprehensive personal freedom, an unfolding that coincides with Virginia Woolf's narrative as a whole. Transformation in this extended sense has much the rhythm of an organic process—the butterfly's evolving declaration of independence. Orlando traces, by her efflorescence, the outlines of an intricate ideal of freedom. This, at all events, is the general view I should like to defend in what follows. The constraint Orlando manages to overthrow is largely intellectual; it consists of certain shibboleths of what we may broadly describe as bourgeois common sense—the dichotomies of the real and the imaginary, the actual and the possible, the masculine and the feminine. I shall proceed by discussing each of these matters in turn and then offering a general assessment of their connections with the central theme of transformation.

Orlando begins his career, as a young Elizabethan patrician, by presuming on a freedom he has not yet achieved: freedom to explore the imaginary without being put out of countenance by the real: "He was describing, as all young poets are forever describing, nature, and in order to match the shade of green precisely, he looked (and here he showed more audacity than most) at the thing itself, which happened to be a laurel bush growing beneath the window. After that, of course, he could write no more. Green in nature is one thing, green in literature another. Nature and letters have a natural antipathy: bring them together and they tear each other to pieces. The shade of green Orlando now saw spoilt his rhyme and split his metre" (16–17).[1] At this point we are evidently being invited by the ironical narrator to suppose that the hero has caught himself out in a silliness to which the antidote is a certain gruff realism; he has been turning love of literature and of its practitioners into an idolatry: "To his imagination it seemed as if even the bodies of those instinct with such divine thoughts must be transfigured. They must have aureoles for hair, incense for breath, and roses must grow between their lips" (82–83). Unfortunately, the love of literature is itself a "disease" whose "fatal nature" is "to substitute a phantom for reality, so that Orlando, to whom fortune had given every gift — plate, linen, houses, men-servants, carpets, beds in profusion — had only to open a book for the whole vast accumulation to turn to mist" (74). Here, for the moment at least, the fantastic prevails and the real betrays an underlying flimsiness; Lamia, in effect, is having her brief revenge.

Yet it is the solidity of Orlando's ancestral domain, we learn, that usually consoles him for the volatility of his phantoms: "He opened his eyes, which had been wide open all the time, but had seen only thoughts, and saw lying in the hollow beneath him, his house" (10–11). It is a little ominous, perhaps, that thoughts and material things are put on a par here as being equally objects of seeing; and indeed it turns out that what Orlando chiefly "sees" in the hollow beneath him is a moralized parade of images:

For after all, he said, kindling as he looked at the great house on the greensward below, the unknown lords and ladies who lived there never forgot to set aside something for those who come after; for the roof that will leak; for the tree that will fall. There was always a warm corner for the old shepherd in the kitchen; always food for the hungry; always their goblets were polished, though they lay sick, and the windows were lit though they were dying. Lords though they were, they were content to go down into obscurity with the mole-catcher and the stonemason. (107)

The landscapes we encounter in Woolf's romance are rarely without such phantom embellishments as the molecatcher and the stonemason. As Orlando moves through his preternaturally slow ripening, each century of English experience somehow generates the setting and conditions required by its characteristic notion of the real.[2] Thus in the Enlightenment "the very landscape outside was less stuck about with garlands and the briars themselves were less thorned and intricate. Perhaps the senses were a little duller and honey and cream less seductive to the palate" (113). In the Renaissance "the weather itself, the heat and cold of summer and winter, was, we may believe, of a different temper altogether. The brilliant amorous day was divided as sheerly from the night as land from water. Sunsets were redder and more intense; dawns were whiter and more auroral. Of our crepuscular half-lights and lingering twilights they knew nothing. The rain fell vehemently or not at all. The sun blazed or there was darkness" (27). The inauguration of the nineteenth century shows once again parallel changes of outer and inner climate: "As the ninth, tenth, and eleventh strokes struck, a huge blackness sprawled over the whole of London. With the twelfth stroke of midnight, the darkness was complete. A turbulent welter of cloud covered the city. All was dark; all was doubt; all was confusion" (225–226). The mocking account of the young poet's discomfiture by "the thing itself," it is eventually borne in on us, was an irony at our expense; things are not to be brought to bay "in themselves," and if nature proves to be no less a phantom of communal prejudice than its poetic image, the charade of Augustan social "reality" virtually cancels itself out: "This is one of the cases where truth does not exist. Nothing exists. The whole thing is a miasma—a mirage" (192). "At one and the same time therefore, society is everything and society is nothing. Society is the most powerful concretion in the world, and society has no existence whatsoever" (193–194).

And reality has its geographical as well as its historical variability, as Orlando unsettlingly discovers during her sojourn among the Turkish gypsies, who cannot abide her transcendentalist inclinations:

It sprang from the sense they had (and their senses are very sharp and much in advance of their vocabulary) that whatever they were doing crumbled like ashes in their hands. An old woman making a basket, a boy skinning a sheep, would be singing contentedly at their work, when Orlando would come into the camp, fling herself down by the fire and gaze into the flames. She need not even look at them, and yet they felt, here is someone who doubts; (we make a rough-and-ready translation from the gipsy language) here is someone who does not do the thing for the sake of doing; nor looks for looking's sake; here is someone who believes neither in sheep-skin nor basket; but sees (here they looked apprehensively about the tent) something else.   (146)

The gypsies disagree profoundly not only with Orlando's refusal to accept nature as the ultimate reality but with what they regard as her vapid sentimentality about nature itself: "The elder men and women thought it probable that she had fallen into the clutches of the vilest and cruelest among all the Gods, which is Nature. Nor were they far wrong. The English disease, a love of Nature, was inborn in her, and here where Nature was so much larger and more powerful than in England, she fell into its hands as she had never done before" (143). "[Rustum el Sadi] had the deepest suspicion that her God was Nature. One day, he found her in tears. Interpreting this to mean that her God had punished her, he told her that he was not surprised. He showed her the fingers of his left hand, withered by the frost; he showed her his right foot, crushed where a rock had fallen" (144).

The root of these quarrels is simply that the disputants hold (or wish to hold) differing theories of appearances on which they substantially agree; so far, at least, reality takes its place among the discredited phantoms of the narrative:

No passion is stronger in the breast of man than the desire to make others believe as he believes. Nothing so cuts at the root of his happiness and fills him with rage as the sense that another rates low what he prizes high. Whigs and Tories, Liberal Party and Labour Party — for what do they battle except their own prestige? It is not love of truth, but desire to prevail that sets quarter against quarter and makes parish desire the downfall of parish. Each seeks peace of mind and subservience rather than the triumph of truth and the exaltation of virtue — But these moralities belong, and should be left to the historian, since they are as dull as ditchwater. "Four hundred and seventy-six bedrooms mean nothing to them," sighed Orlando. "She prefers a sunset to a flock of goats," said the gipsies.   (149)

As Lycius under Lamia's tutelage awakens from one trance into another, Orlando congratulates herself paradoxically at one point on her spiritual progress: " 'I am growing up,' she thought . . . 'I am losing some illusions . . . perhaps to acquire others' " (174).

The moral that Orlando eventually draws from these reflections is emphatically not the lotus-eating romanticism that the narrator mercilessly parodies at one point, and that rather suggests a caricature of Keats's diatribe against Apollonius:

A man who can destroy illusions is both beast and flood. Illusions are to the soul what atmosphere is to the earth. Roll up that tender air and the plant dies, the colour fades. The earth we walk on is a parched cinder. It is marl we tread and fiery cobbles scorch our feet. By the truth we are undone. Life is a dream. 'Tis waking that kills us. He who robs us of our dreams robs us of our life — (and so on for six pages if you will, but the style is tedious and may well be dropped).   (203)

Orlando is little less adroit than the gypsies in getting her bearings among physical objects — sheepskins, baskets, or mountains; on an elementary level, her inventory of such objects matches that of her hosts. What she comes to reject is the interpretation of such reassuring agreements embodied in realism, whether the naive realism of the gypsies or the sophisticated version purveyed to Bloomsbury by G. E. Moore.

In Moore's version, which is a useful foil to Orlando's emerging view, all objects of perception, including sensible qualities, are outside the mind:

Whenever I have a mere sensation or idea, the fact is that I am then aware of something which is equally and in the same sense *not* an inseparable aspect of my experience. The awareness which I have maintained to be included in sensation is the very same unique fact which constitutes every kind of knowledge; "blue" is as much an object, and as little a content of my experience, when I experience it, as the most exalted and independent real thing of which I am ever aware. There is, therefore, no question of how we are to "get outside the circle of our own ideas and sensations." Merely to have a sensation is already to *be* outside the circle. It is to know something [for example, "blue"] which is as truly and really not a part of my experience as anything which I can ever know.

To say that an expanse of sensible color is "outside" or is "not a part" of its respective sensation is to deny any necessity for such expanses to be sensed in order to exist; for what would such a necessity be like? Not, surely, the necessity with which the incidence of evenness depends on that of number, or of loudness on that of sounds. It may be that properties like evenness or loudness are necessarily restricted to qualifying some kinds of things and cannot otherwise occur, but there is no useful analogy to be drawn from this fact. For the object of an awareness is not a property of the awareness at all. A sensation of blue, for example, need not itself be blue. Perhaps, indeed, it *cannot* be blue, for a sensation is simply an act of sensing, and there is room at least for doubt that one can sense bluely. It is, for Moore, a fallacy to consider that sensations are not acts but images — images whose likeness or unlikeness to external objects is a plausible subject for dispute. "We have no reason for supposing that there are such things as mental images at all."[3]

Orlando's evolving view is very nearly the denial of all this, and the heart of it is the conviction that our mental images all too eloquently vindicate their own existence, though their role in sensations is not quite the one Moore so easily dismisses. If one were to distill a formal position from the meditative passages I shall be considering in a moment, the result, I think, would be roughly as follows. Sensations, to be sure, are not acts varying somehow by color and shape; but this is because they are not acts at all, with objects whose independence of being acted on could serve to show the ease with which we may get outside the circle of our experience. When we say that someone has a sensation of a round blue patch we mean that he is in a particular state of mind — for that is the sort of thing a sensation is — and that this particular species of sensation accompanies one's seeming to see the round blue surface of a physical object. *Being of a round blue patch* is the analogue in sensation of *being round and blue* in physical appearance. For these appearances the only evidence is the sensations that accompany them, but conceptually the appearances have priority; reports about physical objects in themselves are simply confidently elliptical reports of appearances. It is these objects, in short, and not images, whose status is in doubt; for the consciousness that encircles us is less diaphanous than Moore allows.[4]

No doubt the sequence of appearances and images that occur to Orlando tallies in part with the experience of others, and defines the order that common sense ascribes to real things. But to dichotomize the world into the real and the apparent or imaginary is to fall into the demoralizing error of regarding consciousness as at best a spyhole into a world from which the mind is essentially excluded. A real object is simply an apparent object that has met a test of coherence with other appearances, and it is as imaginary as any hallucination in the radical sense that, as it happens, without images there are no appearances—no conceptual episodes of seeming to see physical objects. The natural environment of such seemings consists of images, and while certain practicalities are served by discounting the latter, an important freedom and an important truth are redeemed, for the artist especially, by surrendering to their ubiquity.

The spiritual transformation by which Orlando reaches this view is, at the outset, embarrassed by realist misgivings. The callow Jacobean poet deprecates his inability to focus on the real: "Every single thing, once he tried to dislodge it from its place in his mind, he found thus cumbered with other matter like the lump of glass which, after a year at the bottom of the sea, is grown about with bones and dragon-flies, and coins and the tresses of drowned women" (101). Even his current thought, Orlando reflects to his annoyance, is encumbered with metaphors expressing the same sort of impertinent matter:

"Why not simply say what one means and leave it?" So then he tried saying the grass is green and the sky is blue and so to propitiate the austere spirit of poetry whom still, though at a great distance, he could not help reverencing. "The sky is blue," he said, "the grass is green." Looking up, he saw that, on the contrary, the sky is like the veils which a thousand Madonnas have let fall from their hair; and the grass fleets and darkens like a flight of girls fleeing the embraces of hairy satyrs from enchanted woods. "Upon my word," he said . . . "I don't see that one's more true than another. Both are utterly false." And he despaired of being able to solve the problem of what poetry is and what truth is and fell into a deep dejection. (101–102)

This odd mixture of compassion and mockery is characteristic of Virginia Woolf's treatment of the adolescent Orlando's
frustrations. The metaphorical turn of mind, as it blesses or af-
flicts the young man, is simply the habit of transcribing the text
of subjective history without the deletions required to make it
intersubjective:

He loved, beneath all this summer transiency, to feel the earth's
spines beneath him; for such he took the hard root of the oak tree to
be; or, for image followed image, it was the back of a horse that he
was riding; or the deck of a tumbling ship — it was anything indeed, so
long as it was hard, for he felt the need of something which he could
attach his floating heart to; the heart that tugged at his side; the heart
that seemed filled with spiced and amorous gales every evening about
this time when he walked out.   (19)

What Orlando feels the need of, at this stage, is the notion of a
physical world that transcends appearances, possible or actual;
it is the need of something he will eventually recognize as
chimerical: "Hair, pastry, tobacco — of what odds and ends are
we compounded . . . What a phantasmagoria the mind is and
meeting place of dissemblables" (176).

The context of the physical items Orlando mentions is the
mind, or minds, of which they are ingredients, and the result of
contemplating physical appearances in their mental context is
phantasmagoria: "Everything was partly something else, and
each gained an odd moving power from this union of itself and
something not itself so that with this mixture of truth and
falsehood her mind became like a forest in which things moved;
lights and shadows changed, and one thing became another"
(323). At least once we are offered an illustration of precisely
how something becomes nothing; when, on her homeward
voyage from Turkey, Orlando surveys the English coast, she is
affected by a puzzling visual image:

There now rose, like a dome of smooth, white marble, something
which, whether fact or fancy, was so impressive to her fevered imagination that she settled upon it as one has seen a swarm of vibrant
dragonflies alight, with apparent satisfaction, upon the glass bell
which shelters some tender vegetable. The form of it, by the hazard of
fancy, recalled that earliest, most persistent memory — the man with

the big forehead in Twitchett's sittingroom . . . The truth was that the image of the marble dome which her eyes had first discovered so faintly that it suggested a poet's forehead and thus started a flock of irrelevant ideas, was no figment, but a reality; and as the ship advanced down the Thames before a favouring gale, the image with all its associations gave place to the truth, and revealed itself as nothing more and nothing less than the dome of a vast cathedral rising among a fretwork of white spires. (164)

Notably, the image does not give way to truth by withdrawing; what it reveals as "reality" is only itself in a new guise or under a new interpretation. It transpires that the "fancy" is of the kind that prompts us by the dense texture of fancies that cohere with it to announce the presence of a "reality."[5]

Licensed by this phenomenalism, Woolf's narrator rejects the view that history — the account of what happens to perceiving selves — is to be restricted to the "objective," and hence to the partial. An epoch of hyperbolic feelings is better and more accurately served by reproducing its own hyperbolic vision of itself, as the narrator serves the Jacobeans in a surreal and rather Ovidian bagatelle:

The Great Frost was, historians tell us, the most severe that has ever visited these islands. Birds froze in mid-air and fell like stones to the ground. At Norwich a young countrywoman . . . was seen by the onlookers to turn visibly to powder and be blown in a puff of dust over the roofs . . . The fields were full of shepherds, ploughmen, and little bird-scaring boys all struck stark in the act of the moment, one with his hand to his nose, another with the bottle to his lips, a third with a stone raised to throw at the raven who sat, as if stuffed, upon the hedge within a yard of him . . . The court was at Greenwich, and the new King seized the opportunity that his coronation gave him to curry favour with the citizens. He directed that the river, which was frozen to a depth of twenty feet and more for six or seven miles on either side, should be swept, decorated, and given all the semblances of a park or pleasure ground, with arbours, mazes, alleys, drinking booths, etc., at his own expense. (33ff.)

Near London Bridge, where the river had frozen to a depth of some twenty fathoms, a wrecked wherry boat was plainly visible, lying on the bed of the river where it had sunk last Autumn, overladen with apples. The old bumboat woman, who was carrying her fruit to market on the Surrey side, sat there in her plaids and farthingales with her lap full of apples, for all the world as if she were about to serve a customer, though a certain blueness about the lips hinted the truth. 'Twas a sight King James liked to look upon, and he would bring a troupe of courtiers to gaze with him.   (36)

Here, at any rate, is the Jacobean myth vividly illuminated: the fascination with freaks and pageants, with life conceived as a brilliant and intricate masque, with death conceived as a dance of grotesquely ornate drollery. And the style of description, a series of pictorial flashes of macabre transformation and elemental caprice, is in the same idiom as Ovid's *jeux d'esprit* on the flood of Deucalion and the effects of the Gorgon's stare. In *Orlando*, however, the idiom is at the disposal not of a despairing ironist but of a chronicler of the imagination for whom accuracy consists, in effect, in framing the sketch of a room with a suspicion of the side of the sketcher's nose, or perhaps (if he is sitting) with a foreground of his hands and lap. To explode the myth of the thing in itself is, for Orlando the poet, to justify the autonomous exercise of the imagination, and hence to regain an essential freedom.

Talk of regaining a freedom runs the risk of misunderstanding, so I shall take this opportunity of emphasizing that the phenomenalist interpretation of experience we have been considering is hardly a piece of cultural subversion, or a precursor of late twentieth-century *anomie*. One might as plausibly cast in that ideological role Prospero's conviction that we are such stuff as dreams are made on. The point, once again, is not so much to dethrone the real as to exalt the imaginary by showing that, for the hardest-headed among us as for the dreamers, the reading of "see" on which "he sees an oak tree" is consistent with the tree's nonexistence is more fundamental than the reading that implies its existence; in either case one has to do with an image. For their own legitimate purposes, common sense and science partition experience into the objective and the subjective, and this proceeding becomes perverse only if it is allowed to impoverish our sense of reality. Common sense, tradition, even conventional social manners (if prevented from tyrannizing) are good things in their place — beside and not over against the creatures of the mythic imagination. *Orlando* is too history-haunted, too private, too libertarian a romance to reflect the iconoclasm of an ideologue. Its mischief has nothing in common with vandalism.

The narrative demonstrates a different sort of freedom, I think, in its ambiguous handling of time; for we are left to contend as best we can with the fact that the central figure, among others, has lived through more than three centuries of varied history by the end of the narrative while growing no older than thirty-six. This is easily enough accounted for if we assume that the years are measured in intersubjective or public time and the centuries in private; the sense of duration, as the narrator delights in reminding us, is wonderfully elastic:

An hour, once it lodges in the queer element of the human spirit, may be stretched to fifty or a hundred times its clock length; on the other hand, an hour may be accurately represented on the timepiece of the mind by one second. This extraordinary discrepancy between time on the clock and time in the mind, is less known than it should be and deserves fuller investigation.   (98)

All which [that is, Orlando's lionization by Victorian society] is properly enclosed in square brackets, as above, for the good reason that a parenthesis it was without any importance in Orlando's life. She skipped it, to get on with the text. For when the bonfires were blazing in the market place, she was in the dark woods with Shelmerdine alone. So fine was the weather that the trees stretched their branches motionless above them, and if a leaf fell, it fell, spotted and gold, so slowly that one could watch it for half an hour fluttering and falling till it came to rest at last on Orlando's foot.   (256)

And indeed, it cannot be denied that the most successful practitioners of the art of life, often unknown people by the way, somehow contrive to synchronise the sixty or seventy different times which beat simultaneously in every human system so that when eleven strikes all the rest chime in unison, and the present is neither a violent disruption nor completely forgotten in the past. Of them we can justly say that they live precisely the sixty-eight or seventy-two years allotted them on the tombstone. Of the rest, some we know to be dead, though they walk among us; some are not yet born, though they go through the forms of life; others are hundreds of years old though they call themselves thirty-six.   (305)

The times not registered by clock or tombstone apparently divide up the units of public time into arbitrary units of private; presumably, the general rule is that the more eventful or highly valued a span of experience, the swifter it seems in the having and the longer in retrospect, and the reverse with empty or oppressive time. On this interpretation, the narrator has simply chosen to ignore the conventional hierarchy of precision or objectivity among measures of duration. The resulting paradox is a variation on Rosalind's metaphysical impudence toward quite another Orlando in *As You Like It*:

Ros. Time travels in divers paces with divers persons. I'll tell you who time ambles withal, who time gallops withal, and who he stands still withal.

Orl. I prithee, who doth he trot withal?

Ros. With a priest that lacks Latin, and a rich man that hath not the gout; for the one sleeps easily because he cannot study, and the other lives merrily because he feels no pain; the one lacking the burthen of lean and wasteful learning, the other knowing no burthen of heavy tedious penury. These time ambles withal.

Orl. Who doth he gallop withal?

Ros. With a thief to the gallows; for though he go as soft as foot can fall he thinks himself too soon there.

Orl. Who stays it withal?

Ros. With lawyers in the vacation; for they sleep between term and term, and then they perceive not how Time moves.

(3.2.308–333)

The operative word, on what we may call the Shakespearean model of the vagaries of time, is "perceive"; and as applied to the narrative attitude toward the real or objective in *Orlando*, we shall understand that the clock is only one measure — the public measure — among others, all rooted in perception and subject to its contingencies.[6]

The difficulty with this approach is that the Shakespearean model clarifies only part of what Virginia Woolf's narrator is enabled to say by his treatment of time; that Orlando's public years are private minutes does not by itself palliate the miracle that she manages to live through three hundred years of public events, beginning as an Elizabethan and still carrying on in the reign of George V, and the historical evocations are too elaborate and highly charged to be the machinery of a pointless joke. I should like to suggest that the subject of the historical part of *Orlando*'s temporal paradox is not the status of *fact*, but the multiple *possibilities* of the central figure. For these are not all-inclusive; we may reasonably entertain not only the innocuous claim that it is logically possible for Orlando to have lived in any one of several epochs, but also the more interesting claim that given Orlando's essential character the roles she would respectively have played in them are as they are represented in the narrative. Construed in this way, the narrator's flight of fancy turns out to have the assurance and complexity typical of informed claims about what would be true in circumstances that happen not to hold.

With its ellipses filled in, the current claim would, I think, take roughly the following form: there are alternative schemes of things, or total states of past, present, and future affairs — possible worlds, shall we say — that are very similar to the actual world in the things they contain, their laws of nature, and what happens in them. In those similar worlds that the narrator, at least, would pick out as especially similar to the actual world, Orlando never figures as an Elizabethan nobleman without also having the experiences we are reading about.[7] On this interpretation, each historical episode in the narrative is the main clause of a conditional sentence contrary to fact with the if-clause and the subjunctive mood suppressed: "Orlando (would have) aspired to piratical adventure (if he had been a young Elizabethan nobleman)." The "biography" is a direct exploration of what we may call Orlando's historical possibilities. But if this reading is sound, why does the narrator drop the prefix "it is possible that" or "it would have been the case that," and dart from one alternative world to another — from one in which Orlando is Elizabethan to another in which she is Augustan — as if they were all on a par with the actual world?

The answer seems to be that this is precisely the insidious point of the narrative; that the dethronement of the actual is part of the same subversive libertarian program as the dethronement of the real. For the entities that are the fundamental bearers of truth and possibility — the so-called propositions — are no respecters of worlds. That Orlando is an Elizabethan nobleman is true in some possible worlds and false in others, just as it is true at some moments and false at others that Orlando is in Turkey. "Now" and "actually" are not (as common sense would have it) the labels of a privileged moment and world; they are not labels at all, but expressions that vary in reference with the moments and worlds in which sentences containing them are uttered. To evaluate a particular utterance of "Orlando is now in Turkey," one notes the time of utterance and then ascertains whether Orlando is in Turkey at that time. Thus the narrator uses "the present moment" archly here and there as if just one date could be so described, but permits the date mentioned to vary ironically (78, 298, 329).

To contemplate the possible truth of a proposition on this view is to enjoy a kind of freedom of which the utterance in some particular world of "now" or "actually" is a crass interruption. To measure truth by reference to such interruptions is to allow them to immure the self in but one of the universes to which it is native, and since "now" names no moment, being taken in by the hallucination of a Present Moment par excellence is an experience of peculiar dread, a confrontation with the void.

The narrative is strewn with such dread confrontations:

Her thoughts became mysteriously tightened and strung up, as if a piano tuner had put his key in her back and stretched the nerves very taut; at the same time her hearing quickened; she could hear every whisper and crackle in the room, so that the clock ticking on the mantelpiece beat like a hammer. And so for some seconds the light went on becoming brighter, and she saw everything more and more clearly, and the clock ticked louder and louder until there was a terrible explosion right in her ear. Orlando leapt as if she had been violently struck in the head. Ten times she was struck. In fact it was ten o'clock in the morning. It was the eleventh of October. It was nineteen twenty-eight. It was the present moment. No one need wonder that Orlando started, pressed her hand to her heart and turned pale. For what more terrifying revelation can there be than that it is the present moment? That we survive the shock at all is only possible because the past shelters us on one side, and the future on the other.   (298)

She saw with disgusting vividness that the thumb of Joe's right hand was without a fingernail and there was a raised saucer of pink flesh where the nail should have been. The sight was so repulsive that she felt faint for a moment, but in that moment's darkness, when her eyelids flickered, she was relieved of the presence of the present. There was something strange in the shadow that the flicker of her eyes cast, something which (as anyone can test for himself by looking now at the sky) is always absent from the present—whence its terror, its nondescript character—something one trembles to pin through the body with a name and call beauty, for it has no body, is as a shadow and without substance or quality of its own, yet has the power to change whatever it adds itself to. This shadow now while she flickered her eye in her faintness in the carpenter's shop stole out, and attaching itself to the innumerable sights she had been receiving, composed them into something tolerable, comprehensible.   (321–322)

The shadow that the self casts on the moment it contemplates, and that subdues its terror, is the sense of unity, of transcending any particular moment or possible state of affairs. The enjoyment of this unity, I think, is ultimately connected with the narrative insistence on counterfactual history, and the strange egalitarianism with which it presents the incompatible worlds it contemplates.

Our way of determining from the outside what shall count as an individual is a matter of convention. If our problem is to decide whether Orlando the Elizabethan courtier and his namesake the Caroline Ambassador are one and the same, we look for a schedule of continuous passage between the point and moment at which the courtier was last located and the point and moment at which the Ambassador was first located such that each point-moment position on the schedule was occupied by one or the other of them. Continuity in space and time will allow us to identify the courtier with the Ambassador even though it would be logically permissible to take two consecutive positions on the schedule as those respectively on which one individual ceases to exist and a second begins; indeed, if the contrast between the courtier and the Ambassador were as catastrophic as that between Gregor and the beetle, an outsider might be tempted to embrace the latter alternative with some enthusiasm. Even the narrator, who knows better, verges once on treating Orlando's change in sex as if it were a question of identifying distinct parts of a whole consisting of two successive individuals:

Orlando had become a woman — there is no denying it. But in every other respect, Orlando remained precisely as he had been. The change of sex, though it altered *their* future, did nothing whatever to alter *their* identity. *Their* faces remained, as *their* portraits prove, practically the same. His memory — but in future we must, for *convention's* sake, say "her" for "his" and "she" for "he" — her memory then, went back through all the events of her past life without encountering any obstacle.[8]   (138; emphasis added)

From the inside, however, from Orlando's perspective, it is simply axiomatic that if she has a memory at all, it is an awareness "of *her* past," the past of an indivisible subject; there is ultimately no danger of her shrinking away, as perceiver, into the nothingness of the present and the actual. Terms like "Elizabeth's favorite courtier" or "the Caroline Ambassador to Turkey" — the terms of merely conventional statements of identity — are descriptions that change their reference from moment to moment or from one possible world to another; in this respect they are no different from "now," "actually," "the English monarch in 1590" (variable from world to world), or "the English monarch" (variable from time to time and world to world). Proper names and their associated pronouns, on the other hand — in the narrator's ordinary usage, at any rate — do not vary at all in the context of "now" or "it is possible (is actually the case) that." The entire point of our being told, concerning Orlando, that "she reviewed . . . the progress of her own self along her own past" (175) depends on our understanding that the reference of the pronouns "she," "her own self," and "her" is identical despite contextual differences in tense and mood. In the current jargon phrase, the terms are all "rigid designators."

It is true that side by side with pronominal "self" or "herself" we find "self" and "Orlando" serving as common nouns in the plural, and that this may suggest a flirtation with anxieties about the unity of the person:

For she had a great variety of selves to call upon, far more than we have been able to find room for, since a biography is considered complete if it merely accounts for six or seven selves, whereas a person may well have as many thousand. Choosing, then, only those selves we have found room for, Orlando may now have called on the boy who cut the nigger's head down; the boy who sat on the hill; the boy who saw the poet; the boy who handed the Queen the bowl of rose water; or she may have called upon the young man who fell in love with Sasha; or upon the Courtier; or upon the Ambassador; or upon the Soldier; or upon the Traveller; or she may have wanted the Woman to come to her; the Gipsy; the Fine Lady; the Hermit; the girl in love with life; the Patroness of Letters . . . All these selves were different, and she may have called on any of them.

Perhaps; but what appeared certain (for we are in the region of "perhaps" and "appears") was that the one she needed most kept aloof; for she was, to hear her talk, changing her selves as quickly as she drove—there was a new one at every corner—as happens when, for some unaccountable reason, the conscious self, which is the uppermost, and has the power to desire, wishes to be nothing but one self. This is what some people call the true self, and it is, they say, compact of all the selves we have it in us to be; commanded and locked up by the Captain self, the Key self, which amalgamates and controls them all. (309–310)

The list of Orlando's "selves" consists not of individuals but of individual concepts or roles satisfied by the same "she" at different times in different possible worlds. They are her possibilities of transformation, the selves she has it in her to be. Certain traits, on the other hand, are essential to the role-*bearer* or "Captain self"; for "through all those changes she had remained, she reflected, fundamentally the same. She had the same brooding meditative temper, the same love of animals and nature, the same passion for the country and the seasons" (237). There is thus an opportunity of choosing to be an essential or "true" self—to play in one's imagination a role that epitomizes the rest; though the motive for such an averaging, is, says the narrator, "unaccountable." To rejoice imaginatively in the rich multiplicity of one's "selves," it is clear, is to celebrate the unity and energy of the protean Self that, by its joint presence in more than one possible world, impersonates them all.[9]

Suppose—to explore the contrasting possibility—that we deny Orlando's axiom, as in effect Stevenson's Dr. Jekyll tries to do, by assuming that one cannot intelligibly ask whether the Jekyll of one moment is literally the same as the Jekyll of the next; they are distinct objects—stages, let us say—that pass our conventional test (of resemblance and continuity) for parts of the whole that is Jekyll *tout court*, a whole that (like a relay race or dynasty) is extended in time as well as space. In Jekyll's exceptional case, unfortunately, the whole is not continuous; stages of Jekyll periodically end in stages of Hyde. To make matters worse, each stage of Jekyll is also a stage of his submerged *alter idem*, of a Hyde in hiding — "the cavern in which [the mountain bandit] conceals himself from pursuit."

It is, indeed, ostensibly with a view to ending this agonizing duality that Jekyll first resorts to chemical means of achieving an antiseptic alternation between respective stages of the "polar twins": "The unjust might go his way . . . and the just could walk steadfastly . . . no longer exposed to disgrace and penitence." But the plan, on Jekyll's account, has gone wrong; as before, Hyde is unadulterated, and Jekyll "a mere polity of multifarious, incongruous, and independent citizens." In another respect, however, on the assumption that Jekyll and Hyde are not and cannot be identical, the experiment appears to be partly successful: though Jekyll concedes that he is guilty of conniving at Hyde's infamy, "even now I can scarce grant that I committed it"; connivance is presumably far less burdensome to conscience than commission. The "depravity," after all, is merely "vicarious."

As the insistent irony of Stevenson's tale makes clear to us, this account will not do. Connivance is itself a form of commission, that "heresy of Cain" to which (in its venial form) the narrative *raisonneur* Utterson confesses in Stevenson's prologue: "I let my brother go to the devil in his own way." But not all such heresies are venial. To release Hyde — to let him go despite the horror of his "way" — is clearly to go with him. But what is worse, Jekyll is lying. His language betrays him. Far from being vicarious, his sadistic pleasures are simply "the secret pleasures that I had enjoyed in the disguise of Hyde." "Hyde," in short, is the name Jekyll goes by in disguise, under the influence of the drug that both disfigures him and relieves him of his inhibitions; he is no more subject to multiplication by the number of his conflicting urges or transformations than is the drunkard with whom he compares himself. The monster whose deeds he remembers performing is *ipso facto* himself, as he fitfully realizes. To sum up "my life as a whole," for Jekyll, is to include the life of Hyde.

And yet the lie of the exculpatory third person persists to

the end: "He, I say—I cannot say, I." The amateur of "transcendental medicine" remains the dupe of his own intellectual quackery, and especially of his muddled ontology of the self as process rather than as the subject of process.[10] But what Jekyll so strenuously denies, his story forbids us to overlook: under whatever name or condition or disguise, Jekyll endures from stage to stage of his history. It is only the stages endured that are necessarily distinct. There is, in short, a crucial difference between the delusive multiplicity of selves in which Jekyll seeks refuge from his responsibility and the imaginative multiplicity of roles in which Orlando and Jekyll himself (to his grief) find opportunities for the exploration of their freedom.

The "biographer" whom Virginia Woolf has provided for Orlando, if I am thus far right, by blithely renouncing conventional narrative fidelity to the real and the actual, demonstrates (to his own satisfaction at least) a more inclusive fidelity to concrete human experience and its alternative possibilities. To achieve liberty, one must take liberties; and of all the conventions with which such liberties are taken in *Orlando*, none is more mischievously derided than the convention that one's sex ordains how one ought properly to think, to behave, and above all to be treated. The allegorical figures who act out their masque of disapproval and departure in the bedchamber where the sleeping Orlando is changing sex are in effect the three goddesses of sexual propriety: Purity, Modesty, and Chastity, supercilious idols of "those who prohibit; those who deny; those who reverence without knowing why; those who praise without understanding; the still very numerous (Heaven be praised) tribe of the respectable; who prefer to see not; desire to know not; love the darkness" (137).[11]

For the "tribe of the respectable," Orlando's sexual transformation is socially null—a case not covered by the gender-specific rules for responding to persons; hence their enthusiasm for finding ways to avoid acknowledging it: "The change seemed to have been accomplished painlessly and completely and in such a way that Orlando herself showed no surprise at it. Many people, taking this into account, and holding that such a change is against nature, have been at great pains to prove (1) that Orlando had always been a woman, (2) that Orlando is at this moment a man" (139). In the same spirit, the legal case against her right to her own inheritance charges her in desperation with being dead as a male and disqualified as a female from holding property: "Thus it was in a highly ambiguous condition, uncertain whether she was alive or dead, man or woman, Duke or nonentity, that she posted down to her country seat, where, pending the legal judgement, she had the Law's permission to reside in a state of incognito or incognita as the case might turn out to be" (168). One is unknown, insoluble, without the conventional label that defines the roles of those one has to do with.

Orlando's new acquaintance with being a woman permits her, of course, to compare the advantages of the feminine and masculine labels. At first, on her sea voyage home from Turkey, she supposes, like Ovid's Teiresias, that in some respects the feminine lot is the more agreeable:

Then she had pursued, now she fled. Which is the greater ecstasy? The man's or the woman's? And are they not perhaps the same? No, she thought, this is the most delicious (thanking the Captain [for the offer of a slice of corned beef] but refusing), to refuse, and see him frown. Well, she would, if he wished it, have the very thinnest, smallest sliver in the world. This was the most delicious, to yield and see him smile. "For nothing," she thought, regaining her couch on deck and continuing the argument, "is more heavenly than to resist and to yield; to yield and to resist. Surely it throws the spirit into such a rapture that nothing else can. So that I'm not sure," she continued, "that I won't throw myself overboard, for the mere pleasure of being rescued by a bluejacket after all." (It must be remembered that she was like a child entering into possession of a pleasaunce or toycupboard; her arguments would not commend themselves to mature women, who have had the run of it all their lives).   (155–156)

The sardonic parenthesis, as it turns out, is grotesquely understated; the game with which Orlando has allowed herself to be beguiled is stultifying to both sides:

"To fall from a mast-head," she thought, "because you see a woman's ankles; to dress up like a Guy Fawkes and parade the streets, so that women may praise you; to deny a woman teaching lest she may laugh at you; to be the slaves of the frailest chit in petticoats, and yet to go about as if you were the Lords of Creation. —Heavens!" she thought, "what fools they make of us — what fools we are!" And here it would seem from some ambiguity in her terms that she was censuring both sexes equally, as if she belonged to neither.   (158)

The full insidiousness of the prescribed roles emerges only when Orlando's critical neutrality wavers and threatens to give way to the delusion that the roles are more than a game: "Do what she would to restrain them, the tears came to her eyes, until, remembering that it is becoming in a woman to weep, she let them flow" (165). "That men cry as frequently and as unreasonably as women, Orlando knew from her own experience as a man; but she was beginning to be aware that women should be shocked when men display emotion in their presence; and so, shocked she was" (180).

All this, it is true, has the makings of comedy, and nowhere more than when Orlando feels obliged by Purity, Modesty, and Chastity to register shock:

Here she turned to present the Archduchess with the salver, and behold—in her place stood a tall gentleman in black. A heap of clothes lay in the fender. She was alone with a man.

Recalled thus suddenly to a consciousness of her sex, which she had completely forgotten, and of his, which was now remote enough to be equally upsetting, Orlando felt seized with faintness.

"La!" she cried, putting her hand to her·side, "how you frighten me!" "Gentle creature," cried the Archduchess, falling on one knee and at the same time pressing a cordial to Orlando's lips, "forgive me for the deceit I have practised on you!"

Orlando sipped the wine and the Archduke knelt and kissed her hand.

In short, they acted the parts of man and woman for ten minutes with great vigour and then fell into natural discourse.   (178–179).

But the comedy takes an acrimonious turn as Orlando comes to see that the convention of femininity entails not only irksome restrictions but deeply insulting dispensations. To get rid of her unwanted lover, Orlando tries to persuade him of her unworthiness by grossly cheating him at a game; to her irritation, she is eventually spared the punishment she has worked so hard to deserve:

To love a woman who cheats at play was, he said, impossible. Here he broke down completely. Happily, he said, recovering slightly, there were no witnesses. She was, after all, a woman, he said. In short, he was preparing in the chivalry of his heart to forgive her and had bent to ask her pardon for the violence of his language, when she cut the matter short, as he stooped his proud head, by dropping a small toad between his skin and his shirt.

In justice to her, it must be said that she would infinitely have preferred a rapier. Toads are clammy things to conceal about one's person a whole morning. But if rapiers are forbidden, one must have recourse to toads.   (183–184)

There is clearly as much outrage as mischief in the bestowal of the toad; it is a substitute for the home thrust of a rapier.

As Orlando proceeds on her tour down the centuries, she pauses at the eighteenth to collect perennial canards about women like a connoisseur of grievances culling specimens. To Addison, we are informed, woman is "a beautiful romantic animal" (10); to Lord Chesterfield, a child "of a larger growth" (213). Another eighteenth-century wit declares that "when they lack the stimulus of the other sex, women can find nothing to say to each other. When they are alone, they do not talk; they scratch" (219). Still another, that "women are incapable of any feeling of affection for their own sex, and hold each other in the greatest aversion" (220). In the nineteenth century, the injustice of sexual convention begins to be somewhat more evenhanded: "Men felt the chill in their hearts; the damp in their minds. In a desperate effort to snuggle their feelings into some sort of warmth one subterfuge was tried after another. Love, birth, and death were all swaddled in a variety of fine phrases. The sexes drew further and further apart. No open conversation was tolerated. Evasions and concealments were sedulously practised on both sides" (229). Victorian marriage in particular is an institution of stifling dependency into which men and women are herded by the morbid roles imposed on them, roles that in the case of women require a wardrobe calculated to constrain free movement and an array of obligatory phobias (such as the fear "lest there should be robbers in the wainscot") with the same effect: "All these things inclined her, step by step, to submit to the new discovery, whether Queen Victoria's or another's, that each man and each woman has another allotted to it for life, whom it supports, by whom it is supported, till death them do part. It would be a comfort, she felt, to lean, to sit down; yes, to lie down; never, never, never to get up again" (245).

And the twentieth-century Lawrentian reaction against propriety, Orlando finds, has scarcely been an improvement; in

METAMORPHOSIS AS THE QUEST FOR FREEDOM

the name of a vital freedom it has merely substituted a new decorum by which the self is confined (especially in the official paradigm of femininity) to harping on the single note of *eros*, and a dehumanized *eros* at that:

Surely since [Orlando] is a woman, and a beautiful woman, and a woman in the prime of life, she will soon give over this pretence of writing and thinking and begin to think, at least, of a gamekeeper (and as long as she thinks of a man, nobody objects to a woman thinking). And then she will write him a little note (and as long as she writes little notes nobody objects to a woman writing, either). And make an assignation for Sunday dusk; and Sunday dusk will come; and the gamekeeper will whistle under the window—all of which is, of course, the very stuff of life and the only possible subject for fiction. Surely Orlando must have done one of these things? Alas,—a thousand times, alas, Orlando did none of them. Must it then be admitted that Orlando was one of those monsters of iniquity that do not love? She was kind to dogs, faithful to friends, generosity itself to a dozen starving poets, had a passion for poetry. But love—as the male novelists define it—and who, after all, speak with greater authority?—has nothing whatever to do with kindness, fidelity, generosity, or poetry. Love is slipping off one's petticoat and—But we all know what love is. (269)

Behavior is not the only slave of the sexual role, whimsical artifact though the latter is; unfortunately for Orlando, one cannot go through the motions of conformity for long without losing one's inner autonomy; the flimsiness of the eighteenth-century gown, the weight of the Victorian crinoline are in the end a very efficient means of subjecting the mind and the body:

Vain trifles as they seem, clothes have, they say, more important offices than merely to keep us warm . . . There is much to support the view that it is clothes that wear us and not we them; we may make them take the mould of arm or breast, but they mould our hearts, our brains, our tongues to their liking . . . If we compare the picture of Orlando as a man with that of Orlando as a woman we shall see that though both are undoubtedly one and the same person, there are certain changes. The man has his hand free to seize his sword; the woman must use hers to keep the satins from slipping from her shoulders. The man looks the world full in the face, as if it were made for his uses and fashioned to his liking. The woman takes a sidelong glance at it, full of subtlety, even of suspicion. Had they both worn the same clothes, it is possible that their outlook might have been the same too. (188)

Each of these costumes carries with it a particular limitation on outlook, on the range of experience. In the eighteenth century, Orlando accordingly defends her freedom by a tactical transvestism: "Her sex changed far more frequently than those who have worn only one set of clothing can conceive; nor can there be any doubt that she reaped a two-fold harvest by this device; the pleasures of life were increasd and its experiences multiplied. From the probity of breeches she turned to the seductiveness of petticoats and enjoyed the love of both sexes equally" (221).

If the identification of probity with being male and of seductiveness with being female is indeed a fiction ordained by convention and subtly reinforced by the symbolism of dress, then the narrator's talk of "the mixture in her of man and woman" can hardly be taken on its face; it is a parody of the same ludicrously false dichotomies that underlie the hesitations of Orlando's friends about how to classify her:

The curious of her own sex would argue how, for example, if Orlando was a woman, did she never take more than ten minutes to dress? And were not her clothes chosen rather at random, and sometimes worn rather shabby? And then they would say, still, she has none of the formality of a man, or a man's love of power. She is excessively tenderhearted. She could not endure to see a donkey beaten or a kitten drowned. Yet again, they noted, she detested household matters, was up at dawn and out among the fields in summer before the sun had risen. No farmer knew more about the crops than she did. She could drink with the best and liked games of hazard. She rode well and drove six horses at a gallop over London Bridge. Yet again, though bold and active as a man, it was remarked that the sight of another in danger brought on the most womanly palpitations. She would burst into tears on slight provocation. She was unversed in geography, found mathematics intolerable, and held some caprices which are more common among women than men, as, for instance, that to travel south is to travel down hill. (190)

For the mentality that regards every strength or weakness of character or intellect as an essential peculiarity of one sex or the other, Orlando's biological nature will hardly determine her sex; her inability or refusal to sustain a consistent role implies the lack of any definite nature at all. Orlando, as her biographer twice warns us, is sometimes a little at odds with our expectations, sometimes "a trifle clumsy" (17): "Yet it is true that there was an absentmindedness about her which sometimes made her clumsy; she was apt to think of poetry when she should have been thinking of taffeta; her walk was a little too much of a stride for a woman, perhaps, and her gestures, being abrupt, might endanger a cup of tea on occasion" (194).

One might gather from all this that the ideal of "clumsiness" being burnished by Orlando's biographer is a kind of bisexual aestheticism in thin disguise. That the suggestion is far too narrow is sufficiently indicated by the pains the biographer takes to provide that clumsiness with a foil in the freakishness of Orlando's admirer and fellow transvestite Harry Archduke of Finster-Aarhorn, who throws off his pretense to confess

that he was a man and always had been one; that he had seen a portrait of Orlando and fallen hopelessly in love with him; that to compass his ends, he had dressed as a woman . . . that he had heard of her change and hastened to offer his services (here he teed and heed intolerably). For to him, said the Archduke Harry, she was and would ever be the Pink, the Pearl, the Perfection of her sex. The three p's would have been more persuasive if they had not been interspersed with tee-hees and haw-haws of the strangest kind. "If this is love," said Orlando to herself, looking at the Archduke on the other side of the fender and now from the woman's point of view, "there is something highly ridiculous about it." (179)

There is something highly ridiculous in a charade of romanticized prurience. It may be, as the biographer speculates, that the romance and the prurience in love are "so strictly joined together that you cannot separate them"; but in the Archduke it is grotesquely obvious which is the directing impulse: "It was Lust the vulture, not Love the Bird of Paradise that flopped, foully and disgustingly, upon [Orlando's] shoulders" (117–118). The egoism and impersonality of the Archduke's obsession are stupidly confining, and so far in sharp contrast to the inclusiveness of experience and sympathy the biographer eventually celebrates on the eve of Orlando's motherhood: "Hail, happiness! kingfisher flashing from bank to bank, and all fulfillment of natural desire, whether it is what the male novelist says it is; or prayer; or denial; hail! in whatever form it comes, and may there be more forms, and stranger" (294).

Orlando's continuing fascination with a person of her own sex, unlike the Duke's harlequinade, is presented to us as something serious, validated by inner kinship, and made tragic by betrayal:

As all Orlando's loves had been women, now, through the culpable laggardry of the human frame to adapt itself to convention, though she herself was a woman, it was still a woman she loved; and if the consciousness of being of the same sex had any effect at all, it was to quicken and deepen those feelings which she had had as a man. For now a thousand hints and mysteries became plain to her that were then dark. Now, the obscurity, which divides the sexes and lets linger innumerable impurities in its gloom, was removed, and if there is anything in what the poet says about truth and beauty, this affection gained in beauty what it lost in falsity.   (161)

Here, as she was fingering the linen abstractedly, one of the swing-doors between the departments opened and let through, perhaps from the fancy-goods department, a whiff of scent, waxen, tinted as if from pink candles, and the scent curved like a shell round a figure — was it a boy's or was it a girl's — furred, pearled, in Russian trousers — young, slender, seductive — a girl, by God! but faithless, faithless!   (303)

The sexual duality (by the conventional standard) of the people Orlando loves — not only of the Elizabethan aristocrat's mistress but of the twentieth-century poet's husband — seems to me to be offered, like Orlando's transformation itself, both as a reversal of the process by which "the sexes drew further and further apart" (229), and more fundamentally as the pattern for a general response to the doubt that behind another's behavior lie feelings like one's own. It is a doubt one cannot plausibly reason away by appealing to the likeness of behavior in the Other to what in oneself invariably accompanies feeling of such and such a kind; this would be to generalize from a single instance (oneself). Perhaps one might proceed by noting that the sum of one's characteristics is clearly *enough* to produce or admit of the pairing of behavior and inner events one observes in oneself and seeks assurance of in others. Among these characteristics some will be necessary to such pairing. The more like oneself the others are, the more likely it is (by the uniformity of nature) that they too satisfy these necessary conditions. If one could eliminate one's differences from a given class of others without finding an alteration in the pairing, then one would know that these differences at least had not disqualified the others from sharing one's feelings, and indeed perhaps had qualified them to have other sorts of feelings as well, of which one had had no suspicion. But of course, most of the changes required by the experiment are quite impossible: "There are a great many properties of which I cannot divest myself and a great many that I cannot acquire; and among them are properties which are peculiar to me, or peculiar to some other person."[12] But an experiment in empathic transformation that cannot be conducted in fact can still (perhaps) be conducted in imagination; and the poet Orlando is peculiarly fitted to conduct it.

For the rest, those who, like Orlando and her husband, have emancipated themselves from artificial norms of sexuality, find that their most fragmentary utterances hold no mystery for their partners — that at a profound level their minds turn out to be formed on the same pattern: " 'Are you positive you aren't a man' he would ask anxiously, and she would echo, 'Can it be possible that you're not a woman?' and then they must put it to the proof without more ado. For each was so surprised at the quickness of the other's sympathy, and it was to each such a revelation that a woman could be as tolerant and free-spoken as a man, and a man as strange and subtle as a woman, that they had to put the matter to the proof at once" (258). The only matter they are putting to the proof here is their physical difference; tolerance and subtlety have turned out not to be criteria of sex at all.[13]

Orlando rebels against the tyranny of the real, the actual, and the sterotypical by casually trespassing on boundaries she comes to regard as artificial; her transformation is simply the temporal emblem of her multiple residence in universes that are held by common sense to be mutually inaccessible. But the sequence of universes we look into is far from arbitrary; they turn out at last to have been framed in the awareness of the twentieth-century woman who alone among Orlando's avatars is able, like Eliot's Teiresias, to achieve a synoptic vision. The worlds in which that vision occurs may not enjoy a privileged status of actuality, but they alone are the scene of Orlando's maturity and fulfillment, and they alone are the measure of likeness among possible worlds that gives meaning to the counterfactual idiom of Orlando's "biography" (in all like worlds in which Orlando enjoys a given form, her experiences in that form are as registered in the world of the mature woman's awareness). In this sense the subject of that "biography" is a woman, and the earlier sequences of the book are perversely misleading. Why is the womanhood of the most inclusive Orlando reserved by the device of transformation as a surprise? Why, for that matter, does the tone of the narrative as a whole mislead us by transforming itself by degrees from fantasy to mimesis, from parody to directness?[14]

The answer, I think, is that part of the subversive function of Orlando's transformation is craftily rhetorical. To be taken seriously, in the face of rooted prejudice, as the heroine of a quest for creative mastery, it is as well for the heroine to begin by introducing herself as a hero; for "the truth is," says her biographer with more than a touch of irony, "that when we write of a woman, everything is out of place — culminations and perorations; the accent never falls where it does with a man" (312). The Shakespearean mistress of an earlier Orlando is able to exercise the full force of her personality, to take command of her play, only after she assumes the disguise of a gentleman, and drops the name of "Rosalind" for the questionable *nom de guerre* of "Ganymede." Virginia Woolf's Orlando refines the stratagem by acting under a far more valiant name — Orlando is Roland — and retaining it even when she has thrown off her disguise. Now, however, it is inalienably the name of a woman. By taking command of a literary kind reserved by prejudice for men, Orlando achieves still another freedom of the imagination for herself and for us.

NOTES
INDEX

NOTES

INTRODUCTION

1. See Fred Sommers, "Predicability," in *Philosophy in America*, ed. Max Black (Ithaca, N.Y.: Cornell University Press, 1965).

2. Thomas Nagel, "What Is It Like to Be a Bat?" *The Philosophical Review* 83 (1974), 438–439.

3. Ibid., p. 442.

4. Herman Melville, *Moby Dick*, chap. 74.

5. Nagel, "What Is It Like to Be a Bat?" p. 448, n. 14.

6. Harold T. P. Hayes, "The Pursuit of Reason," *The New York Times Magazine*, June 12, 1977, pp. 75, 78.

7. Ibid., pp. 23, 78.

8. Lawrence H. Davis, "Disembodied Brains," *Australasian Journal of Philosophy* 52 (1974), 121–122, 128.

9. Ibid., p. 129.

10. Ibid., pp. 131–132.

11. I have found no studies of transformation that quite coincide with mine in aim or approach; but every student of the subject is indebted to the pioneering and magisterial survey by Clemens Heselhaus, "Metamorphose-Dichtungen und Metamorphose-Anschauungen," *Euphorion* 46 (1952), 121–146. For another sort of approach to a somewhat different range of illustrative texts, the reader may wish to consult Irving Massey, *The Gaping Pig* (Berkeley: University of California Press, 1976).

12. See, for example, Marshall Edelson, *Language and Interpretation in Psychoanalysis* (New Haven: Yale University Press, 1975), pp. 23–24, 69.

1. CIRCE AND ODYSSEUS

1. *Eustathii Commentarii ad Odysseam*, ed. Gottfried Stallbaum (Leipzig: J. A. G. Weigel, 1825), I, 379 (hereafter cited as *Ad Odysseam*); *Scholia Graeca in Homeri Odysseam*, ed. Wilhelm Dindorf (Oxford, 1855), II, 469–470 (Hereafter cited as Dindorf, *Scholia*). See Horace, *Epod*. 17.17–18: "tunc mens et sonus relapsus."

2. Kurt von Fritz, "*Nóos* and *Noeîn* in the Homeric Poems," *Classical Philology* 38 (1943), 85b, 87b, 90b.

3. *Iliad* 15.80ff., *Odyssey* 2.92, *Iliad* 1.363.

4. Von Fritz, "*Nóos* and *Noeîn*," p.83a.

5. Ibid., p. 82a.

6. Renzo Vitale, "Il *nóos* di Parmenide," *Vichiano* 6 (1969), 232. Translation mine.

7. Erwin Rohde, *Psyche* (New York: Harcourt, Brace, 1925), p. 30.

8. *Iliad* 6.234, 17.470.

9. *Iliad* 23.103–104.

10. Rohde, *Psyche*, p. 41.

11. Dindorf, *Scholia* II, 463; Denys Page, *Poetae Melici Graeci* (Oxford: Clarendon Press, 1962), p. 473. See Euripides, *Hippolytus* 925–931.

12. Denys Page, *Folktales in Homer's Odyssey* (Cambridge, Mass.: Harvard University Press, 1973), pp. 56, 67–68. See Rhys Carpenter, *Folktale, Fiction, and Saga in the Homeric Epics* (Berkeley: University of California Press, 1958), p. 20; Cyrus Gordon, *The Common Background of Greek and Hebrew Civilizations* (New York: Norton, 1965), pp. 87–88; Robert Brown, *The Myth of Kirke* (London: Longmans-Green, 1883), pp. 51–88.

13. I am assuming here, with Saul Kripke, that, as we use terms like "pain" and "C-fiber excitation," it makes no sense to say, "Pain *happens* to be identical with C-fiber excitation, but it might *not* have been" — as if "pain" were synonymous with a description like "the cause of this sensation" that fluctuates in reference from one possible world to another, in some of which worlds a neural state is not the cause of the indicated sensation. Unlike this cause, neither C-fiber excitation nor pain might have been anything but what it actually is; so if they are identical in any possible world they are identical in all. See Saul Kripke, "Identity and Necessity," in *Identity and Individuation*, ed. Milton K. Munitz (New York: New York University Press, 1971), pp. 135–164.

14. Eustathius, *Ad Odysseam* I, 368–369.

15. J. G. Frazer, *Spirits of the Corn and of the Wild* (London: Macmillan, 1912), 2.18–19. See Rohde, *Psyche*, p. 200, n.4; W. K. C. Guthrie, *The Greeks and Their Gods* (Boston: Beacon Press, 1961), pp. 193, 221.

16. Eustathius, *Ad Odysseam* I, 382.

17. Commentary (in *Miqra'oth Gᵉdoloth*) on Daniel 4:33.

18. Page, *Folktales*, p. 55.

19. Eustathius, *Ad Odysseam* II, 381.

20. In the ancient religion of whose sacrament I am supposing the enchantress to be a minister, blessedness and cursedness are conditions nearly allied, and the blessedness of being transformed does not escape this painful

contradiction. (Even a transformation to godhead, such as awaits the heroes of the *Trachiniae* and *Oedipus at Colonus*, is not attended by any softening of their old familiar harshness and obduracy.) To have been a sacred animal in that religion is to have been given a second chance of sorts, like the Gregorius of Christian legend, but—unlike Gregorius—not the slightest hint of sainthood.

2. OVID'S EPIC

1. The text on which I base my translations is Hugo Magnus, ed., *Ovidi Metamorphoseon libri XV* (Berlin: Weidmann, 1914); but in several crucial places I have preferred the readings of R. Merkel (Leipzig, 1888).

2. Brooks Otis, *Ovid As an Epic Poet* (Cambridge: Cambridge University Press, 1966), pp. 262, 229.

3. Ibid., pp. 136, 117.

4. Ibid., p. 107.

5. See A. J. Ayer, *The Problem of Knowledge* (Baltimore: Penguin, 1956), pp. 220-221.

6. Otis, *Ovid As Epic Poet*, p. 158.

7. See Stewart Candlish, "The Inexplicability of Identity," *Australasian Journal of Philosophy* 49 (1971), 23-37.

8. Bruce Langtry, "Similarity, Continuity, and Survival," *Australasian Journal of Philosophy* 53 (1975), 13-14. Emphasis added, as in my translations of Plautus, *Amphitruo* 1.1.245, 286-293, 301-304.

9. Roland Crahay, "La Vision poétique d'Ovide et l'esthétique baroque," *Atti del Convegno internazionale ovidiano* (Rome: Istituto di studi romani, 1956), p. 103. Translation mine.

10. *Medea* 1078, 1056.

11. Bruno Snell, *The Discovery of the Mind*, trans. T. G. Rosenmeyer (Oxford: Basil Blackwell, 1953), p. 14; E. R. Dodds, *The Greeks and the Irrational* (Boston: Beacon Press, 1957), pp. 15-16.

12. For the soliloquies see (1) *Iliad* 11.403, 407; (2) 17.90, 97; (3) 21.552, 562; (4) 22.98, 122.

13. Mary-Kay Gamel Orlandi ("Playfulness and Seriousness in Ovid's *Metamorphoses*," Ph.D. diss., University of California, Berkeley, 1973) seems to reach similar conclusions, pointing to the moral confusion that prevails in the Ovidian world (p. 90), and its suggestion of "the relativity of all value systems" (p. 208). But she blurs this point by arguing (mistakenly, in my view) that Ovid's poem implies the truth of certain moral propositions (pp. 95, 208, 213, 215, 219-220, 221, 223-224, 229-230). Ovid's despair, on the contrary, seems to me to consist in having moral attitudes for which he can find no objective grounds. It is a despair of the existence of any moral sentence, however moving, that is not literally absurd.

14. See Orlandi, "Playfulness and Seriousness," p. 207.

15. Otis, *Ovid As Epic Poet*, pp. 161, 165. See Orlandi, "Playfulness and Seriousness," p. 62.

16. Crahay, *La Vision poétique d'Ovide*, p. 103. Translation mine.

17. Otis, *Ovid As Epic Poet*, p. 140.

18. W. Dement, "An Essay on Dreams," in *New Directions in Psychology*, ed. W. Edwards et al. (New York: Holt, Rinehart, and Winston, 1965), vol. 2, p. 205; quoted in E. M. Curley, "Dreaming and Conceptual Revision," *Australasian Journal of Philosophy* 53 (1975), 140.

19. See Orlandi, "Playfulness and Seriousness," p. 44.

20. Otis, *Ovid As Epic Poet*, pp. 198, 88.

21. Ibid., p. 205.

22. Ibid., pp. 125-126, 194, 266.

23. Ibid., pp. 256, 272, 263, 262-263.

24. Aristotle, *Politica* 1314a34-38, 1314b18ff., 1315a4ff., 1315b9-10; Cicero, *De re publica* 1.33.

25. Otis, *Ovid As Epic Poet*, pp. 125, 145.

26. Ibid., pp. 247, 258-259.

27. Ibid., pp. 145, 166, 184, 225.

28. Ibid., pp. 246, 240, 251.

29. Walther Ludwig, *Struktur und Einheit der Metamorphosen Ovids* (Berlin: de Gruyter, 1965), pp. 80-81. Translation mine.

30. See Orlandi, "Playfulness and Seriousness," pp. 206, 232.

31. See Orlandi, "Playfulness and Seriousness," p. 206.

32. G. Karl Galinski, "The Cipus Episode," *Transactions of the American Philological Association* 98 (1967), 184.

33. Ibid., p. 185.

34. Luigi Alfonsi, "L'inquadramento filosofico delle Metamorfosi ovidiane," in *Ovidiana*, ed. N. I. Herescu (Paris: Belles Lettres, 1958), p. 272; Roland Crahay and Jean Hubaux, "Sous la masque de Pythagore," in *Ovidiana*, p. 290. Translations mine.

35. Douglas Little, "The Speech of Pythagoras in *Metamorphoses* 15 and the Structure of the *Metamorphoses*," *Hermes* 98 (1970), 360; Otis, *Ovid As Epic Poet*, p. 302; Little, "The Speech of Pythagoras," pp. 354, 343; Hermann Fränkel, *Ovid: A Poet between Two Worlds* (Berkeley: University of California Press, 1945), p. 110.

36. Georges Lafaye, *Les Métamorphoses d'Ovide et leurs modèles grecs* (Paris: F. Alcan, 1904), pp. 12-17, 208.

37. Seneca, *Epistulae morales* 107.20. Emphasis added.

38. Ibid., 107.18, 21.

39. Lafaye, *Les Métamorphoses d'Ovide*, p. 199; Modestus van Straaten, *Panetius* (Amsterdam: H. J. Paris, 1946), pp. 70, 76n2. For Posidonius see Max Pohlenz, *Die Stoa* (Göttingen: Vandenhoek und Ruprecht, 1948), 1.230. Translations mine.

40. Cicero, *De re publica* 3.18-19; Lactantius, *Divinae institutiones* 6.9.2-4.

41. Plutarch, *De sollertia animalium* 963F; Pohlenz, *Die Stoa*, 1.39, 85, 227-228.

42. Charles Segal, "Myth and Philosophy in the *Metamorphoses*," *American Journal of Philology* 15 (1969), 283.

43. Horace, *Sermones* 2.6.63; Aelian, *De natura animalium* 12.7.

44. Segal, "Myth and Philosophy," p. 281.

3. THE GOLDEN ASS

1. The basis of my translations is Rudolfus Helm, ed., *Apulei Madaurensis Metamorphoseon libri XI* (Leipzig: Teubner, 1955), but I have sometimes preferred the readings of Jan van der Vliet (Leipzig: Teubner, 1897).

2. Pseudo-Lucian, *Lucius, or the Ass* 581.

3. Ibid., 582, 617.

4. But cf. Fritz Norden, *Apuleius von Madaura und das Römische Privatrecht* (Leipzig: Teubner, 1912): "And yet what this scene releases in his breast is not compassion at all. The Roman aristocrat is thinking only of himself. For if he cries out 'dii boni!' in anguish, it is only because he thinks with a shudder that he himself, or rather the hero of his first-person novel, will no doubt presently find himself in the same situation" (p. 70). The false premise of this line of argument is that the speaker's selfish despondency has nothing to do with compassion. One might more plausibly argue that the two emotions are essentially connected: "Take physic, pomp!/Expose thyself to feel what wretches feel,/That thou mayst shake the superflux to them,/And show the heavens more just" (*King Lear* 3.4.33–36). Lucius' "dii boni!" in fact is extorted from him, *before* his selfish fears intrude, by the discovery of something monstrous: the spectacle of kindred beings turned into travesties of themselves by circumstances that, as he later sees to his dread, are soon to claim another victim. Without the sense of kinship, surely, there would be no such acute sense of monstrosity, and no agonized "dii boni!" Here as elsewhere, to be sure, the author maintains an unsentimental narrative reticence; but indifference is quite another matter.

5. For *bipes*, see 4.10.

6. With the ridicule of Syro-Phoenician ritual self-mutilation, compare Elijah's mockery of the Canaanite priests who cut themselves with swords and lances in a vain attempt to propitiate Baal and Ashtoreth, 1 Kings 18:28. See also Deut. 14:1.

7. Plutarch, *De Iside et Osiride* 369A, 372A.

8. Plutarch, *De fato* 574D–F; Albinus, *Didascalicus* 16, 26.

9. *De dogmate Platonis* 1.12.

10. *Apologia* 64. On Isiac monotheism see R. E. Witt, *Isis in the Graecoroman World* (Ithaca, N.Y.: Cornell University Press, 1970), p. 129.

11. A. Salac, "Inscriptions de Kymé, d'Éolide, de Phocée, de Tralles," *Bulletin de correspondance hellénique* (1927), 379–380; quoted in Patrick G. Walsh, *The Roman Novel* (Cambridge: Cambridge University Press, 1970), p. 253.

12. *De Iside et Osiride* 354C, 367A, 369B, 371A, 372F, 377F–378A.

13. *De dogmate Platonis* 2.23.

14. *De dogmate Platonis* 2.20. See the definition of wisdom, ibid. 2.23.

15. James Tatum, "The Tales in Apuleius" *Metamorphoses*," *Proceedings of the American Philological Association* 100 (1969), 526.

16. Walsh, *The Roman Novel*, p. 184. This is the usual modern view; see the references in Claudio Moreschini, "La demonologia medioplatonica e le *Metamorfosi* di Apuleio," *Maia* 17 (1965), 39; and also in Walsh, p. 177.

17. Walsh, *The Roman Novel*, p. 178.

18. Ibid., pp. 180, 179n4.

19. *Apology* 11; 9-10.

20. *De Iside et Osiride* 372D, 377A, 356A, 358B, 365B, 371F. See also Witt, *Isis in the Graecoroman World:* "Roman poets regard Isis . . . as a lady of easy virtue, countenancing the sexual enjoyments and lovemaking" (p. 138). "Isis alone claimed an infinity of titles: and became all things to all men. She could be 'chaste' and yet raise high the phallus" (p. 121). "Pompeii provides proof of the existence of two contrasted elements in the cult of Isis, the spiritual and holy and the frankly erotic" (p. 85).

21. *De curiositate* 515D.

22. Ibid., 517CD, 521A.

23. *Apology* 27.

24. *Georgics* 2.490ff.

25. *Apology* 457.

26. *Odyssey* 9.414; see also 9.410. To be precise, the two words are close enough to allow a pun, but are in fact distinctly accented.

27. *De finibus* 5.49.

28. Walsh, *The Roman Novel*, p. 143. Cf. Moreschini, "La demonologia medioplatonica," who inclines to regard the alleged incoherence as a virtue: "The diverse experiences coexist alongside that religious one that comprehends them all, just as Apuleius was able to be mystic and magician, philosopher and orator, connoisseur of lore and votary of sensual pleasure" (p. 41). Translation mine.

29. *De deo Socratis* 6.

30. *Apology* 42-43; see *De deo Socratis* 15. For divination with children at the temple of Apis, see Xenophon, *Ephesiaca* 5.4. For the identification of Isis with Io and Apis with Epaphus, see Herodotus 2.41 and Witt, *Isis in the Graecoroman World*, pp. 247-248. Carl Schlam, "Platonica in the *Metamorphoses* of Apuleius," *TAPA* 101 (1970), argues that the romance discredits Lucius' magical aspiration as an "attempt to manipulate the divine for human ends" (p. 479). But it is hardly obvious that Lucius' "ends" are at variance with those of *daemones*.

31. *Apology* 1, 15. See Norden, *Apuleius von Madaura*, pp. 49, 52-53.

32. Plutarch, *Quomodo quis suos in virtute sentiat profectus* 75F-76B; Albinus, *Didascalicus* 30.

33. *De dogmate Platonis* 2.21, 22, 19.

34. *De Iside et Osiride* 360DE, 361E; see also 361CD, and *De deo Socratis* 12-15.

35. *Apology* 12; See Walsh, *The Roman Novel*, p. 183.

36. *De dogmate Platonis* 2.14. These phrases attributed to Apuleius again simply reproduce a tripartition defended by his contemporary Albinus, *Didascalicus* 33. One must avoid condemning all impure loves alike because purity, strictly understood, is not to be had.

37. *De Iside et Osiride* 362E (ass ritually hurled from cliff); 362E, 363C, 371C (redhaired and unteachable, like Typhon); 363B (impure beasts avatars of sinners).

38. *De Iside et Osiride* 372E.

39. For the identification of Isis with Io see note 30 above. For Habrocomes' dream, see Xenophon, *Ephesiaca* 2.8.

40. *De Iside et Osiride* 380D.

41. *De Iside et Osiride* 382 AB.

42. *De sollertia animalium* 961A, 964D.

43. *Apology* 64; see *De dogmate Platonis* 1.9: "Animam vero animantium omnium [dicit Plato] non esse corpoream nec sane perituram cum corpore fuerit absoluta." On metonymic reading see Plutarch, *De Iside et Osiride* 355B, 374E.

44. *De communibus notitiis* 1064AB.

4. THE WEREWOLF OF MARIE DE FRANCE

1. The text on which I base my translations is *Les Lais de Marie de France*, ed. Jean Rychner (Paris: Champion, 1966). I have also consulted the edition of Karl Warnke and Reinhold Köhler (Halle: Max Niemeyer, 1900).

2. *Ethica Nicomachea* 1148b19-30, 1149a9-15.

3. *Yonec*, 105-118.

4. Leo Spitzer, "Marie de France — Dichterin von Problem-märchen," *Zeitschrift für romanische Philologie* 50 (1930), 48n. Translation mine, as in note 8 below.

5. I shall use Marie's word "baron" throughout in its threefold sense of man, husband, and lord.

6. For the common noun, see ll. 3, 14, 63 [cf. 292], 138, 140, 162, 197. For the proper noun, see ll. 125, 227, 231, 274.

7. See ll. 157, 241, 257, 274.

8. In this respect, it seems to me, Spitzer's dismissive generalization is seriously misleading: "The 'wonders' are unproblematic, trimming, stage decoration for the tale, ways of setting the tale in order; what are problematic in Marie are the realistic *données*" ("Marie de France," p. 41).

9. See Ernest Hoepffner, ed., *Les Lais de Marie de France* (Paris: Boivin, 1935), p. 146.

10. *Yonec*, 155-164.

11. In *Yonec*, "deceive" is the regular meaning of *faire semblant*: see ll. 161, 181, 227, 247, 258.

12. *Guigemar*, 483-492.

13. In the sense of inclination, *talent* seems to betray a metaphorical derivation from its Greek etymon *talanton* (a weight; hence, a torque or potentiality for tipping the balance). But see below, note 17; and cf. Gianni Mombello, *Les Avatars de "Talentum"* (Turin: Società Editrice Internazionale, 1976).

14. *Guigemar*, 57-68.

15. The inhibition the lady has failed to overcome is thus not merely aesthetic or instinctual. But see Manfred Bambeck, "Das Werwolf-motif im 'Bisclavret,' " *Zeitschrift für romanische Philologie* 89 (1973), 132, 136.

16. Prologue 10-16. See Mortimer J. Donovan, *The Breton Lay: A Guide*

to Varieties (Notre Dame, Ind.: University of Notre Dame Press, 1969), pp. 1-56.

17. *Sen* and (in some of its meanings) *talent* discharge much the same function as *noûs* and *mens* in the classical texts I have already considered. There is no sign in the text that in his mute appeal for the king's mercy the *bisclavret*'s humanity has been partially restored, or its partial disclosure made possible, by royal charisma (Bambeck, "Das Werwolf-motif," pp. 128, 136, 146); the deformed baron singles out his master, and the only man with the authority to break off the hunt at its climactic moment. Note that the baron's human behavior is far from enough to identify him as human; indeed, he risks being destroyed as a demon or witch (*pace* Bambeck, pp. 130-131). The behavioral data are ambiguous if not interpreted by a "gnadenhafte Intuition" (Bambeck, p. 135).

18. It is too much to say (with Bambeck, "Das Werwolf-motif," p. 133) that the councillor's argument implies the beast's humanity. Selective resentment in beasts is not inconsistent with the natural history current in the twelfth century. A particularly apt case in point is Pliny's story of a dog who picks his master's murderer out of a crowd and mangles him until he confesses (*Naturalis Historia* 8.142). See also *Naturalis Historia* 8.50 (the lion's discriminating retaliation).

19. *The Faerie Queene*, 1.8.40.

20. For *devenir* see ll. 27, 63, 254, 270; for *aventure*, ll. 61, 99, 269.

21. *Vita nuova*, 42.

5. THIEVES AND SUICIDES IN THE *INFERNO*

1. The basis of my translations from *La Divina Commedia* is the edition of G. A. Scartazzini and G. Vandelli (Milan: Hoepli, 1958).

2. See *Purgatorio* 25.88-108.

3. *Ethica Nicomachea* 1150b32ff. For evidence of a particular concern with the Aristotelian discussion of incontinence, see *Inferno* 11.79-84.

4. *Metamorphoses* 15.422-430, 233ff., 165-168.

5. *Phoenix* 78: "se tamen ipsa creat."

6. Thomas Aquinas, *Summa theologica* 1.104.1 (hereafter cited as *STh*).

7. Ibid., 1.76.2 *ad* 2.

8. Ettore Paratore, *Tradizione e struttura in Dante* (Florence: G. C. Sansoni, 1968), pp. 250-251, joins Mattalia in reading the thieves' transformations as implying a comparison between the principle of individuation and private property (with an equivocation on *proprietas*). But the formal properties fused or exchanged by the thieves' souls are ordinary universals of which individuals can partake without theft; it is only in this *bolgia* that to achieve a human form one must deprive someone else of it.

9. *STh* 3.2.1; Boethius, *De persona et natura* 7 (*in calce*). It is, I think, a mistake to see in the thieves' mingling a feature of the mystery itself rather than of various heretical interpretations of it; for the former view see Diana Darby Chapin, "Metamorphosis As Punishment and Reward: Pagan and Christian Perspectives" (Ph.D. diss., Cornell University, 1971), pp. 117-118.

The passage she appeals to in fact supports the contrary view; for in Dante's visionary treatment the transmutation or mingling of natures is only in the *concept*, and not in the *reality*, of Christ's double nature (*Purgatorio* 31.126). This is the canonical view; that the two natures really mingle (like those of the thieves) is a form of the Eutychean heresy.

10. *Metamorphoses* 4.362–365.

11. *STh* 1,2.27.1 *ad* 2.

12. *STh* 2,2.66.6. Vittorio Russo, "La pena dei ladri," *Sussidi di esegesi dantesca* (Naples: Liguori, 1966), p. 138, refers the thieves' loss of their human *nature* to Aquinas' argument that possession of external things is *natural* to men because they are created in the image of God (*STh* 2,2.66.1). But in this passage Aquinas is discussing only men's *public* use of external things, not their private control and allotment of such things, which alone is subject to theft and which is ordained not by nature but by the fiat and the interests of particular societies (2,2.66.2). (Here Aquinas seems to dissent from *Digesta* 47.2.1 in favor of *Digesta* 1.1.5.)

13. See *Paradiso* 25.113 and Psalms 101:7 (Vulg.).

14. Benvenuto de Rambaldis de Imola, *Comentum super Dantis Aldigherii Comoediam*, ed. Giacopo Filippo Lacaita (Florence: G. Barbèra, 1877), 2,249. Translation mine.

15. See *STh* 1,2.27.3 *ad* 4.

16. *STh* Suppl. 3.92.1 *ad* 7; 1.57.4 *ad* 1.

17. *STh* 1,2.111.4.

18. Benvenuto, *Comentum*, 2,435. Translation mine.

19. *Inferno* 31.55ff.; *Ethica Nicomachea* 1150a1–8.

20. Augustine, *De civitate Dei* 1.17.

21. Benvenuto, *Comentum*, 2,448.

22. *Digesta* 31.7.1–2.

23. *Digesta* 7.1.6.

24. *STh* 2,2.64.5 *ad* 5.

25. *STh* 2,2.119.3 *obiectio prima* (this is the part of the *obiectio* that Aquinas will not disallow; he is quoting *Ethica Nicomachea* 1120a1ff.).

26. *STh* 2,2.119.2 *ad* 3.

27. See *Metamorphoses* 3.215 (where Harpyia is one of Actaeon's dogs); Servius on *Aeneid* 3.209; *Aen.* 3.252. Such beings, both at *Aen.* 3.225–226, 234, 244 and at *Aen.* 6.606, keep their victims from eating in the abstract sense in which "misers are imagined to endure the Furies because they abstain from their winnings" (Servius on *Aen.* 3.209). They also cause insomnia (Servius on *Aen.* 3.209) and are characterized as "triste monstrum," "saeva pestis" (3.214–215), and "infelix vates" (3.246). In Dante too they are *tristes*—"fanno lamenti"—by metonymy of effect for cause. For the voracity of *tristitia* see, for example, Prov. 25:20.

28. *STh* 2,2.64.5.

29. Benvenuto, *Comentum*, 2,425–426. Translation mine.

30. Ibid., 2,442. Translation mine. See also Paratore, *Tradizione e struttura*, pp. 208–209.

31. *STh* 2,2.64.5.

32. Augustine, *Homiliae* 1.8.

33. Augustine, *De civitate Dei* 1.20.

34. *STh* 2,2.20.3; 2,2.35.1. Mattalia (according to Paratore, *Tradizione e struttura*, pp. 182–183) argues that the imprisonment of the soul in a plant portrays self-hatred as self-love inverted, by turning inside out the rational soul's absorption of the vegetable and animal souls that precede it in the embryo. But absorption in this sense would require a plant with organs of sense and motion.

35. Richard Terdiman, "Problematical Virtuosity: Dante's Depiction of the Thieves," *Dante Studies* 91 (1973), 38–39, 42–43.

36. *STh* 2,2.162.1; 2,2.132.1; 2,2.129.3 *ad* 4; 2,2.132.1.

6. SPENSER'S MALBECCO

1. I quote from the edition of J. C. Smith and E. de Selincourt (Oxford: Oxford University Press, 1912).

2. *Metamorphoses* 11.782–795.

3. For knowledge of this correspondence (though not for the interpretation of it) I am indebted to Waldo F. McNeir, "Ariosto's Sospetto, Gascoigne's Suspicion, and Spenser's Malbecco," in *Festschrift für Walther Fischer* (Heidelberg: Carl Winter, 1952), pp. 34–48.

4. *Cinque canti* 2.16. The basis of my translations is the text in *Orlando Furioso*, ed. Nicola Zingarelli (Milan: Hoepli, 1959).

5. I quote from *A Hundreth Sundrie Posies*, ed. C. T. Prouty (Columbia, Mo.: University of Missouri, 1942), p. 83.

6. *Romeo and Juliet* 2.2.186–187. See *Anthologia Palatina* 5.173. For the topos see also *Anth. Pal.* 5.82, 83, 170; and Ovid, *Amores* 2.15.

7. "In body each of us would be remote from Essence, but in soul and in what we chiefly are, we partake of Essence and *are* an essence . . . the sovereign part of us is what, in a manner, we are" (Plotinus, *Enneades* 6.8.12). "The soul of man is man" (*Enneades* 3.5.5). "The individual would seem to be this [the best of what he comprises], since what is sovereign is also superior" (Aristotle, *Ethica Nicomachea* 1178a2–3). "Sometimes what is principal in man is called man" (Aquinas, *Summa Theologica* 1.4 *ad* 1). Translations mine.

8. Aquinas, *Summa Theologica* 1.3.3.

7. DONNE'S "SULLEN WRIT"

1. The text from which I quote is *The Poems of John Donne*, ed. Herbert Grierson (Oxford: Oxford University Press, 1912).

2. Aquinas, *Summa Theologica* 1.98.1 (hereafter cited as *STh*); Marsilio Ficino, scholium at *Enneades* 4.4.39, reproduced in *Plotini Enneades cum Marsilii Ficini interpretatione*, ed. Friedrich Creuzer and Georg Heinrich Moser (Paris: Didot, 1855).

3. This is the received wisdom about sparrows in general; see Pliny, *Natural History* 10.107.

4. *As You Like It* 2.5.26–27, 2.1.57; Holy Sonnet 9.

5. Aquinas, *Compendium Theologiae* 142.

6. Aristotle, *Metaphysics* 986a23–26; *Ethica Nicomachea* 1106b29f.

7. Epistle.

8. Erasmus, "Puerpera," in *Colloquia*, ed. C. Schrevel (Amsterdam: Blauw, 1693), pp. 402, 394–395, 401–402.

9. Wesley Milgate, ed., *The Satires, Epigrams, and Verse Letters of John Donne* (Oxford: Clarendon Press, 1967), p. 191.

10. Richard Hooker, *On the Laws of Ecclesiastical Polity* 1.8.8; *STh* 1.79.12.

11. Aristotle, *Ethica Nicomachea* 1112a7–8.

12. Milgate, *Satires, Epigrams, and Verse Letters*, p. 189.

13. Janel M. Mueller, "Donne's Epic Venture in the *Metempsychosis*," *Modern Philology* 70 (1972), 109–137, traces the philosophy implicit in Donne's poem to the heretical teaching of the second-century Gnostic libertine Carpocrates and his son Epiphanes. But each of the four alleged grounds for this pedigree seems to me to point in another direction.

(1) Mueller identifies as Manichean Donne's reference to "Destiny the Commissary of God" (31), and especially to "Fate, which God made, but doth not controule" (2). But these phrases do not preclude a Providential theory of history. Destiny is God's "Commissary" because of the duties entrusted to her, just as earthly goods are said by Dante to be "commessi" (committed) to Fortuna (*Inferno* 7.62) with specific instructions as to their disposition (7.78ff.). And Fate (the preordained course of events) is not overruled ("controuled") by God only in the sense that it is overruled by no one, its unerring Author least of all; there is no suggestion here that Fate somehow takes the initiative. This is all traditional; for both doctrine and nomenclature see Boethius *Cons. phil.* 4.6; *STh* 1.23.6; *STh* 1.23.6 *ad* 2; *STh* 1.117.3

(2) There is nothing heretical (despite Mueller, p. 128b) in the speaker's assumption that free will is cancelled out by Fate. This reflects the theological outlook of Donne's contemporaries as he himself interprets it when he writes that free will is "wounded and maimed . . . in the Roman Church," and "dead in our Church" (*Letters*, ed. Charles Merrill [New York: Sturgis and Walton, 1910], p. 231).

(3) The main incentive to follow Mueller is his claim that Carpocratean metempsychosis admits of vegetable incarnations, as in Donne's poem. But this claim is supported by the modern English version of Tertullian quoted by Mueller, not by Tertullian's Latin text. The translation: "The transmigration of human souls, therefore, into any kind of heterogeneous bodies, he thought by all means indispensable whenever any depravity whatever had not been fully perpetrated in the early stage of life's passage" (Peter Holmes; quoted by Mueller, p. 124a). Tertullian: "Itaque metempsychosin necessarie imminere, si non in primo quoque vitae huius commeatu omnibus inlicitis satisfiat" (*De anima* 35, ed. Franz Öhler [Leipzig: T. O. Weigel, 1854]). The purpose of reincarnation asserted by Carpocrates—to fulfill a duty to sin neglected in previous incarnations—would hardly be served by the means of acting available to a plant. (See Irenaeus, *Contra haereses* 2.32, in Migne, *Patrologia Graeca* 5 [1846], 742.) Moreover, the Carpocratean souls endure an

elaborate ordeal between incarnations that Donne could hardly have ignored had he set himself the task of emulating the teaching of the Gnostic sect (see Irenaeus, 1.25, in Migne, *PG* 5.602).

(4) Carpocrateans do, like Donne's speaker (518-519), use the formulas of moral nihilism (Tertullian, *De anima* 35). But they hold no monopoly on such formulas among the philosophical sects of antiquity; see Sextus Empiricus, *Pyrrhoniae hypotyposes* 3.179, 190, 205 (the last citation being a reference to Zeno's and Chrysippus' defense of incest—a teaching not paralleled in the extant fragments of Carpocrates but conspicuous in Donne's poem).

14. Milgate, *Satires, Epigrams, and Verse Letters*, p. 178.

15. Mueller's argument ("Donne's Epic Venture") for a community of genre is unconvincing. (1) It is not true that both poems are "epics on a comprehensive historic plan" (p. 119a). There are no equivalents in Donne's narrative to Ovid's Achilles or Ulysses or Jason; Donne keeps his protagonist in the wings of history. (2) There is no portrait in either poem of "the falling away of man from the harmonious simplicity of the Golden Age" (p. 116b). Man in Ovid is not descended from the rational beings of the Golden Age but from the stones of Deucalion and Pyrrha. Donne presents no Golden Age at all. We watch mankind already in exile, on the eve of the first murder, and unlike the Hesiodic and Ovidian pattern, the Soul's moral descent is not linear; the ape, for example, is guilty neither of the mouse's envy nor of the wolf's treachery, nor of the sparrow's filial ingratitude. (3) Donne's attack on human predacity owes far less to the ironic amusement of Ovid than to Juvenal's sarcastic indignation. See Juvenal 15, in which the satirist uses the epic style of narrative to expose a human vice he assumes to be general and beyond cure. Jonson's cloacal epic on the navigation of Fleet Ditch ("On the Famous Voyage") is, like Donne's, a satire on a kind of baseness in human nature for which there is no obvious remedy, and like Donne's and Juvenal's mock-epic it uses Pythagoras' doctrine as an opportunity for a bitter joke (see Jonson, 133-144).

16. See Mueller, "Donne's Epic Venture," p. 116n24: "[Donne] parallels broadly the famous lines on cultural relativism from Myrrha's soliloquy in defense of incest (10.321-325) in stanzas 20-21 and 52 of the *Metempsychosis*."

17. Calvin, *Institutes* 3.23.2 (quoted from the translation of F. L. Battles [Philadelphia: Westminster Press, 1960]); Donne, *Biathanatos* (London: Henry Sayle, 1646), p. 145.

8. LAMIA AND THE SOPHIST

1. I am quoting from the edition of H. W. Garrod (Oxford: Oxford University Press, 1939).

2. J. Lempriere, *Bibliotheca Classica* (London: T. Cadell and W. Davies, 1797), s.v. "Mercury."

3. *The Squire's Tale,* 478-479.

4. Earl Wasserman, *The Finer Tone* (Baltimore: Johns Hopkins University Press, 1953), p. 160.

5. Walter Jackson Bate, *John Keats* (Cambridge, Mass. Harvard University Press, 1963), p. 553.

6. Barry Allan Gradman, "Dying into Life: Metamorphosis in Keat's Poetry" (Ph.D. diss., Cornell University, 1972), p. 287.

7. David Perkins, "Lamia," in *Keats*, ed. Walter Jackson Bate (Englewood Cliffs, N.J.: Prentice-Hall, 1961), pp. 147, 144.

8. Ibid., p. 144

9. Donald H. Reiman, "Keats and the Humanistic Paradox: Mythological History in *Lamia*," *Studies in English Literature* 11 (1971), 665.

10. Wasserman, *The Finer Tone*, p. 165.

11. *A Midsummer Night's Dream* 3.2.388, 4.1.95–96; *The Merchant's Tale* 2038–2039.

12. Perkins, "Lamia," p. 145.

13. Ibid., p. 146.

14. Lempriere, *Bibliotheca Classica*, Dd4^r, Dd3^r, L3^r.

15. Bate, *John Keats*, pp. 552–553; see also p. 560.

16. Perkins, "Lamia," p. 151.

17. Lempriere, *Bibliotheca Classica*, Q1^r.

18. Gradman, "Dying into Life," p. 297.

19. Perkins, "Lamia," p. 148.

20. Bate, *John Keats*, p. 545.

21. Ibid., pp. 547–548.

22. Gradman, "Dying into Life," p. 294.

23. Reiman, "Keats and the Humanistic Paradox," p. 664.

24. Gradman, "Dying into Life," p. 299.

25. Gradman, "Dying into Life," p. 303; Perkins, "Lamia," p. 148.

26. Perkins, "Lamia," p. 151.

27. Ibid., p. 149.

9. THE ORDEAL OF GREGOR SAMSA

1. F. D. Luke, "The Metamorphosis," in *Franz Kafka Today*, ed. Angel Flores and Harvey Swander (Madison: University of Wisconsin Press, 1958), p. 28; Paul L. Landsberg, "The Metamorphosis," in *Franz Kafka Today*, p.132. See also Hartmut Binder, *Motiv und Gestaltung bei Franz Kafka* (Bonn: Bouvier, 1966), pp. 296, 359.

2. Walter H. Sokel, *Franz Kafka — Tragik und Ironie: zur Struktur seiner Kunst* (Vienna: George Müller, 1964), pp. 96, 79, 80. All translations from this work are mine.

3. I refer here and hereafter to the pages of Franz Kafka, *Erzählungen*, ed. Max Brod (Hamburg: S. Fischer, 1967). This text is the basis of my translations.

4. Sokel, *Franz Kafka*, p. 78.

5. Ibid., p. 82.

6. Though Kafka's story does not illustrate a character's use of metamorphosis as a ground for disclaiming responsibility, it is instructive to contrast Gregor Samsa's ingenuousness with the evasions of just such a character. Stevenson's Dr. Jekyll, in his posthumous confession, undertakes to convince us, and no doubt himself, that someone spatiotemporally continuous with him and identical in memory is none the less another person—that Jekyll is not

Hyde. The latter, we are told, began by treating his inhibited *alter idem* to a vicarious experience of rakish naughtiness and ended, to Jekyll's horror, by committing atrocities. But it is clear from Jekyll's account that he has simply been using an addictive drug to alter his appearance and wipe away his inhibitions—in short, that "Hyde" names, not a wayward surrogate of Jekyll, but Jekyll himself. (Jekyll's pretentious metaphysical argument for diminished moral accountability is of a piece with the metaphysical rhapsodies of his approach to science, and it is a crucial subtlety of Stevenson's portrait that the *soi-disant* chemist turns out to have no notion of chemistry at all.) "Hyde," of course, says nothing to spoil "Jekyll's" alibi—unlike Kafka's monstrous insect, who would be only too glad to be accepted as none other than Gregor, and who is condemned in the name of a metaphysical theory akin to Dr. Jekyll's. See G. K. Chesterton, *Robert Louis Stevenson* (London: Hodder and Stoughton, 1927), pp. 72ff.; Irving S. Saposnik, "The Anatomy of *Dr. Jekyll and Mr. Hyde*," *Studies in English Literature* 11 (1971), 715–731; Joseph J. Egan, "The Relationship of Theme and Art in *The Strange Case of Dr. Jekyll and Mr. Hyde*," *English Literature in Transition 1880–1920* 9 (1966), 28-32.

7. Sokel, *Franz Kafka*, p. 84.

8. Ibid., p. 89.

9. See Mark Spilka, "Kafka's Sources for the 'Metamorphosis,'" *Comparative Literature* 11 (1959), p. 305.: "[Kafka] connects Gregor with one person who is not repelled by his appearance, who is even willing to speak to him (as none of his family will except in anger) . . . words 'which apparently she took to be friendly.' And they are friendly, since they include and absorb deformity in the larger acceptance of human worth." These words, on the contrary, exasperate Gregor with some justice; they are unmistakably contemptuous, like the charwoman's later obituary on him: "It's croaked." For the charwoman, an intelligent dungbeetle is still a dungbeetle.

10. See Benno von Wiese, *Die deutsche Novelle* (Düsseldorf: August Bagel, 1965), p. 329: "The picture, which has already been mentioned at the outset of the narrative . . . occurs here obviously as representing the sphere of the Thou, but still in the erotic-sexual sense." (All translations from this work are mine.)

11. Sokel, *Franz Kafka*, p. 90.

12. Ibid., p. 91.

13. Ibid., pp. 92, 98.

14. Benno von Wiese, *Die deutsche Novelle*, p. 328.

15. Ibid., pp. 325, 334.

16. Norman Malcolm, "Wittgenstein's Philosophical Investigations," in *Meaning and Knowledge*, ed. Ernest Nagel and Richard B. Brandt (New York: Harcourt, Brace, 1965), p. 450; Ludwig Wittgenstein, *Philosophical Investigations* (New York: Macmillan, 1953), I, sec. 360. See Landsberg, "The Metamorphosis," p. 126: "In our customary certainty of the identity of our being and world in general, there is just enough of artificiality, enough will, enough fragility so that Kafka's fiction touches an unacknowledged reality." See also Spilka, "Kafka's Sources," p. 297: "There are other parts of Dostoevsky's story [*The Double*] which would have attracted Kafka. Among them is Golyadkin's

curious remark that his colleagues might have turned him into a rag without much trouble—but that rag would have possessed both dignity and feelings, 'even though dignity was defenseless and feelings could not assert themselves, and lay hidden deep-down in the filthy folds of the rag.' "

17. In effect he resigns himself to the narrator's taxonomy; see Peter U. Beicken, *Franz Kafka: eine kritische Einführung in die Forschung* (Frankfurt: Athenaion, 1974), p. 267: "Gregor is not *like* a monstrous insect, he *is* this insect." (Translation mine.)

18. See Landsberg, "The Metamorphosis," p. 130: "At the very moment that we are impressed with a spiritual metamorphosis of the self, we feel a certain stability in our being . . . At a given moment I am myself and yet another. Every physical manifestation sooner or later becomes unfaithful to my person, but my intimate unity emanates from a buried source." Contrast Norbert Kassel, *Das Groteske bei Franz Kafka* (München: Wilhelm Fink, 1969), p. 164: "The problem of human fellowship and the question of help not granted by one's fellow human beings form the real theme of the story. We come to see that Gregor, in the measure that he loses human contact with his family, sinks more and more into the apathy of the beast." (Translation mine.)

10. VIRGINIA WOOLF'S *ORLANDO*

1. My references are to the pages of Virginia Woolf, *Orlando: A Biography* (New York: Harcourt, Brace, 1929).

2. It would be an exaggeration to claim, with Avrom Fleishman, *The English Historical Novel* (Baltimore: Johns Hopkins University Press, 1971), that "In *Orlando* . . . the hero-heroine is a personification not only of his family but also of his time . . . Such consistent parallelism implies a constant relationship between the individual and his environment which in the esthetic realm functions as symbolism but in the philosophic can only be considered determinism" (pp. 238-239). I shall try to show that, on the contrary, determinism is what the romance fervently resists, but Fleishman is in any case nearer the mark when he recognizes that "Orlando is not a pale reflector of historical periods, but a being with enough vitality to insure his individuality, sometimes in the teeth of the age" (p. 329). See Jean Guiguet, *Virginia Woolf et son oeuvre* (Paris: Didier, 1963): "Thus, despite his multiple love affairs and despite the throngs Orlando goes through, we are led perforce to his solitude; not that in which he shuts himself up sometimes, and that gives him a chance to attempt the big themes favored by Virginia Woolf: Sea, Air, Woods, Earth, in the manner of parody, to be sure, but not without the insinuation of a clandestine satisfaction—but a solitude fundamentally characteristic of the Stranger" (p. 275). (Translation mine, as in notes 5 and 6 below.) The solitude Guiguet so acutely describes is, I think, indispensable to Orlando's freedom, or at least her capacity to achieve it.

3. G. E. Moore, *Philosophical Studies* (Paterson, N.J.: Littlefield, Adams, 1959), pp. 27, 24.

4. An argument for attributing a realism like Moore's to Virginia Woolf is presented by S. P. Rosenbaum, "The Philosophical Realism of Virginia

Woolf," in *English Literature and British Philosophy*, ed. S. P. Rosenbaum (Chicago: University of Chicago Press, 1971). Unfortunately the argument turns on such specious equations as the following: "By attending only to material reality both [literary and philosophical materialists] overlook that other reality that Moore called 'transparent' and 'diaphanous' and that Virginia Woolf described as 'a luminous halo, a semi-transparent envelope' " (p. 322). But these "realities" are hardly equivalent. With its inherent perceptual qualities (the luminosity that keeps it from being fully transparent), Virginia Woolf's "envelope" or "halo" necessarily modifies what it transmits, precisely in the manner of the sense-images whose existence Moore is disposed to reject. And that is because their existence is something Virginia Woolf herself is very much disposed to affirm.

5. It is tempting, but I think mistaken, to draw a realist moral from this kind of sequence in the author's work. See Rosenbaum, "Philosophical Realism": "The point of view in the story ['The Mark on the Wall'], the personality of the narrator who speculates on the impossibility of knowing anything because she cannot be troubled to stand up and see just what exactly is the mark on the wall, is an element in the story that should not be overlooked. Sanity and sense involve the interrelations of thought *and* external reality, of consciousness *and* the objects of consciousness" (p. 325). But this is to suppose, falsely, that philosophical idealism excludes the possibility of "standing up and seeing" when in fact it simply offers an account of such experiences alternative to realism. In this respect Guiguet's reading of the same story is more satisfactory: "That the mark was a snail — and it was enough to get up, to correct the visual datum by the tactile datum, in order to assure oneself of this — is at once laughable and unimportant. It is at bottom pure accident that the original sensation and this object coincide. What is essential is everything that has occupied the mind between the sensation and the perception: it is this content that is the reality, that is the mark on the wall" (*Virginia Woolf*, p. 379).

6. A number of critics have concluded, with Guiguet, that for the author time is "relative" and "subjective," without a "common measure" (*Virginia Woolf*, p. 381). Avrom Fleishman, "Woolf and McTaggart," *ELH* 36 (1969), goes so far as to have the author follow McTaggart in insisting that there is "no time-series" and "no series of events" (p. 729). James Hafley, *The Glass Roof* (New York: Russell and Russell, 1963), remarks that in the last chapter of *Orlando* "there is no past, no present, no future, but only pure duration itself, one and undivided (p. 97). But this will not do; in *Orlando* and elsewhere the author's characters live by many measures of time, one of which (public or clock time) they have in common. The objective domain is not merely annulled but (as in Kant) replaced by the intersubjective. Guiguet, at least, appears to acknowledge this in his discussion of *Jacob's Room*: "It is a question of the multiple times and spaces in the midst of multiple consciousnesses. In the first pages, for example, there are those of Betty Flanders, Charles Steele, Archer, Jacob, so many circles covering different areas, different periods, circles in which everything has different proportions and different aspects, and circles whose *intersections* in some sort cross-hatch a *common zone* and thereby

make it stand out from the arabesques in which it is concealed" (p. 381; emphasis added). "Experience shows," says Guiguet, "that today will be like yesterday, Tuesday like Monday. That is, the moment we occupy now, then seesawing into the past, will be lost" (p. 389). But this is to admit the reality of temporal succession, even if the events it orders are consecutive states of mind. As for the last chapter of *Orlando*, it is just such a succession, a diffuse meditation beginning and ending with an intersubjective or public event (shopping and driving home respectively). The order of the heroine's intervening memories does not correspond to the order of the events remembered, but this surely does not imply that either order is illusory.

7. See David Lewis, *Counterfactuals* (Cambridge, Mass.: Harvard University Press, 1973). One is tempted to say that such exploration is trivially verbal. Isn't possibility mere consistency? If so, the possibility of Orlando's being male (for example) is nothing more than the lack of a contradiction in the sentence "Orlando is male" or some such. But this trivialization of the narrative enterprise will not do; the possibility in question is Orlando's being male, and it is surely false that Orlando's being male is the same as some sentence expressing it. One may perhaps avoid this objection by admitting that possibility is not consistency but going on to deny that there are any such exotic objects as the meanings of expressions — as (for example) the proposition expressed by "Orlando is male" — and hence to recommend that "It is logically possible that Orlando is male" be taken as a mere form of words reporting the consistency of a sentence. But this tactic is hardly plausible. The meanings of sentences have at least enough existence for particular sentences to have more than one; when we count the alternative meanings of a sentence, surely we are not simply parsing it. It seems clear that one can believe it possible that Orlando should have been male (even if she happens not to be) without having beliefs about some sentence — but not without believing that there is a conceivable state of affairs in which Orlando is male. I think we can safely conclude that when Virginia Woolf's narrator explores, in other but similar schemes of things, the consequences of the logical possibility that Orlando was a sixteenth-century gentleman, he is not passing judgment on the syntax of a piece of English but rather contemplating a proposition that (like all propositions) varies in its truth or falsity from one possible world to another.

8. See Fleishman, *The Historical Novel*: "All the Orlando-figures are one Orlando under various guises, just as each Sackville embodies the abstract title of earl or duke for a time" (p. 240). This is a confusion. If "Orlando" is to be treated by analogy with "Earl of Dorset," then the "figures" named by the former term are not one but many (in succession).

9. See Nancy Topping Bazin, *Virginia Woolf and the Androgynous Vision* (New Brunswick, N.J.: Rutgers University Press, 1973): "Making [Jacob's] presence incidental helps to suggest that the reality (the soul or essence) of Jacob exists apart from the actuality (or facts) of his life, yet that one must somehow get at his 'reality' through these facts" (p. 93). "The whole [that Bernard, in *The Waves*, strives to express] must include . . . himself as defined by his many selves and the selves he might have been but wasn't" (p. 143).

10. Robert Louis Stevenson, *Strange Case of Dr. Jekyll and Mr. Hyde*, in *The Merry Men* (Boston: Turner, 1906), pp. 385, 375, 374, 381, 307, 385, 387, 391, 372 respectively.

11. See Herbert Marder, *Feminism and Art: A Study of Virginia Woolf* (Chicago: University of Chicago Press, 1968): "This whole sequence . . . illustrates a movement from repression to freedom" (p. 114).

12. A. J. Ayer, *The Problem of Knowledge* (Baltimore: Penguin, 1956), p. 220.

13. See Hafley, *The Glass Roof*, p. 104.

14. John Graham, "The 'Caricature Value' of Parody and Fantasy in *Orlando*," *University of Toronto Quarterly* 30 (1961), 345–366, sees inconsistency and enervation in the passage from fantasy to mimesis, from parody to seriousness; but the change is not arbitrary. The whole point of the festive opening is the necessity to entrap — by gaiety into gravity, by easy acceptance of masculine quest into unresisting belief in feminine.

INDEX

243